PRIVACY AND CIVIL LIBERTIES OVERSIGHT BOARD

Report on the Telephone Records Program

Conducted under Section 215

of the USA PATRIOT Act and on the

Operations of the Foreign Intelligence Surveillance Court

JANUARY 23, 2014

PRIVACY & CIVIL LIBERTIES OVERSIGHT BOARD

Report on the Telephone Records Program Conducted under Section 215 of the USA PATRIOT Act and on the Operations of the Foreign Intelligence Surveillance Court

Part 1:
INTRODUCTION

On June 5, 2013, the British newspaper *The Guardian* published the first of a series of articles based on unauthorized disclosures of classified documents by Edward Snowden, a contractor for the National Security Agency ("NSA").[1] The article described an NSA program to collect millions of telephone records, including records about purely domestic calls. Over the course of the next several days, there were additional articles regarding this program as well as another NSA program referred to in leaked documents as "PRISM."

These disclosures caused a great deal of concern both over the extent to which they damaged national security and over the nature and scope of the surveillance programs they purported to reveal. Subsequently, authorized disclosures from the government confirmed both programs. Under one, the NSA collects telephone call records or metadata — but not the content of phone conversations — covering the calls of most Americans on an ongoing basis, subject to renewed approvals by the Foreign Intelligence Surveillance Court ("FISC" or "FISA court"). This program was approved by the FISC pursuant to Section 215 of the USA PATRIOT Act ("Patriot Act"). Under the second program, the government collects the content of electronic communications, including phone calls and emails, where the targets are reasonably believed to be non-U.S. persons located outside the United States.[2] Section 702 of the FISA Amendments Act is the basis for this program.[3]

Immediately following the press revelations, the public and many policymakers began asking questions about the scope and nature of these NSA programs. Central among the issues raised was the degree to which the programs included appropriate safeguards for privacy and civil liberties. One week after the first news article appeared, a bipartisan group of thirteen U.S. Senators asked the recently reconstituted Privacy and Civil Liberties Oversight Board ("PCLOB") to investigate the two NSA programs and to provide an unclassified report "so that the public and the Congress can have a long overdue debate" about the privacy issues raised.[4] A July 11, 2013, letter from House Minority Leader Nancy Pelosi requested that the Board also consider the operations of the FISC, which approved

---

[1]   *See* Glenn Greenwald, *NSA Collecting Phone Records of Millions of Verizon Customers Daily*, THE GUARDIAN (June 5, 2013).

[2]   Even when the target is a non-U.S. person, collections of communications involving U.S. persons may still occur, either where those individuals are in communication with non-U.S. persons or where they are mistakenly believed to be non-U.S. persons.

[3]   This is the program inaccurately referred to in early reports as the PRISM program. PRISM is actually the database in which such communications are compiled.

[4]   Letter from Senator Tom Udall *et al.* to the Privacy and Civil Liberties Oversight Board (June 12, 2013), *available at* http://www.pclob.gov/.

the two programs. On June 21, 2013, the Board met with President Obama and his senior staff at the White House, and the President asked the Board to review "where our counterterrorism efforts and our values come into tension."[5]

In response to the congressional and presidential requests, the Board immediately initiated a study of the 215 and 702 programs and the operation of the FISA court. This Report contains the results of the Board's 215 program study as well as our analysis and recommendations regarding the FISC's operation.

I.   Background

The PCLOB is an independent bipartisan agency within the executive branch established by the Implementing Recommendations of the 9/11 Commission Act of 2007.[6] The Board is comprised of four part-time members and a full-time chairman, all appointed by the President and confirmed by the Senate. The Board's authorizing statute gives it two primary responsibilities:

1) To analyze and review actions the executive branch takes to protect the Nation from terrorism, ensuring that the need for such actions is balanced with the need to protect privacy and civil liberties; and

2) To ensure that liberty concerns are appropriately considered in the development and implementation of laws, regulations, and policies related to efforts to protect the Nation against terrorism.[7]

This Report arises out of the Board's responsibility to provide oversight by analyzing and reviewing executive branch actions, in this case the operation of the Section 215 telephone records program.

The Board today is in its third iteration. In July 2004, the National Commission on Terrorist Attacks on the United States (known as the 9/11 Commission) recommended that "there should be a board within the executive branch to oversee adherence to the guidelines we recommend and the commitment the government makes to defend our civil

---

5   *See* Letter from Democratic Leader Nancy Pelosi to Chairman David Medine (July 11, 2013), *available at* http://www.pclob.gov/; Remarks by the President in a Press Conference at the White House (Aug. 9, 2013), *available at* http://www.whitehouse.gov/the-press-office/2013/08/09/remarks-president-press-conference.

6   Pub. L. No. 110-53, § 801(a), 121 Stat. 266, 352-58 (2007).

7   *See* Pub. L. No. 110-53, § 801(a) (codified at 42 U.S.C. § 2000ee).

liberties."[8] In August 2004, President George W. Bush created the President's Board on Safeguarding Americans' Civil Liberties by executive order.[9] The President's Board ceased to meet upon the enactment of the Intelligence Reform and Terrorism Prevention Act of 2004, which created a Privacy and Civil Liberties Oversight Board within the Executive Office of the President.[10]

In 2007, the Implementing Recommendations of the 9/11 Commission Act reconstituted the Board in its current form as an independent agency within the executive branch.[11] The Act requires that all five Board members be appointed by the President, by and with the advice and consent of the Senate, for staggered six-year terms. The Act further requires that the Board be bipartisan in composition. No more than three of the five members may be from the same political party, and before appointing members who are not from the President's political party, the President must consult with the leadership of the opposing party.

With the reconstitution of the Board, the 9/11 Commission Act terminated, effective January 30, 2008, the terms of the individuals then serving as Board members within the Executive Office of the President. From that time until August 2012, the Board did not function, as none of the positions on the Board were filled. Then, in August 2012, the Board's current four part-time members were confirmed by the Senate, providing the reconstituted Board with its first confirmed members and a quorum to begin operations.[12]

---

[8]   THE 9/11 COMMISSION REPORT: FINAL REPORT OF THE NATIONAL COMMISSION ON TERRORIST ATTACKS UPON THE UNITED STATES, at 395 (2004). The 9/11 Commission was a bipartisan panel established to "make a full and complete accounting of the circumstances surrounding" the September 11, 2001, terrorist attacks, and to provide "recommendations for corrective measures that can be taken to prevent acts of terrorism." Intelligence Authorization Act for Fiscal Year 2003, Pub. L. No. 107-306, § 602(4), (5), 116 Stat. 2383, 2408 (2002).

[9]   See Exec. Order No. 13353, 69 Fed. Reg. 53,585 (Aug. 27, 2004). The President's Board was chaired by the Deputy Attorney General and consisted of twenty-two representatives from the Departments of State, Defense, Justice, Treasury, Health and Human Services, and Homeland Security; the Office of Management and Budget; and the Intelligence Community. During its tenure, the President's Board met six times.

[10]   See Pub. L. No. 108-458, § 1061(b), 118 Stat. 3638, 3684 (2004). As chartered under IRTPA, the Board was comprised of two Board members appointed by the President, by and with the advice and consent of the Senate, and three additional Board members appointed by the President. Id. § 1061(e)(1).

[11]   See Pub. L. No. 110-53, § 801(a), 121 Stat. 266, 352-58 (2007).

[12]   The Board's four part-time members were confirmed by the Senate on August 2, 2012, and were appointed by the President and sworn into office later that month for the following terms:

- Rachel L. Brand, for a term ending January 29, 2017;

- Elisebeth Collins Cook, for a term ending January 29, 2014. On January 6, 2014, Ms. Cook was nominated for a second term ending January 29, 2020. Under the Board's authorizing statute, as a result of this nomination, Ms. Cook can continue to serve through the end of the Senate's current session and, if confirmed before then, through January 29, 2020.

- James X. Dempsey, for a term ending January 29, 2016; and

The Board's chairman, its only full-time member, was confirmed on May 7, 2013, and sworn in on May 29, five days before news stories based upon the NSA leaks began to appear.

Since the PCLOB began operations as an independent agency in August 2012, it has released two semi-annual reports to Congress and the President summarizing the agency's start up activities.[13] This Report represents the Board's first comprehensive study of a government program.

II.   Study Methodology

In response to the congressional and presidential requests, the PCLOB undertook an in-depth study of the Section 215 and 702 programs as well as the operations of the FISA court.[14] This study included classified briefings with officials from the Office of the Director for National Intelligence ("ODNI"), NSA, Department of Justice, Federal Bureau of Investigation ("FBI"), and Central Intelligence Agency ("CIA"). Board members also met with White House staff, a former presiding judge of the FISA court, academics, privacy and civil liberties advocates, technology and communications companies, and trade associations. The Board also received a demonstration of the Section 215 program's operation and capabilities at the NSA. The Board has been provided access to classified opinions by the FISC, various inspector general reports, and additional classified documents relating to the operation and effectiveness of the programs. At every step of the way, the Board has received the full cooperation of the intelligence agencies. Board staff have conducted a detailed analysis of applicable statutory authorities, the First and Fourth Amendments to the Constitution, and privacy and civil liberties policy issues.

As part of its study, and consistent with our statutory mandate to operate publicly where possible, the Board held two public forums. The first was a day-long public workshop held in Washington, D.C., on July 9, 2013, comprised of three panels addressing

---

- Patricia M. Wald, for a term ending January 29, 2013. On December 12, 2013, the Senate confirmed Ms. Wald for a second term ending January 29, 2019.

The Board's chairman and only full-time member, David Medine, was originally nominated by the President on December 15, 2011, and was re-nominated on January 22, 2013. The Senate confirmed Mr. Medine on May 7, 2013, and he was sworn in on May 29, 2013, for a term ending January 29, 2018.

[13]   *See* Privacy and Civil Liberties Oversight Board, Semi-Annual Report, September 2012 to March 2013 (June 27, 2013); Privacy and Civil Liberties Oversight Board, Semi-Annual Report, March 2013 to September 2013 (Nov. 3, 2013), *available at* http://www.pclob.gov/.

[14]   Prior to the confirmation of the chairman, the four part-time members had identified implementation of the FISA Amendments Act as a priority for oversight; in other words, the Section 702 Program already was familiar to the majority of the Board in June 2013.

different aspects of the Section 215 and 702 programs.[15] The panelists provided input on the legal, constitutional, technology, and policy issues implicated by the two programs. The first panel addressed the legality of the programs, and included comments from a former FISC judge regarding the operation of that court. Because technological issues are central to the operations of both programs, the second panel was comprised of technology experts. The third panel included academics and members of the advocacy community; panelists were invited to provide views on the policy implications of the NSA programs and what changes, if any, would be appropriate.

As the Board's study of the NSA surveillance programs moved forward, the Board began to consider possible recommendations for program changes. At the same time, the Board wanted to try to identify any unanticipated consequences of reforms it was considering. Accordingly, on November 4, 2013, the Board held a public hearing in Washington, D.C.[16] The hearing began with a panel of current government officials who addressed the value of the programs and the potential impact of proposed changes. The second panel, designed to explore the operation of the FISA court, consisted of another former FISC judge, along with a former government official and a private attorney who both had appeared before the FISC. Finally, the Board heard from a diverse panel of experts on potential Section 215 and 702 reforms.

The Board provided its draft description of the operations of the FISA court (but not our recommendations) to court's staff to ensure that this description accurately portrayed the court's operations. The Board also provided draft portions of its analysis regarding the effectiveness of the Section 215 program (but not our conclusions and recommendations) to the U.S. Intelligence Community to ensure that our factual statements were correct and complete. While the Board's Report was subject to classification review, none of the changes resulting from that process affected our analysis or recommendations. There was no outside review of the substance of the Board's analysis and recommendations.

During the time the PCLOB has been conducting this study, members of Congress have introduced a variety of legislative proposals to address the Section 215 and 702 programs, the government has engaged in several internal reviews of the programs, and several lawsuits have been filed challenging the programs' legitimacy. To ensure that the PCLOB's recommendations may be considered as part of this ongoing debate, the Board divided this study into two parts. The first part, this Report, covers the PCLOB's analysis and recommendations regarding operation of the 215 program and the FISA court. The second part will be a subsequent unclassified report containing PCLOB's analysis and recommendations concerning the 702 program.

---

[15]   *See* Annex C.

[16]   *See* Annex D.

In addition, proposals for modifications to the Section 215 program and the operation of the FISC were under active consideration by the White House while we were conducting our study. Pursuant to the Board's statutory duty to advise the President and elements of the executive branch to ensure that privacy and civil liberties are appropriately considered in the development and implementation of legislation and policies and to provide advice on proposals to retain or enhance a particular power, the PCLOB briefed senior White House staff on the Board's tentative conclusions on December 5, 2013. The PCLOB provided a near final draft of the Board's conclusions and recommendations on Section 215 and the operations of the FISA court (Parts 5, 7 and 8 of this Report) to the White House on January 3, the transparency section (Part 9) on January 8, 2014, and additional statutory analysis on January 14, 2014 (Part 5). On January 8, the full Board met with the President, the Vice President and senior officials to present the Board's conclusions and the views of individual Board members.

III.   Report Organization

The body of this Report consists of seven sections, five of which address the Section 215 telephone records program. After this introduction and the executive summary, Part 3 describes in detail how the telephone records program works. To put the present-day operation of the program in context, Part 4 reviews its history, including its evolution from predecessor intelligence activities. An analysis of whether the telephone records program meets applicable statutory requirements follows in Part 5. Part 6 addresses the constitutional issues raised by the telephone records program under both the First and Fourth Amendments. The final section discussing the Section 215 program, Part 7, examines the potential benefits of the program, its efficacy in achieving its purposes, the impact of the program on privacy and civil liberties, and the Board's conclusions that reforms are needed.

After considering the 215 program, the Report addresses the operations of the Foreign Intelligence Surveillance Court. That section, Part 8, concludes by proposing an approach that, in appropriate cases, would allow the FISC judges to hear from a Special Advocate. Part 9, the final section of the Report, addresses the issue of transparency, which has been a priority of this Board since it began operations.[17]

---

[17]   *See* Privacy and Civil Liberties Oversight Board, Minutes of Open Meeting of March 5, 2013, at 6-7, *available at* http://www.pclob.gov/.

IV. What's Next?

While this Report includes a number of detailed conclusions and recommendations, it does not purport to answer all questions. The Board welcomes the opportunity for further dialogue within the executive branch and with Congress about the issues raised in this Report and how best to implement the Board's recommendations.

The Board's next report will consider the Section 702 program, addressing whether, in the Board's view, the program is consistent with statutory authority, complies with the Constitution, and strikes the appropriate balance between national security and privacy and civil liberties. That report will also be made available to the public.

Part 2:
EXECUTIVE SUMMARY

The statute creating the Privacy and Civil Liberties Oversight Board ("PCLOB" or "Board") directs the Board to analyze and review actions taken by the executive branch to protect the nation from terrorism, "ensuring that the need for such actions is balanced with the need to protect privacy and civil liberties."[18] In pursuit of this mission, the PCLOB has conducted an in-depth analysis of the bulk telephone records program operated by the National Security Agency ("NSA") under Section 215 of the USA PATRIOT Act ("Patriot Act"). The Board's examination has also included a review of the operation of the Foreign Intelligence Surveillance Court ("FISC" or "FISA court"). This Executive Summary outlines the Board's conclusions and recommendations.

I. Overview of the Report

A. Background: Description and History of the Section 215 Program

The NSA's telephone records program is operated under an order issued by the FISA court pursuant to Section 215 of the Patriot Act, an order that is renewed approximately every ninety days. The program is intended to enable the government to identify communications among known and unknown terrorism suspects, particularly those located inside the United States. When the NSA identifies communications that may be associated with terrorism, it issues intelligence reports to other federal agencies, such as the FBI, that work to prevent terrorist attacks. The FISC order authorizes the NSA to collect nearly all call detail records generated by certain telephone companies in the United States, and specifies detailed rules for the use and retention of these records. Call detail records typically include much of the information that appears on a customer's telephone bill: the date and time of a call, its duration, and the participating telephone numbers. Such information is commonly referred to as a type of "metadata." The records collected by the NSA under this program do not, however, include the content of any telephone conversation.

After collecting these telephone records, the NSA stores them in a centralized database. Initially, NSA analysts are permitted to access the Section 215 calling records only through "queries" of the database. A query is a search for a specific number or other selection term within the database. Before any specific number is used as the search target or "seed" for a query, one of twenty-two designated NSA officials must first determine that

---

18   42 U.S.C. § 2000ee(c)(1).

there is a reasonable, articulable suspicion ("RAS") that the number is associated with terrorism. Once the seed has been RAS-approved, NSA analysts may run queries that will return the calling records for that seed, and permit "contact chaining" to develop a fuller picture of the seed's contacts. Contact chaining enables analysts to retrieve not only the numbers directly in contact with the seed number (the "first hop"), but also numbers in contact with all first hop numbers (the "second hop"), as well as all numbers in contact with all second hop numbers (the "third hop").

The Section 215 telephone records program has its roots in counterterrorism efforts that originated in the immediate aftermath of the September 11 attacks. The NSA began collecting telephone metadata in bulk as one part of what became known as the President's Surveillance Program. From late 2001 through early 2006, the NSA collected bulk telephony metadata based upon presidential authorizations issued every thirty to forty-five days. In May 2006, the FISC first granted an application by the government to conduct the telephone records program under Section 215.[19] The government's application relied heavily on the reasoning of a 2004 FISA court opinion and order approving the bulk collection of Internet metadata under a different provision of FISA.[20]

On June 5, 2013, the British newspaper *The Guardian* published an article based on unauthorized disclosures of classified documents by Edward Snowden, a contractor for the NSA, which revealed the telephone records program to the public. On August 29, 2013, FISC Judge Claire Eagan issued an opinion explaining the court's rationale for approving the Section 215 telephone records program.[21] Although prior authorizations of the program had been accompanied by detailed orders outlining applicable rules and minimization procedures, this was the first judicial opinion explaining the FISA court's legal reasoning in authorizing the bulk records collection. The Section 215 program was reauthorized most recently by the FISC on January 3, 2014.

Over the years, a series of compliance issues were brought to the attention of the FISA court by the government. However, none of these compliance issues involved significant intentional misuse of the system. Nor has the Board seen any evidence of bad faith or misconduct on the part of any government officials or agents involved with the program.[22] Rather, the compliance issues were recognized by the FISC — and are

---

[19]   *See* Order, *In re Application of the Federal Bureau of Investigation for an Order Requiring the Production of Tangible Things*, No. BR 06-05 (FISA Ct. May 24, 2006).

[20]   *See* Opinion and Order, No. PR/TT [*redacted*] (FISA Ct.).

[21]   *See* Amended Memorandum Opinion, *In re Application of the Federal Bureau of Investigation for an Order Requiring the Production of Tangible Things*, No. BR 13-109 (FISA Ct. Aug. 29, 2013).

[22]   Neither has the Board seen any evidence that would suggest any telephone providers did not rely in good faith on orders of the FISC when producing metadata to the government.

recognized by the Board — as a product of the program's technological complexity and vast scope, illustrating the risks inherent in such a program.

B. Legal Analysis: Statutory and Constitutional Issues

Section 215 is designed to enable the FBI to acquire records that a business has in its possession, as part of an FBI investigation, when those records are relevant to the investigation. Yet the operation of the NSA's bulk telephone records program bears almost no resemblance to that description. While the Board believes that this program has been conducted in good faith to vigorously pursue the government's counterterrorism mission and appreciates the government's efforts to bring the program under the oversight of the FISA court, the Board concludes that Section 215 does not provide an adequate legal basis to support the program.

There are four grounds upon which we find that the telephone records program fails to comply with Section 215. First, the telephone records acquired under the program have no connection to any specific FBI investigation at the time of their collection. Second, because the records are collected in bulk — potentially encompassing all telephone calling records across the nation — they cannot be regarded as "relevant" to any FBI investigation as required by the statute without redefining the word relevant in a manner that is circular, unlimited in scope, and out of step with the case law from analogous legal contexts involving the production of records. Third, the program operates by putting telephone companies under an obligation to furnish new calling records on a daily basis as they are generated (instead of turning over records already in their possession) — an approach lacking foundation in the statute and one that is inconsistent with FISA as a whole. Fourth, the statute permits only the FBI to obtain items for use in its investigations; it does not authorize the NSA to collect anything.

In addition, we conclude that the program violates the Electronic Communications Privacy Act. That statute prohibits telephone companies from sharing customer records with the government except in response to specific enumerated circumstances, which do not include Section 215 orders.

Finally, we do not agree that the program can be considered statutorily authorized because Congress twice delayed the expiration of Section 215 during the operation of the program without amending the statute. The "reenactment doctrine," under which Congress is presumed to have adopted settled administrative or judicial interpretations of a statute, does not trump the plain meaning of a law, and cannot save an administrative or judicial interpretation that contradicts the statute itself. Moreover, the circumstances presented here differ in pivotal ways from any in which the reenactment doctrine has ever been applied, and applying the doctrine would undermine the public's ability to know what the law is and hold their elected representatives accountable for their legislative choices.

The NSA's telephone records program also raises concerns under both the First and Fourth Amendments to the United States Constitution. We explore these concerns and explain that while government officials are entitled to rely on existing Supreme Court doctrine in formulating policy, the existing doctrine does not fully answer whether the Section 215 telephone records program is constitutionally sound. In particular, the scope and duration of the program are beyond anything ever before confronted by the courts, and as a result of technological developments, the government possesses capabilities to collect, store, and analyze data not available when existing Supreme Court doctrine was developed. Without seeking to predict the direction of changes in Supreme Court doctrine, the Board urges as a policy matter that the government consider how to preserve underlying constitutional guarantees in the face of modern communications technology and surveillance capabilities.

C. Policy Implications of the Section 215 Program

The threat of terrorism faced today by the United States is real. The Section 215 telephone records program was intended as one tool to combat this threat — a tool that would help investigators piece together the networks of terrorist groups and the patterns of their communications with a speed and comprehensiveness not otherwise available. However, we conclude that the Section 215 program has shown minimal value in safeguarding the nation from terrorism. Based on the information provided to the Board, including classified briefings and documentation, we have not identified a single instance involving a threat to the United States in which the program made a concrete difference in the outcome of a counterterrorism investigation. Moreover, we are aware of no instance in which the program directly contributed to the discovery of a previously unknown terrorist plot or the disruption of a terrorist attack. And we believe that in only one instance over the past seven years has the program arguably contributed to the identification of an unknown terrorism suspect. Even in that case, the suspect was not involved in planning a terrorist attack and there is reason to believe that the FBI may have discovered him without the contribution of the NSA's program.

The Board's review suggests that where the telephone records collected by the NSA under its Section 215 program have provided value, they have done so primarily in two ways: by offering additional leads regarding the contacts of terrorism suspects already known to investigators, and by demonstrating that foreign terrorist plots do *not* have a U.S. nexus. The former can help investigators confirm suspicions about the target of an inquiry or about persons in contact with that target. The latter can help the intelligence community focus its limited investigatory resources by avoiding false leads and channeling efforts where they are needed most. But with respect to the former, our review suggests that the Section 215 program offers little unique value but largely duplicates the FBI's own information gathering efforts. And with respect to the latter, while the value of proper resource allocation in time-sensitive situations is not to be discounted, we question whether the American public should accept the government's routine collection of all of its telephone records because it helps in cases where there is no threat to the United States.

The Board also has analyzed the Section 215 program's implications for privacy and civil liberties and has concluded that they are serious. Because telephone calling records can reveal intimate details about a person's life, particularly when aggregated with other information and subjected to sophisticated computer analysis, the government's collection of a person's entire telephone calling history has a significant and detrimental effect on individual privacy. The circumstances of a particular call can be highly suggestive of its content, such that the mere record of a call potentially offers a window into the caller's private affairs. Moreover, when the government collects *all* of a person's telephone records, storing them for five years in a government database that is subject to high-speed digital searching and analysis, the privacy implications go far beyond what can be revealed by the metadata of a single telephone call.

Beyond such individual privacy intrusions, permitting the government to routinely collect the calling records of the entire nation fundamentally shifts the balance of power between the state and its citizens. With its powers of compulsion and criminal prosecution, the government poses unique threats to privacy when it collects data on its own citizens. Government collection of personal information on such a massive scale also courts the ever-present danger of "mission creep." An even more compelling danger is that personal information collected by the government will be misused to harass, blackmail, or intimidate, or to single out for scrutiny particular individuals or groups. To be clear, the Board has seen no evidence suggesting that anything of the sort is occurring at the NSA and the agency's incidents of non-compliance with the rules approved by the FISC have generally involved unintentional misuse. Yet, while the danger of abuse may seem remote, given historical abuse of personal information by the government during the twentieth century, the risk is more than merely theoretical.

Moreover, the bulk collection of telephone records can be expected to have a chilling effect on the free exercise of speech and association, because individuals and groups engaged in sensitive or controversial work have less reason to trust in the confidentiality of their relationships as revealed by their calling patterns. Inability to expect privacy vis-à-vis the government in one's telephone communications means that people engaged in wholly lawful activities — but who for various reasons justifiably do not wish the government to know about their communications — must either forgo such activities, reduce their frequency, or take costly measures to hide them from government surveillance. The telephone records program thus hinders the ability of advocacy organizations to communicate confidentially with members, donors, legislators, whistleblowers, members of the public, and others. For similar reasons, awareness that a record of all telephone calls is stored in a government database may have debilitating consequences for communication between journalists and sources.

To be sure, detailed rules currently in place limit the NSA's *use* of the telephone records it collects. These rules offer many valuable safeguards designed to curb the intrusiveness of the program. But in our view, they cannot fully ameliorate the implications for privacy, speech, and association that follow from the government's ongoing *collection* of virtually all telephone records of every American. Any governmental program that entails such costs requires a strong showing of efficacy. We do not believe the NSA's telephone records program conducted under Section 215 meets that standard.

D. Operation of the Foreign Intelligence Surveillance Court

Congress created the FISA court in 1978 in response to concerns about the abuse of electronic surveillance. This represented a major restructuring of the domestic conduct of foreign intelligence surveillance, with constitutional implications. Prior to then, successive Presidents had authorized national security wiretaps and other searches solely on the basis of their executive powers under Article II of the Constitution. The Foreign Intelligence Surveillance Act ("FISA") of 1978 provided a procedure under which the Attorney General could obtain a judicial warrant authorizing the use of electronic surveillance in the United States for foreign intelligence purposes.

Over time, the scope of FISA and the jurisdiction of the FISA court have evolved. Initially, the FISC's sole role was to approve individualized FISA warrants for electronic surveillance relating to a specific person, a specific place, or a specific communications account or device. Beginning in 2004, the role of the FISC changed when the government approached the court with its first request to approve a program involving what is now referred to as "bulk collection." In conducting this study, the Board was told by former FISA court judges that they were quite comfortable hearing only from government attorneys when evaluating individual surveillance requests but that the judges' decision making would be greatly enhanced if they could hear opposing views when ruling on requests to establish new surveillance programs.

Upon the FISC's receipt of a proposed application, a member of the court's legal staff will review the application and evaluate whether it meets the legal requirements under FISA. The FISC's legal staff are career employees who have developed substantial expertise in FISA, but they serve as staff to the judges rather than as advocates. While their role includes identifying any flaws in the government's statutory or constitutional analysis, it does not reach to contesting the government's arguments in the manner of an opposing party. The FISA court process for considering applications may include a hearing, and FISC judges have the authority to take testimony from government employees familiar with the technical details of an application. FISA does not provide a mechanism for the court to invite non-governmental parties to provide views on pending government applications or otherwise participate in FISC proceedings prior to approval of an application.

FISA also established a Foreign Intelligence Court of Review ("FISCR"), comprised of three judges drawn from U.S. district courts or courts of appeals. Appeals to the FISCR have been rare: thus far there have been only two decisions issued by the court. Electronic communications service providers have some limited ability to appeal FISC orders, but FISA does not provide a way for the FISCR to receive the views of other non-governmental parties on appeals pending before it.[23]

The FISC's *ex parte*, classified proceedings have raised concerns that the court does not take adequate account of positions other than those of the government. It is critical to the integrity of the process that the public has confidence in its impartiality and rigor. Therefore, the Board believes that some reforms are appropriate and would help bolster public confidence in the operation of the court. The most important reforms proposed by the Board are: (1) creation of a panel of private attorneys, Special Advocates, who can be brought into cases involving novel and significant issues by FISA court judges; (2) development of a process facilitating appellate review of such decisions; and (3) providing increased opportunity for the FISC to receive technical assistance and legal input from outside parties.

E. Transparency Issues

In a representative democracy, the tension between openness and secrecy is inevitable and complex. The challenges are especially acute in the area of intelligence collection, where the powers exercised by the government implicate fundamental rights and our enemies are constantly trying to understand our capabilities in order to avoid detection. In this context, both openness and secrecy are vital to our survival, and we must strive to develop and implement intelligence programs in ways that serve both values.

Transparency is one of the foundations of democratic governance. Our constitutional system of government relies upon the participation of an informed electorate. This in turn requires public access to information about the activities of the government. Transparency supports accountability. It is especially important with regard to activities of the government that affect the rights of individuals, where it is closely interlinked with redress for violations of rights. In the intelligence context, although a certain amount of secrecy is necessary, transparency regarding collection authorities and

---

[23]   However, the court has in one instance accepted amicus, or "friend of the court," briefs on a significant legal question pending before it.

their exercise can increase public confidence in the intelligence process and in the monumental decisions that our leaders make based on intelligence products.

In the aftermath of the Snowden disclosures, the government has released a substantial amount of information on the leaked government surveillance programs. Although there remains a deep well of distrust, these official disclosures have helped foster greater public understanding of government surveillance programs. However, to date the official disclosures relate almost exclusively to specific programs that had already been the subject of leaks, and we must be careful in citing these disclosures as object lessons for what additional transparency might be appropriate in the future.

The Board believes that the government must take the initiative and formulate long-term solutions that promote greater transparency for government surveillance policies more generally, in order to inform public debate on technology, national security, and civil liberties going beyond the current controversy. In this effort, all three branches have a role. For the executive branch, disclosures about key national security programs that involve the collection, storage and dissemination of personal information — such as the operation of the National Counterterrorism Center — show that it is possible to describe practices and policies publicly, even those that have not been otherwise leaked, without damage to national security or operational effectiveness.

With regard to the legislative process, even where classified intelligence operations are involved, the purposes and framework of a program for domestic intelligence collection should be debated in public. During the process of developing legislation, some hearings and briefings may need to be conducted in secret to ensure that policymakers fully understand the intended use of a particular authority. But the government should not base an ongoing program affecting the rights of Americans on an interpretation of a statute that is not apparent from a natural reading of the text. In the case of Section 215, the government should have made it publicly clear in the reauthorization process that it intended for Section 215 to serve as legal authority to collect data in bulk on an ongoing basis.

There is also a need for greater transparency regarding operation of the FISA court. Prospectively, we encourage the FISC judges to continue the recent practice of writing opinions with an eye to declassification, separating specific sensitive facts peculiar to the case at hand from broader legal analyses. We also believe that there is significant value in producing declassified versions of earlier opinions, and recommend that the government undertake a classification review of all significant FISC opinions and orders involving novel interpretations of law. We realize that the process of redacting opinions not drafted for public disclosure will be more difficult and will burden individuals with other pressing duties, but we believe that it is appropriate to make the effort where those opinions and orders complete the historical picture of the development of legal doctrine regarding matters within the jurisdiction of the FISA court. In addition, should the government adopt our recommendation for a Special Advocate in the FISC, the nature and extent of that advocate's role must be transparent to be effective.

It is also important to promote transparency through increased reporting to the public on the scope of surveillance programs. We urge the government to work with Internet service providers and other companies to reach agreement on standards allowing reasonable disclosures of aggregate statistics that would be meaningful without revealing sensitive government capabilities or tactics. We recommend that the government should also increase the level of detail in its unclassified reporting to Congress and the public regarding surveillance programs.

II.   Overview of the PCLOB's Recommendations

A. Section 215 Program

Recommendation 1: *The government should end its Section 215 bulk telephone records program.*

The Section 215 bulk telephone records program lacks a viable legal foundation under Section 215, implicates constitutional concerns under the First and Fourth Amendments, raises serious threats to privacy and civil liberties as a policy matter, and has shown only limited value. As a result, the Board recommends that the government end the program.

Without the current Section 215 program, the government would still be able to seek telephone calling records directly from communications providers through other existing legal authorities. The Board does not recommend that the government impose data retention requirements on providers in order to facilitate any system of seeking records directly from private databases.

Once the Section 215 bulk collection program has ended, the government should purge the database of telephone records that have been collected and stored during the program's operation, subject to limits on purging data that may arise under federal law or as a result of any pending litigation.

The Board also recommends against the enactment of legislation that would merely codify the existing program or any other program that collects bulk data on such a massive scale regarding individuals with no suspected ties to terrorism or criminal activity. Moreover, the Board's constitutional analysis should provide a message of caution, and as a policy matter, given the significant privacy and civil liberties interests at stake, if Congress seeks to provide legal authority for any new program, it should seek the least intrusive alternative and should not legislate to the outer bounds of its authority.

The Board recognizes that the government may need a short period of time to explore and institutionalize alternative approaches, and believes it would be appropriate for the government to wind down the 215 program over a brief interim period. If the government does find the need for a short wind-down period, the Board urges that it should follow the procedures under Recommendation 2 below.

Recommendation 2: *The government should immediately implement additional privacy safeguards in operating the Section 215 bulk collection program.*

The Board recommends that the government immediately implement several additional privacy safeguards to mitigate the privacy impact of the present Section 215 program. The recommended changes can be implemented without any need for congressional or FISC authorization. Specifically, the government should:

(a) reduce the retention period for the bulk telephone records program from five years to three years;

(b) reduce the number of "hops" used in contact chaining from three to two;

(c) submit the NSA's "reasonable articulable suspicion" determinations to the FISC for review after they have been approved by NSA and used to query the database; and

(d) require a "reasonable articulable suspicion" determination before analysts may submit queries to, or otherwise analyze, the "corporate store," which contains the results of contact chaining queries to the full "collection store."

B. FISA Court Operations

Recommendation 3: *Congress should enact legislation enabling the FISC to hear independent views, in addition to the government's views, on novel and significant applications and in other matters in which a FISC judge determines that consideration of the issues would merit such additional views.*

Congress should authorize the establishment of a panel of outside lawyers to serve as Special Advocates before the FISC in appropriate cases. The Presiding Judge of the FISC should select attorneys drawn from the private sector to serve on the panel. The attorneys should be capable of obtaining appropriate security clearances and would then be available to be called upon to participate in certain FISC proceedings.

The decision as to whether the Special Advocate would participate in any particular matter should be left to the discretion of the FISC. The Board expects that the court would invite the Special Advocate to participate in matters involving interpretation of the scope of surveillance authorities, other matters presenting novel legal or technical questions, or matters involving broad programs of collection. The role of the Special Advocate, when invited by the court to participate, would be to make legal arguments addressing privacy, civil rights, and civil liberties interests. The Special Advocate would review the government's application and exercise his or her judgment about whether the proposed surveillance or collection is consistent with law or unduly affects privacy and civil liberties interests.

Recommendation 4: *Congress should enact legislation to expand the opportunities for appellate review of FISC decisions by the FISCR and for review of FISCR decisions by the Supreme Court of the United States.*

Providing for greater appellate review of FISC and FISCR rulings will strengthen the integrity of judicial review under FISA. Providing a role for the Special Advocate in seeking that appellate review will further increase public confidence in the integrity of the process.

Recommendation 5: *The FISC should take full advantage of existing authorities to obtain technical assistance and expand opportunities for legal input from outside parties.*

FISC judges should take advantage of their ability to appoint Special Masters or other technical experts to assist them in reviewing voluminous or technical materials, either in connection with initial applications or in compliance reviews. In addition, the FISC and the FISCR should develop procedures to facilitate amicus participation by third parties in cases involving questions that are of broad public interest, where it is feasible to do so consistent with national security.

C. Promoting Transparency

Recommendation 6: *To the maximum extent consistent with national security, the government should create and release with minimal redactions declassified versions of new decisions, orders and opinions by the FISC and FISCR in cases involving novel interpretations of FISA or other significant questions of law, technology or compliance.*

FISC judges should continue their recent practice of drafting opinions in cases involving novel issues and other significant decisions in the expectation that declassified versions will be released to the public. The government should promptly create and release declassified versions of these FISC opinions.

> **Recommendation 7:** *Regarding previously written opinions, the government should perform a declassification review of decisions, orders and opinions by the FISC and FISCR that have not yet been released to the public and that involve novel interpretations of FISA or other significant questions of law, technology or compliance.*

Although it may be more difficult to declassify older FISC opinions drafted without expectation of public release, the release of such older opinions is still important to facilitate public understanding of the development of the law under FISA. The government should create and release declassified versions of older opinions in novel or significant cases to the greatest extent possible consistent with protection of national security. This should cover programs that have been discontinued, where the legal interpretations justifying such programs have ongoing relevance.

> **Recommendation 8:** *The Attorney General should regularly and publicly report information regarding the operation of the Special Advocate program recommended by the Board. This should include statistics on the frequency and nature of Special Advocate participation in FISC and FISCR proceedings.*

These reports should include statistics showing the number of cases in which a Special Advocate participated, as well as the number of cases identified by the government as raising a novel or significant issue, but in which the judge declined to invite Special Advocate participation. The reports should also indicate the extent to which FISC decisions have been subject to review in the FISCR and the frequency with which Special Advocate requests for FISCR review have been granted.

> **Recommendation 9:** *The government should work with Internet service providers and other companies that regularly receive FISA production orders to develop rules permitting the companies to voluntarily disclose certain statistical information. In addition, the government should publicly disclose more detailed statistics to provide a more complete picture of government surveillance operations.*

The Board urges the government to pursue discussions with communications service providers to determine the maximum amount of information that companies could voluntarily publish to show the extent of government surveillance requests they receive per year in a way that is consistent with protection of national security. In addition, the government should itself release annual reports showing in more detail the nature and scope of FISA surveillance for each year.

Recommendation 10: *The Attorney General should fully inform the PCLOB of the government's activities under FISA and provide the PCLOB with copies of the detailed reports submitted under FISA to the specified committees of Congress. This should include providing the PCLOB with copies of the FISC decisions required to be produced under Section 601(a)(5).*[24]

Recommendation 11: *The Board urges the government to begin developing principles and criteria for transparency.*

The Board urges the Administration to commence the process of articulating principles and criteria for deciding what must be kept secret and what can be released as to existing and future programs that affect the American public.

Recommendation 12: *The scope of surveillance authorities affecting Americans should be public.*

In particular, the Administration should develop principles and criteria for the public articulation of the legal authorities under which it conducts surveillance affecting Americans. If the text of the statute itself is not sufficient to inform the public of the scope of asserted government authority, then the key elements of the legal opinion or other documents describing the government's legal analysis should be made public so there can be a free and open debate regarding the law's scope. This includes both original enactments such as 215's revisions and subsequent reauthorizations. While sensitive operational details regarding the conduct of government surveillance programs should remain classified, and while legal interpretations of the application of a statute in a particular case may also be secret so long as the use of that technique in a particular case is secret, the government's interpretations of statutes that provide the basis for ongoing surveillance programs affecting Americans can and should be made public.

---

[24] Section 601(a)(5), which is codified at 50 U.S.C. § 1871(a)(5), requires the congressional intelligence and judiciary committees to be provided with decisions, orders, and opinions from the FISC, and from its companion appellate court, that include significant construction or interpretation of FISA provisions.

Part 3:
DESCRIPTION OF THE NSA SECTION 215 PROGRAM

I.   Telephone Calling Records

When a person completes a telephone call, telephone company equipment generates a record of certain details about that call. These "call detail records" typically include much of the information that appears on a customer's telephone bill: the date and time of a call, its duration, and the participating telephone numbers. Such records also can include a range of technical information about how the call was routed from one participant to the other through the infrastructure of the telephone companies' networks. Telephone companies create these records in order to bill customers for their calls, detect fraud, and for other business purposes.

While calling records provide information about particular telephone calls, they do not include the contents of any telephone conversations. Because these records provide information about a communication but not the communication itself, they often are referred to as a form of "metadata," a word sometimes defined as "data about data." Call detail records often are called "telephony metadata."

After generating calling records in the normal course of business, telephone companies keep them on file for varying periods of time. Federal regulations presently require the companies to retain toll billing records for a minimum of eighteen months.[25]

II.   What the NSA Collects under Section 215 of the Patriot Act

The Foreign Intelligence Surveillance Act ("FISA") includes a "business records" provision that allows the FBI to obtain books, records, papers, documents, and other items that may be relevant to a counterterrorism investigation. To obtain such records under this provision, the FBI must file an application with the Foreign Intelligence Surveillance Court ("FISC" or "FISA court") requesting that the court issue an order directing a person or entity to turn over the items sought.[26] The business records provision of FISA was significantly expanded by Section 215 of the Patriot Act in 2001, and as a result it frequently is referred to as Section 215.[27] Under a program authorized by the FISA court pursuant to Section 215, the NSA is permitted to obtain all call detail records generated by

---

25   *See* 47 C.F.R. § 42.6.

26   *See* 50 U.S.C. § 1861(a)(1), (b)(2)(A). See also pages 40 to 42 of this Report for a more detailed discussion of FISA's business records provision.

27   *See* Pub. L. No. 107-56, § 215, 115 Stat. 272, 287 (2001) (codified as amended at 50 U.S.C. § 1861).

certain telephone companies in the United States. The FISA court has determined that Section 215 provides a legal basis to order the telephone companies to facilitate this program by supplying the NSA with their calling records.[28]

Under the FISA court's orders, certain telephone companies must provide the NSA with "all call detail records" generated by those companies.[29] Because the companies are directed to supply virtually all of their calling records to the NSA, the FISA court's orders result in the production of call detail records for a large volume of telephone communications; the NSA has described its program as enabling "comprehensive" analysis of telephone communications "that cross different providers and telecommunications networks."[30] The vast majority of the records obtained are for purely domestic calls, meaning those calls in which both participants are located within the United States, including local calls.

The calling records provided to the NSA do not identify which individual is associated with any particular telephone number: they do not include the name, address, or financial information of any telephone subscriber or customer. (Such information can be obtained by the government through other means, however, including reverse telephone directories and subpoenas issued to the telephone companies.) Nor do the records, as noted, include the spoken contents of any telephone conversation.[31] In other words, the NSA is not able to listen to any telephone calls under the authority provided by these orders.

In addition, the calling records that the NSA collects under its Section 215 program do not currently include "cell site location information." That information, unique to mobile phones, is a component of a call detail record that shows which cell phone tower a mobile phone is connecting with. Thus it can be used to track the geographic location of a mobile phone user at that time the user places or receives a call. At the NSA's request, telephone companies remove that information from their calling records before transmitting the

---

[28]   *See* Amended Memorandum Opinion, *In re Application of the Federal Bureau of Investigation for an Order Requiring the Production of Tangible Things*, No. BR 13-109 (FISA Ct. Aug. 29, 2013); Memorandum, *In re Application of the Federal Bureau of Investigation for an Order Requiring the Production of Tangible Things*, No. BR 13-158 (FISA Ct. Oct. 11, 2013). See pages 40 to 46 of this Report for a description of the FISA court's initial approval of the NSA's telephone records program under Section 215.

[29]   Primary Order at 3, *In re Application of the Federal Bureau of Investigation for an Order Requiring the Production of Tangible Things*, No. BR 13-158 (FISA Ct. Oct. 11, 2013) ("Primary Order"). At least one telephone company presently is ordered to provide less than all of its call detail records. *See id.* at 3-4.

[30]   *See* Declaration of Teresa H. Shea, Signals Intelligence Director, National Security Agency, ¶¶ 59-60, *ACLU v. Clapper*, No. 13-3994 (S.D.N.Y. Oct. 1, 2013) ("Shea Decl.").

[31]   *See* Primary Order at 3 n.1 (noting that "[t]elephony metadata does not include the substantive content of any communication, as defined by 18 U.S.C. § 2510(8)"). Section 2510(8) defines "content" as "any information concerning the substance, purport, or meaning of that communication." 18 U.S.C. § 2510(8).

records to the NSA.[32] In the past, the NSA has collected a limited amount of cell site location information to test the feasibility of incorporating such information into its Section 215 program, but that information has not been used for intelligence analysis, and the government has stated that the agency does not now collect it under this program.

Some information obtained by the NSA under Section 215 could nevertheless provide a general indication of a caller's geographic location. For instance, the area code and prefix of a landline telephone number can indicate the general area from which a call is sent. The same may be true of the "trunk identifier" associated with a telephone call, which pinpoints a segment of the communication line that connects two telephones during a conversation.[33]

III.   Delivery of Calling Records from Telephone Companies to the NSA

Approximately every ninety days, the government files an application with the FISA court requesting that the telephone companies be ordered to continue providing their calling records to the NSA for another ninety days. These applications are signed by officials from the FBI, as required by Section 215, but they typically note that the FBI is seeking the production of telephone records to the NSA. Accordingly, the FISA court's orders direct the telephone companies to "produce to NSA" their calling records.[34]

When the FISA court approves the government's applications to renew the program, the court issues a "primary order" outlining the scope of what each telephone company must furnish to the NSA and the conditions under which the government can use, retain, and disseminate the data. At the same time, the court issues individual "secondary orders" separately addressed to each telephone company, directing it to comply with those terms and produce its records to the NSA.[35] After receiving a secondary order, a telephone company must continue the production of its records "on an ongoing daily basis" for the

---

[32]   Amended Memorandum Opinion, *In re Application of the Federal Bureau of Investigation for an Order Requiring the Production of Tangible Things*, at 4 n.5, No. BR 13-109 (FISA Ct. Aug. 29, 2013); *see also* Declaration of Acting Assistant Director Robert J. Holley, Federal Bureau of Investigation, ¶ 5, *ACLU v. Clapper*, No. 13-3994 (S.D.N.Y. Oct. 1, 2013) ("Holley Decl.") (stating that metadata obtained under the orders does not include cell site location information). Agency personnel check this portion of incoming records to ensure that cell site location information has been removed.

[33]   *See* Primary Order at 3 n.1 (noting that for purposes of the order, "telephony metadata" includes the "trunk identifier" for a call).

[34]   Primary Order at 3.

[35]   *See, e.g.*, Secondary Order, *In re Application of the Federal Bureau of Investigation for an Order Requiring the Production of Tangible Things*, No. BR 13-80 (FISA Ct. Apr. 25, 2013) ("Secondary Order").

ninety-day duration of the order.[36] The company may not disclose to anyone that it has received such an order.[37]

Each telephone company must furnish the NSA with "an electronic copy" of its calling records.[38] Companies transmit those records to the NSA, which stores them "in repositories within secure networks."[39]

Telephone companies must provide their calling records to the NSA on a daily basis until the expiration date of each FISA court order. In other words, when the companies are served with an order from the FISC, they do not hand over to the NSA the calling records they have in their possession at that time. Instead, over the next ninety days, they must provide the NSA with the new calling records that they generate each day.

IV.   How the NSA Stores and Handles the Telephone Records

When the records of particular telephone calls reach the NSA, the agency stores and processes those records in repositories within secure networks under its control.[40] Upon the arrival of new records at the NSA, agency technical personnel perform a number of steps to ensure that the records, which come from different telephone companies, are in a standard format compatible with the NSA's databases. The agency is permitted to duplicate the data it receives for storage in recovery back-up systems.[41]

---

[36]   Primary Order at 3-4; *id.* at 17 (indicating duration of the order).

[37]   Every "secondary order" delivered to the telephone companies directing them to provide calling records to the NSA prohibits the companies from publicly disclosing the existence of the order and tightly limits the persons with whom that information may be shared. Specifically, the secondary orders direct that, with three exceptions, "no person shall disclose to any other person that the FBI or NSA has sought or obtained tangible things under this Order." Secondary Order at 2. The personnel who receive a secondary order on behalf of the telephone companies are permitted to disclose its existence only to (1) "those persons to whom disclosure is necessary to comply with such Order," (2) "an attorney to obtain legal advice or assistance with respect to the production of things in response to the Order," and (3) "other persons as permitted by the Director of the FBI or the Director's designee." *Id.* Any person to whom disclosure is made under one of these exceptions must be informed of the limitations set forth above. *Id.* at 3. Furthermore, any person who makes or intends to make a disclosure under the first or third exception above (*i.e.*, a disclosure to anyone except to an attorney for legal assistance) must, at the request of the FBI director or his designee, "identify to the Director or such designee the person to whom such disclosure will be made or to whom such disclosure was made prior to the request." *Id.* at 3.

[38]   Primary Order at 3-4.

[39]   Primary Order at 4.

[40]   Primary Order at 4.

[41]   *See* Primary Order at 4-5 n.2. Should it ever be necessary to recover data that is stored in these back-up systems, "in the event of any natural disaster, man-made emergency, attack, or other unforeseen event," the FISA court's orders appear to require that any access or use of the back-up data be conducted in compliance with the same rules that ordinarily govern utilization of the records. *Id.*

Once the calling records are properly formatted, NSA houses them within its data repositories. At this point, technical personnel may take additional measures to make the calling records usable for intelligence analysis, including removing "high volume" telephone identifiers and other unwanted data.[42]

The NSA is required to limit who has access to the calling records it obtains. The agency must restrict access to authorized personnel who have received training on the use of those records. [43] Such personnel can include both NSA employees and other individuals who are working under the NSA Director's control on Signals Intelligence.[44] The calling records are routed to dedicated portions of NSA's systems and are required to carry unique data markings enabling software and other controls to restrict access to the authorized personnel who have received the proper training and guidance.[45] Training is required both for intelligence analysts and for the technical personnel who access the data to make it usable for analysis.[46]

Calling records must be deleted from the NSA's repositories no later than five years after the agency receives them.[47] If a calling record shows up in a "query" performed by an analyst, however — a process described below — the information about that call need not be destroyed after five years.

V. How the NSA Analyzes the Telephone Records

The NSA uses the calling records it obtains under Section 215 to attempt to identify communications among known and unknown terrorism suspects, particularly those located inside the United States.[48] When the NSA identifies communications or telephone numbers of interest, it issues intelligence reports to other federal agencies, such as the FBI,

---

[42]   Primary Order at 6.

[43]   Primary Order at 5.

[44]   *See* Primary Order at 6 n.5 (requiring that all personnel engaged in signals intelligence operations be "under the direction, authority, or control" of the director of the NSA).

[45]   Primary Order at 4-5.

[46]   Primary Order at 5. The training requirements do not, however, extend to all technical personnel who might have access to the records, including those responsible for "NSA's underlying corporate infrastructure and the transmission of the BR metadata from the specified persons to NSA." *Id.* at 5 n.3.

[47]   Primary Order at 14.

[48]   *See* Shea Decl. ¶ 8 (stating that "by analyzing telephony metadata based on telephone numbers associated with terrorist activities, trained expert intelligence analysts can work to determine whether known or suspected terrorists have been in contact with individuals in the U.S."). The records of domestic and international calls — where one or both participants are inside the United States — are viewed as the most "analytically significant" by the agency, which sees them as "particularly likely" to identify suspects in the United States who are planning domestic attacks. Shea Decl. ¶ 9.

that work to prevent terrorist attacks. In carrying out this endeavor, the NSA is required by the FISA court to adhere to certain "minimization" requirements, described below, that govern the manner in which the calling records may be used within the agency and disseminated outside of it.[49]

The NSA is prohibited from using the calling records it obtains under the FISA court's orders except as specified in those orders.[50] The vast majority of the records the NSA collects are never seen by any person.[51]

The rules governing the NSA's access to the calling records under the FISA court's orders are set forth below.

A. Contact Chaining and the Query Process

Analysis of calling records under this program begins with telephone numbers that already are suspected of being associated with terrorism. The NSA then searches for other telephone numbers that have been in contact with a suspected number, or in contact with those who have been in contact with a suspected number.[52]

Initially, NSA analysts are permitted to access the Section 215 calling records only through "queries" of the database. A query is a software-enabled search for a specific number or other selection term within the database.[53] When an analyst performs a query of a telephone number, for instance, the software interfaces with the database and provides results to the analyst that include a record of calls in which that number participated.

Analysts perform these queries to facilitate what is called "contact chaining" — the process of identifying the connections among individuals through their calls with each other.[54] The goals of contact chaining are to identify unknown terrorist operatives through

---

[49]   *See* Primary Order at 4.

[50]   *See* Primary Order at 4.

[51]   Shea Decl. ¶ 23.

[52]   Calling records may be searched or identified using numbers other than a "telephone number" as that term is normally used — *i.e.*, a number associated with a specific telephone that another caller can dial in order to reach that phone. The records may also include other unique numbers that are associated with a particular telephone user or a particular communications device. Among these are a telephone calling card number, which is used to pay for individual telephone calls, and an International Mobile station Equipment Identity ("IMEI") number, which is uniquely associated with a particular mobile telephone. *See* Primary Order at 3 n.1 (explaining that telephony metadata includes IMEI numbers, IMSI numbers, and calling card numbers).

[53]   Analysts can search the database using numbers, words, or symbols that uniquely identify a particular caller or device, like a telephone number or a calling card number. These types of selection terms are referred to as "identifiers." But analysts also can search for selection terms that are not uniquely associated with any particular caller or device.

[54]   Primary Order at 6.

their contacts with known suspects, discover links between known suspects, and monitor the pattern of communications among suspects.[55] Presently, the only purpose for which NSA analysts are permitted to search the Section 215 calling records housed in the agency's database is to conduct queries as described above, which are designed to build contact chains leading outward from a target to other telephone numbers.[56] The NSA has stated that it does not conduct pattern-based searches. Instead, every search begins with a specific telephone number or other specific selection term.[57]

B. Standards for Approving Queries

A telephone number (or other selection term) used to search the calling records is referred to as a "seed."[58] Before analysts can search the records with that seed, one of twenty-two designated NSA officials must give approval.[59] Such approval can be granted only if the official determines that there is reasonable, articulable suspicion that the selection term is associated with terrorism: in the words of the FISA court orders, a term can be approved for use as a seed only after the designated official has determined that, "based on the factual and practical considerations of everyday life on which reasonable and prudent persons act, there are facts giving rise to a reasonable, articulable suspicion" that the number "is associated with" a terrorist organization identified in the FISA court's orders.[60]

The requirement that analysts have "reasonable articulable suspicion" before searching the database with a particular number is often referred to as the "RAS" standard. It is designed in part "to prevent any general browsing of data."[61] Government lawyers have characterized this standard as "the cornerstone minimization procedure" that "ensures the overall reasonableness" of the program.[62]

---

[55]   *See* Shea Decl. ¶ 8.

[56]   Primary Order at 6.

[57]   As described below, however, different standards govern how NSA analysts may access and analyze the *results* of these searches.

[58]   Primary Order at 6.

[59]   Primary Order at 7.

[60]   Primary Order at 7. NSA analysts may also perform queries of the calling records using numbers that are, at the time, the subject of electronic surveillance authorized by the FISA court, based on the court's finding of probable cause to believe that the number is used by an agent of a specified terrorist organization. Primary Order at 9. Analysts may query only those numbers that have received an individual probable cause determination by the FISA court, not numbers that are being monitored with FISA court approval pursuant the broader authorities conferred by Sections 702, 703, or 704 of the FISA Amendments Act. *Id.* at 9-10.

[61]   Shea Decl. ¶ 20.

[62]   Report of the United States at 23, *In re Application of the Federal Bureau of Investigation for an Order Requiring the Production of Tangible Things*, No. BR 09-09 (FISA Ct. Aug. 17, 2009).

The FISA court orders approving the Section 215 program do not explain what it means for a selection term, like a telephone number, to be "associated with" a designated terrorist organization. The NSA has developed internal criteria to implement this standard, however. To take a simple example illustrating one of these criteria, intelligence reports might indicate that a particular person has communicated by email with a known terrorism suspect in furtherance of terrorist activity. Other intelligence reports might provide a telephone number believed to be used by that person. Together, these pieces of information would provide reasonable articulable suspicion that the telephone number is associated with terrorism.

If a telephone number or other selection term is "reasonably believed" to be used by a U.S. person, the FISA court's orders specify that it may not be regarded as associated with a terrorist organization solely "on the basis of activities that are protected by the First Amendment to the Constitution."[63] In implementing this requirement, the NSA presumes that, absent information to the contrary, any U.S. telephone number is used by a U.S. person. Because this restriction prohibits the NSA only from using First Amendment–protected activity as the *sole* basis for regarding a number as associated with terrorism, the agency may consider activities such as participating a public rally, attending a particular place of worship, expressing political views on the Internet, or buying a particular book — as long as those activities are not the *exclusive* basis for the agency's assessment.

The information on which the NSA's RAS determinations are based comes from several sources, including other federal agencies. In some instances, other agencies specifically request that the NSA conduct analysis of particular telephone numbers.[64]

After a selection term has been approved for use as a "seed" — based on a determination that it is reasonably suspected of being associated with a specified terrorist organization — that approval is effective for one year, meaning that repeated queries using that seed can be made for the next year. Approval lasts only six months, however, if the term is reasonably believed to be used by a U.S. person.[65]

C. How Queries Are Conducted and What They Produce

There are two methods through which the NSA is permitted to "query" the Section 215 calling records for analytic purposes with approved selection terms.

The first method is a manual process performed by individual analysts. In a "manual analyst query," an individual analyst working at a computer terminal personally enters an approved seed term into the agency's database software. The software searches the

---

[63]   Primary Order at 9.

[64]   *See, e.g.*, Holley Decl. ¶ 16 (referring to information requests by the FBI).

[65]   Primary Order at 10.

records obtained by the agency under Section 215 and returns those records that are within one "hop" of the seed (*i.e.*, all of the telephone numbers directly in contact with the seed). The analyst may then review the telephone numbers found to be in contact with a first-hop number (*i.e.*, within two hops of the seed) and the telephone numbers found to be in contact with a second-hop number (*i.e.*, within three hops of the seed).[66]

If analysts try to look beyond the third hop of a query, or to perform a query of a selection term that has not been RAS approved, the NSA's software is designed to prevent the action from being completed.[67]

The results gathered by the NSA's software show the web of telephone connections emanating outward from the seed, up to three links away from it. For every connection that is represented in these links, the software provides the associated information about the telephone calls involved, such as their date, time of day, and duration.

An analyst's query, therefore, provides access to more than the calling records of a seed number that is reasonably suspected being associated with terrorism. The query also gives the analyst access to the complete calling records of every number that has been in direct contact with the seed number. It further gives the analyst access to the complete calling records of every number that has been in contact with one of those numbers. To put it another way, an analyst who performs a query of a suspected number is able to view the records of calls involving telephone numbers that had contact with a telephone number that had contact with another telephone number that had contact with the original target.

If a seed number has seventy-five direct contacts, for instance, and each of these first-hop contact has seventy-five new contacts of its own, then each query would provide the government with the complete calling records of 5,625 telephone numbers. And if each of those second-hop numbers has seventy-five new contacts of its own, a single query would result in a batch of calling records involving over 420,000 telephone numbers.

Calling records that fall within the results of a query are not deleted after five years. The results can be stored by the analyst who performed the query and may then be analyzed for intelligence purposes and shared with others, inside and outside the NSA, under rules described below. The results may be searched using terms that are not RAS-approved, subjected to other analytic methods or techniques besides querying, or integrated with records obtained by the NSA under other authorities.

---

[66]   *See* Shea Decl. ¶ 22.

[67]   The NSA is directed by the FISA court to "ensure, through adequate and appropriate technical and management controls, that queries of the BR metadata for intelligence analysis purposes will be initiated using only a selection term that has been RAS-approved." Primary Order at 6-7. NSA's technical controls are designed to preclude any query for intelligence analysis purposes using a seed that lacks RAS approval.

In 2012, the FISA court approved a new and automated method of performing queries, one that is associated with a new infrastructure implemented by the NSA to process its calling records.[68] The essence of this new process is that, instead of waiting for individual analysts to perform manual queries of particular selection terms that have been RAS approved, the NSA's database periodically performs queries on all RAS-approved seed terms, up to three hops away from the approved seeds. The database places the results of these queries together in a repository called the "corporate store."

The ultimate result of the automated query process is a repository, the corporate store, containing the records of all telephone calls that are within three "hops" of every currently approved selection term.[69] Authorized analysts looking to conduct intelligence analysis may then use the records in the corporate store, instead of searching the full repository of records.[70]

According to the FISA court's orders, records that have been moved into the corporate store may be searched by authorized personnel "for valid foreign intelligence purposes, without the requirement that those searches use only RAS-approved selection terms."[71] Analysts therefore can query the records in the corporate store with terms that are not reasonably suspected of association with terrorism. They also are permitted to analyze records in the corporate store through means other than individual contact-chaining queries that begin with a single selection term: because the records in the corporate store all stem from RAS-approved queries, the agency is allowed to apply other analytic methods and techniques to the query results.[72] For instance, such calling records may be integrated with data acquired under other authorities for further analysis. The FISA court's orders expressly state that the NSA may apply "the full range" of signals intelligence analytic tradecraft to the calling records that are responsive to a query, which includes every record in the corporate store.[73]

If the NSA queries around 300 seed numbers a year, as it did in 2012, then based on the estimates provided earlier about the number of records produced in response to a

---

[68]   This "automated query process" was first approved for use by the FISA court in late 2012. Primary Order at 11 n.11.

[69]   *See* Primary Order at 11.

[70]   Under the manual query process, by contrast, analysts access the main collection repository, which contains all telephone records obtained under Section 215, but software controls are designed to prevent analysts from viewing records not linked to an RAS-approved number.

[71]   Primary Order at 11.

[72]   *See* Primary Order at 13 n.15.

[73]   Primary Order at 13 n.15.

single query, the corporate store would contain records involving over 120 million telephone numbers.[74]

The FISA court's orders call for audit capability with respect to all queries of the call detail records.[75] This requirement of an auditable record does not apply, however, "to the results of RAS-approved queries."[76] Therefore, when analysts access records that have turned up within three hops of a selection term — whether through a manual analyst query or by searching the corporate store — the court's orders do not impose a requirement that their actions be recorded or subject to audit, though other rules governing the NSA may impose this requirement.

VI.   What the NSA Does with Information Obtained from the Telephone Records

By analyzing telephone calling records obtained under Section 215, the NSA seeks to identify counterterrorism information that is of investigative value to other intelligence and law enforcement agencies such as the FBI.[77] Such information could indicate that there have been communications between known or suspected terrorist operatives overseas and persons within the United States, or among suspects within the United States, which could assist in detecting people in the United States who may be acting in furtherance of a foreign terrorist organization.[78]

Information obtained by NSA analysts through querying the calling records — the telephone connections, the associated details of each telephone call identified, and other intelligence gleaned derived from these sources — may be shared for intelligence purposes among NSA analysts who have received "appropriate and adequate training and guidance regarding the procedures and restrictions for the handling and dissemination of such information," according to the FISA court.[79]

Once the NSA has identified information believed to have potential counterterrorism value, it passes that information on to other federal agencies, including the FBI. Before the NSA may share information it obtains from the calling records outside

---

[74]   While fewer than 300 identifiers were used to query the call detail records in 2012, that number "has varied over the years." Shea Decl. ¶ 24.

[75]   *See* Primary Order at 7 ("Whenever the BR metadata is accessed for foreign intelligence analysis purposes or using foreign intelligence analysis query tools, an auditable record of the activity shall be generated.").

[76]   Primary Order at 7 n.6.

[77]   Shea Decl. ¶ 26.

[78]   Shea Decl. ¶¶ 16, 28.

[79]   Primary Order at 12-13.

the agency, it must apply to that information the minimization procedures of Section 7 of United States Signals Intelligence Directive SP0018 ("USSID 18"), which prescribes rules for the dissemination of information about U.S. persons in order to ensure that the NSA's activities are conducted consistent with law and the Fourth Amendment to the Constitution.[80]

Additionally, before the NSA may disseminate any "U.S. person information" outside the agency, one of five designated high-level NSA officials must determine that the information "is in fact related to counterterrorism information" and that it "is necessary to understand the counterterrorism information or assess its importance."[81]

The FBI can use the information it receives from the NSA to guide its investigations into terrorist operatives and threats inside the United States. When the FBI receives information that was obtained through Section 215, the Bureau is ordered by the FISA court to follow the minimization procedures set forth in the *Attorney General's Guidelines for Domestic FBI Operations* (Sept. 29, 2008).[82]

Other federal agencies also receive information from the NSA that was obtained through Section 215, but the FISA court's orders do not establish rules for how those agencies must handle the information they receive.[83] In addition, the government has informed the FISA court that it may provide telephone numbers derived from the program to "appropriate . . . foreign government agencies."[84]

The NSA tracks the number of reports it provides to other agencies and the number of telephone numbers identified as investigative leads in those reports. During the first three years in which the telephone records program was authorized by the FISA court (between May 2006 and May 2009), the NSA "provided to the FBI and/or other intelligence

---

[80]   Primary Order at 13; *see* United States Signals Intelligence Directive SP0018 (Jan. 25, 2011), *available at* http://icontherecord.tumblr.com/.

[81]   Primary Order at 13. The agency also may share such information with "Executive Branch personnel" for specific oversight purposes, namely in order to (1) permit those personnel "to determine whether the information contains exculpatory or impeachment information or is otherwise discoverable in legal proceedings," or (2) permit those personnel "to facilitate their lawful oversight functions." *Id.* at 13-14.

[82]   *See* Primary Order at 4.

[83]   *See* Primary Order; *see also* Shea Decl. ¶ 26 (reporting that the agency analyzes the call detail records to find information that would be of investigative value to the FBI "or other intelligence agencies"). The text of Section 215 appears to require that all federal officers and employees who receive information acquired from the calling records adhere to the Attorney General's guidelines, *see* 50 U.S.C. § 1861(h), but such a requirement is not explicit in the FISA court's orders.

[84]   *See* Memorandum of Law in Support of Application for Certain Tangible Things for Investigations to Protect Against International Terrorism, at 15, *In re Application of the Federal Bureau of Investigation for an Order Requiring the Production of Tangible Things*, No. BR 06-05 (FISA Ct. May 23, 2006).

agencies a total of 277 reports containing approximately 2,900 telephone identifiers that the NSA had identified."[85]

VII.　Internal Oversight and Reporting to the FISA Court

Monitoring of the NSA's compliance with the FISA court's orders is undertaken by the NSA and the National Security Division of the Department of Justice, which periodically must report certain information to the court. The details of these oversight requirements are set forth below.

First, the NSA must enforce rules on which of its personnel have access to the calling records and information extracted from the calling records. Both groups of personnel must receive training tailored to their respective privileges. Specifically, the NSA's Office of General Counsel and its Office of the Director of Compliance are ordered to "ensure that personnel with access to the BR metadata receive appropriate and adequate training and guidance regarding the procedures and restrictions for collection, storage, analysis, dissemination, and retention of the BR metadata and the results of queries of the BR metadata."[86] Those two offices "shall further ensure that all NSA personnel who receive query results in any form first receive appropriate and adequate training and guidance regarding the procedures and restrictions for the handling and dissemination of such information."[87] The NSA is directed to maintain records of all such training and to provide the Justice Department ("DOJ") with copies of "all formal briefing and/or training materials" used to "brief/train NSA personnel."[88]

Second, the NSA must take certain steps to ensure the effectiveness of the measures it has put in place to limit access to the calling records. Specifically, the agency's Office of the Director of Compliance is tasked with monitoring the software and other technical controls that restrict the work of NSA personnel, as well as the agency's logging, for auditing purposes, of instances in which personnel access the records.[89]

Third, the NSA must cooperate with the DOJ regarding how it interprets and implements the FISA court's orders authorizing the program. Specifically, the NSA's Office

---

[85]　　Shea Decl. ¶ 26.

[86]　　Primary Order at 14. The government uses the term "BR metadata" to refer to the business records metadata acquired under the Section 215 program.

[87]　　Primary Order at 14.

[88]　　Primary Order at 14-15. The FISA court's orders do not specify what this training must consist of, stating instead that "[t]he nature of the training that is appropriate and adequate for a particular person will depend on the person's responsibilities and the circumstances of his access to the BR metadata or the results from any queries of the metadata." *Id.* at 14 n.17.

[89]　　Primary Order at 15.

of General Counsel is to consult with the Department of Justice on "all significant legal opinions that relate to the interpretation, scope, and/or implementation" of the program. [90] At least once during every ninety-day authorization period, NSA and DOJ representatives are required to meet "for the purpose of assessing compliance" with the FISA court's orders, including "a review of NSA's monitoring and assessment to ensure that only approved metadata is being acquired." The results of this meeting must be put in writing and submitted to the FISA court as part of any request to renew or reinstate authority for the program.[91] During every authorization period, DOJ personnel also must meet with the inspector general of the NSA "to discuss their respective oversight responsibilities and assess NSA's compliance with the Court's orders."[92] And at least once during each authorization period, officials from the DOJ and the NSA's Office of General Counsel must review a sample of the justifications that were used by the NSA to approve the querying of particular telephone numbers within the database of calling records.[93]

Fourth, during each ninety-day period for which the program is authorized by the FISA court, the government must file monthly reports with the court on its execution of the program. Approximately every thirty days, the NSA must submit a report that "includes a discussion" of the agency's application of the RAS standard and its implementation of the new automated query process.[94] Each report also must state the number of instances since the last report "in which NSA has shared, in any form, results from queries of the BR metadata that contain U.S. person information, in any form, with anyone outside NSA."[95] For every instance in which information about a U.S. person was shared in this manner, the report must include an attestation that one of the officials authorized to approve such disseminations determined, in advance, "that the information was related to counterterrorism information and necessary to understand counterterrorism information or to assess its importance."[96] In practice, these monthly reports typically provide (1) a short description of some of the considerations that go into the agency's RAS determinations, (2) the number of selection terms currently approved for querying the database, (3) a paragraph describing a single example of an RAS determination made during the previous month, and (4) a list of the instances during the prior month in which information extracted from the calling records was shared with other agencies (including

---

[90]   Primary Order at 15.

[91]   Primary Order at 15.

[92]   Primary Order at 15.

[93]   Primary Order at 16.

[94]   Primary Order at 16.

[95]   Primary Order at 16.

[96]   Primary Order at 16-17.

the date and recipients of the dissemination and the required attestation about the need to share such information). NSA officials sign the reports under penalty of perjury.[97]

The NSA has implemented an extensive array of internal procedures designed to ensure that its actions comply with the rules described above.

VIII. Congressional Reporting Requirements

In addition to the reporting obligations contained in the FISA court's orders, which require that designated information periodically be supplied to the court, the FISA statute requires the executive branch to report particular matters to the intelligence and judiciary committees in Congress. Certain developments in the NSA's Section 215 program, including changes proposed by the government or approved by the FISA court, would trigger these reporting requirements.

The executive branch must provide four congressional committees with significant orders and opinions of the FISA court and information about the ramifications of the FISA court's orders. Specifically, twice a year, the Attorney General is required to submit to the House and Senate intelligence and judiciary committees "a summary of significant legal interpretations" of FISA involving matters before the FISA court or its companion appellate court, the Foreign Intelligence Surveillance Court of Review, "including interpretations presented in applications or pleadings" filed with those courts.[98] This summary must be accompanied by "copies of all decisions, orders, or opinions" of the two courts "that include significant construction or interpretation" of the provisions of FISA.[99] For the preceding six-month period, the Attorney General's report also must set forth the aggregate number of persons targeted for orders issued under FISA, including a breakdown of those targeted for access to records under Section 215.[100]

In addition, on an annual basis the Attorney General must "inform" the House and Senate intelligence committees and the Senate Judiciary Committee "concerning all requests" for the production of items under Section 215.[101] The Attorney General must submit a report to the intelligence and judiciary committees setting forth, with respect to

---

[97]   If the government seeks to renew its authority to collect calling records at the end of a ninety-day authorization period, it must include in its most recent thirty-day report "a description of any significant changes proposed in the way in which the call detail records would be received from the Providers and any significant changes to the controls NSA has in place to receive, store, process, and disseminate the BR metadata." Primary Order at 16.

[98]   50 U.S.C. § 1871(a)(4).

[99]   50 U.S.C. § 1871(a)(5).

[100]   50 U.S.C. § 1871(a)(1)(D).

[101]   50 U.S.C. § 1862(a).

the previous calendar year, statistical information about the applications filed with the FISA court under Section 215 and the orders issued by the court granting, modifying, or denying such applications. [102] An unclassified report must also be provided to Congress containing a subset of this statistical information.[103]

---

[102]   50 U.S.C. § 1862(b).

[103]   50 U.S.C. § 1862(c).

Part 4:
HISTORY OF THE NSA SECTION 215 PROGRAM

I.   The NSA's Initiation of Bulk Telephone Records Collection Under the President's Surveillance Program

The telephone records program that the NSA operates today under Section 215 of the Patriot Act evolved out of counterterrorism efforts that began shortly after the attacks of September 11, 2001. In October 2001, President George W. Bush issued a highly classified presidential authorization directing the NSA to collect certain foreign intelligence by electronic surveillance in order to prevent acts of terrorism within the United States, based upon a finding that an extraordinary emergency existed because of the September 11 attacks. Under this authorization, electronic surveillance was permitted within the United States for counterterrorism purposes without judicial warrants or court orders for a limited number of days.[104] President Bush authorized the NSA to: (1) collect the contents of certain international communications, a program that was later referred to as the Terrorist Surveillance Program ("TSP"), and (2) collect in bulk non-content information, or "metadata," about telephone and Internet communications.[105]

The President renewed the authorization for the NSA's activities in early November 2001. Thereafter, the authorization was renewed continuously, with some modifications in the scope of the authorized collection, approximately every thirty to sixty days until 2007. Each presidential authorization included the finding that an extraordinary emergency continued to exist justifying ongoing warrantless surveillance. Key members of Congress and the presiding judge of the Foreign Intelligence Surveillance Court were briefed on the existence of the program. The collection of communications content and bulk metadata under these presidential authorizations became known as the President's Surveillance Program. According to a 2009 report by the inspectors general of several defense and intelligence agencies, over time, "the program became less a temporary response to the September 11 terrorist attacks and more a permanent surveillance tool."[106]

---

[104]   *See* DNI Announces the Declassification of the Existence of Collection Activities Authorized by President George W. Bush Shortly After the Attacks of September 11, 2001 (Dec. 21, 2013), http://icontherecord.tumblr.com/.

[105]   *See id.* With respect to telephone communications, metadata includes information about the participating telephone numbers and the date, time, and duration of a call. With respect to Internet communications, metadata includes, among other things, addressing information that helps route a message to the proper destination, such as the "to" and "from" lines attached to an email.

[106]   *See* Unclassified Report on the President's Surveillance Program, prepared by the Office of Inspectors General of the Department of Defense, Department of Justice, Central Intelligence Agency, National Security Agency, and Office of the Director of National Intelligence, at 31 (July 10, 2009) ("OIGs Rpt.").

II. Reassessment of Legal Basis for President's Surveillance Program

In 2003, the Office of Legal Counsel in the Department of Justice ("OLC") began a comprehensive reassessment of the legal basis for the President's Surveillance Program. The OLC conducted a new legal analysis that supported much of the program authorized by the President, but it became concerned that this revised analysis would not be sufficient to support the legality of certain aspects of the program.[107] After extensive debate within the Administration, in March 2004 the President decided to modify certain intelligence-gathering activities under the program, discontinuing the bulk collection of Internet metadata.[108]

III. Transition of Internet Metadata Collection to FISA Court Authority

The Foreign Intelligence Surveillance Act of 1978 ("FISA") created, for the first time, a legislative structure governing executive branch efforts to conduct surveillance within the United States to obtain foreign intelligence. The Act established a special court, comprised of sitting federal judges, to review and grant or deny applications made by the executive branch to conduct electronic surveillance for foreign intelligence purposes — the Foreign Intelligence Surveillance Court ("FISC" or "FISA court").[109]

One of FISA's provisions allows the government to seek permission from the FISA court to monitor communications by installing a "pen register" or "trap and trace device" to capture information sent from a communications instrument or facility.[110] A pen register records the "dialing, routing, addressing, or signaling information" transmitted through wire or electronic communication, but does not capture the contents of communications.[111] Early versions of pen registers simply recorded the numbers dialed from a telephone, but later developments allowed the devices to capture information such as the "to" line in an email. A "trap and trace device" records information about *incoming* telephone calls or other electronic communications. [112] Sometimes combined in a single instrument, pen registers and trap and trace devices are often referred to as pen/trap or PR/TT devices.

---

[107]   OIGs Rpt. at 20.

[108]   *See* OIGs Rpt. at 29; DNI Announces the Declassification of the Existence of Collection Activities Authorized by President George W. Bush Shortly After the Attacks of September 11, 2001 (Dec. 21, 2013), http://icontherecord.tumblr.com/.

[109]   See Part 8 of this Report for a discussion of the FISA court and its operations.

[110]   *See* 50 U.S.C. § 1842.

[111]   18 U.S.C. § 3127(3).

[112]   18 U.S.C. § 3127(4).

In 2004, the Administration sought FISA court approval for NSA to collect large amounts of Internet metadata in bulk under FISA's pen/trap provisions. Judge Kollar-Kotelly granted the government's application in July 2004.[113] Her order approved the government's request while requiring the government to comply with certain additional restrictions and procedures.[114] As proposed by the government, Judge Kollar-Kotelly's order permitted Internet metadata to be acquired only if it travelled through certain designated communications channels that were relatively likely to contain messages of counterterrorism interest, "in order to build a meta data archive that will be, in relative terms, richly populated" with terrorism-related communications.[115]

Once in the possession of the NSA, the Internet metadata collected under the FISA court's order could be accessed by NSA personnel only through queries targeting particular Internet accounts or addresses, and only after the NSA concluded there was a "reasonable articulable suspicion" that the account or address was "associated with" a target.[116] The NSA was permitted to employ only the specific analytical methods described in the court's opinion. Under these rules, it could engage in "contact chaining" to identify Internet users directly in contact with a target account or address, or directly in contact with a user who was directly in contact with the target. In other words, the agency could search for Internet users who were up to two steps removed from a target.[117]

Judge Kollar-Kotelly issued a lengthy opinion with her order approving the Internet metadata program, discussing the statutory and constitutional issues raised by the government's request and the "exceptionally broad form of collection" it entailed.[118] The opinion concluded that the Internet metadata to be obtained by the government was "relevant to an ongoing investigation," as required by the statute, "even though only a very small percentage of the information obtained" would be "directly relevant to such an investigation." This was so, the opinion said, because large-scale collection was "necessary to identify the much smaller number" of terrorism-related communications.[119] Emphasizing that "senior responsible officials, whose judgment on these matters is entitled to deference, have . . . also explained why they seek to collect the particular meta data . . .

---

[113]   *See* Opinion and Order, No. PR/TT [*redacted*] (FISA Ct.) ("PR/TT Op.").

[114]   *See* PR/TT Op. at 84-85.

[115]   PR/TT Op. at 47.

[116]   PR/TT Op. at 83.

[117]   PR/TT Op. at 42-45. See pages 26 to 31 of this Report for an explanation of contact chaining within the context of telephone metadata analysis.

[118]   PR/TT Op. at 23.

[119]   PR/TT Op. at 47-49.

identified in the application," the opinion stated: "Based on these explanations, the proposed collection appears to be a reasonably effective means to this end."[120]

After several years of operation, which included significant incidents of noncompliance with the FISA court's orders, the bulk collection of Internet metadata under FISA court approval was terminated. Upon concluding that the program's value was limited, the NSA did not seek to renew it. The government's successful transition of this collection authority from the President's Surveillance Program to the FISA court, however, served as a model for a similar transition in the NSA's bulk collection of telephone records.

IV.   Transition of Telephone Records Collection to FISA Court Authority

In December 2005, the *New York Times* published articles revealing the portion of the President's Surveillance Program that involved intercepting the contents of international emails and telephone calls. This article caused concern for the telephone companies that were providing records under the program. Although their concerns about the interception of communications content were somewhat assuaged by the issuance of a Department of Justice "white paper" outlining the legal argument in favor of those interceptions, the companies remained concerned about providing telephone metadata (calling records) to the government. The *New York Times* had not revealed that aspect of the program, but reporters at *USA Today* were investigating it in early 2006. As a result, the government began to explore options for obtaining an order issued by the FISA court compelling assistance with the collection of telephone metadata, similar to the orders compelling assistance with the Internet metadata program. Ultimately, in May 2006 the government moved to transition the telephone records program from the President's Surveillance Program to a section of FISA known as the "business records" provision.

FISA's business records provision was first enacted in 1998.[121] Titled "Access to certain business records for foreign intelligence and international terrorism investigations," the provision originally permitted the FBI to apply to the FISA court for an order requiring a business "to release records in its possession for an investigation to gather foreign intelligence information or an investigation concerning international terrorism."[122] The FISA court could issue such orders to only four types of businesses: "a common carrier, public accommodation facility, physical storage facility, or vehicle rental facility."[123] Any application for such an order was required to attest that there were

---

[120]   PR/TT Op. at 53-54.

[121]   *See* Pub. L. No. 105-272, § 602, 112 Stat. 2396, 2410-12 (Oct. 20, 1998).

[122]   50 U.S.C. § 1862(a) (2000).

[123]   50 U.S.C. § 1862(a) (2000).

"specific and articulable facts giving reason to believe that the person to whom the records pertain is a foreign power or an agent of a foreign power."[124]

The Patriot Act, passed in 2001, significantly extended the reach of FISA's business records provision.[125] Section 215 of the Patriot Act made two fundamental changes to the law. First, the FBI was no longer limited to seeking records from common carriers, public accommodation facilities, physical storage facilities, or vehicle rental facilities. Instead, the FBI could apply to the FISA court for an order requiring the production of "any tangible things (including books, records, papers, documents, and other items) for an investigation to protect against international terrorism."[126] Second, the FBI no longer needed to demonstrate "specific and articulable facts" showing that a person to whom the records pertained was a foreign power or an agent of a foreign power. Instead, the FBI only needed to specify that the records concerned were being sought "for an authorized investigation" conducted under guidelines approved by the Attorney General.[127]

Section 215 became one of the most controversial features of the Patriot Act, criticized by some lawmakers and others for the potentially wide scope of the record-gathering it authorized, as well as for its nondisclosure provision, which prevented recipients of an order from telling anyone about the order. It was one of several Patriot Act provisions that were not made permanent by the Act but were set to expire in 2005 (later extended to 2006).

Beginning in 2005, numerous bills were introduced in Congress to reauthorize Section 215 and the other "sunsetting" provisions of the Patriot Act, while making certain changes to those provisions. Congressional debate over these competing proposals extended into the spring of 2006. Thus, legislative debate about the reauthorization of Section 215, including proposals to limit its scope and impose additional safeguards, was occurring at the same time that executive branch lawyers were formulating a strategy to use that statute as the legal basis for the NSA's bulk telephone records collection. The collection of telephone records under the President's Surveillance Program was classified, however, and the government's plans to seek new legal authority for that collection were not made public. Thus, congressional debates about the terms on which Section 215 should be renewed included no public discussion of the fact that the executive branch was planning to place the NSA's bulk calling records program under the auspices of the reauthorized statute.

---

124   50 U.S.C. § 1862(b)(2)(B) (2000).

125   *See* Pub. L. No. 107-56, § 215, 115 Stat. 272, 287 (2001).

126   50 U.S.C. § 1861(a)(1) (2002).

127   50 U.S.C. § 1861(b)(2) (2002).

In March 2006, the President signed the USA PATRIOT Improvement and Reauthorization Act of 2005, which made a number of changes to the business records provision of FISA (by then commonly referred to as Section 215).[128] Among other changes, the new law required that before granting a business records application, FISA court judges had to determine that the records being sought were likely "relevant" to an FBI investigation. Specifically, the law now demanded that each application contain "a statement of facts showing that there are reasonable grounds to believe that the tangible things sought are relevant to an authorized investigation (other than a threat assessment)."[129]

The new law made other modifications to Section 215 as well. One such change explicitly limited the items that could be obtained under the statute to those that were obtainable through grand jury subpoenas, administrative subpoenas, or court orders.[130] Certain proposals to restrict the scope of Section 215 even further were rejected.

By May 2006, Congress had renewed Section 215, and government lawyers were finalizing their application to the FISA court seeking permission to conduct the NSA's telephone records program under the auspices of the amended statute.

The government's application, filed in May 2006, requested an order directing certain U.S. telephone companies to provide the NSA with call detail records created by those companies. It requested that the companies be ordered to produce these records "on an ongoing daily basis to the extent practicable for a period of ninety days." In other words, the application sought to put the companies under a continuing obligation, for a period of ninety days, to provide the NSA with all of their newly created calling records on a daily basis, rather than direct the companies to turn over records already in their possession at the time an order was served on them. The government sought telephone records so that the NSA could analyze them and disseminate intelligence from those records to "the FBI, CIA, or other appropriate U.S. Government and foreign government agencies."[131]

The government's application included a proposed set of rules for NSA's handling, analysis, and dissemination of the calling records it received.[132] The application and its

---

[128]   *See* Pub. L. No. 109-177, 120 Stat. 192 (2006).

[129]   50 U.S.C. § 1861(b)(2)(A); *see id.* § 1861(c)(1) (requiring FISA court judge to find that an application meets this requirement before entering an order).

[130]   *See* 50 U.S.C. § 1861(c)(2)(D) (stating that an order issued under Section 215 "may only require the production of a tangible thing if such thing can be obtained with a subpoena duces tecum issued by a court of the United States in aid of a grand jury investigation or with any other order issued by a court of the United States directing the production of records or tangible things").

[131]   Memorandum of Law in Support of Application for Certain Tangible Things for Investigations to Protect Against International Terrorism, at 15, *In re Application of the Federal Bureau of Investigation for an Order Requiring the Production of Tangible Things*, No. BR 06-05 (FISA Ct. May 23, 2006) ("2006 Mem.").

[132]   *See* 2006 Mem. at 21-22.

supporting memorandum of law explained that the telephone records were being sought "by the FBI on behalf of NSA" so that the NSA could use metadata analysis "to identify and find operatives" of terrorist organizations. The application was supported by two declarations: one from NSA Director Lieutenant General Keith Alexander, describing the requested calling records and how the NSA would treat them, and one from National Counterterrorism Center Director Vice Admiral John Scott Redd, describing the threat to the United States posed by Al Qaeda.

The government's memorandum of law argued, among other things, that the application was "completely consistent with this Court's ground breaking and innovative decision" that had approved the collection of "bulk e-mail metadata" under FISA's pen register provision.[133] The memorandum extensively cited that 2004 decision in discussing one of the key statutory prerequisites of FISA's business records section — the requirement that any records sought be "relevant" to an authorized FBI investigation.

As noted above, Section 215 requires any application to include "a statement of facts showing that there are reasonable grounds to believe" that the records sought "are relevant to an authorized investigation" conducted in accordance with certain criteria.[134] To show that this requirement was met, the government argued: "All of the business records to be collected here are relevant to FBI investigations . . . because the NSA can effectively conduct metadata analysis only if it has the data in bulk."[135] Echoing the arguments made in its 2004 Internet metadata application, the government stated that "although investigators do not know *exactly* where the terrorists' communications are hiding in the billions of telephone calls flowing through the United States today, we do know that they *are there*, and if we archive the data now, we will be able to use it in a targeted way to find the terrorists tomorrow."[136]

The government's legal memorandum relied heavily on the FISA court's 2004 decision approving the NSA's bulk Internet metadata program, arguing that the interpretation of the word "relevant" in Section 215 should incorporate "deference . . . to the fully considered judgment of the executive branch in assessing and responding to national security threats and in determining the potential significance of intelligence-related information."[137] It further argued that the statute "does not expressly impose any requirement to tailor a request for tangible things precisely to obtain solely records that

---

[133]   2006 Mem. at 3.

[134]   50 U.S.C. § 1861(b)(2)(A).

[135]   2006 Mem. at 2.

[136]   2006 Mem. at 8 (emphasis in original).

[137]   2006 Mem. at 16-17.

are strictly relevant to the investigation."[138] Even if it did, the memorandum argued, to interpret the word "relevant" in the statute it was "appropriate to use as a guideline the Supreme Court's 'special needs' jurisprudence, which balances any intrusion into privacy against the government interest at stake to determine whether a warrant or individualized suspicion is required."[139] In sum, the government argued: "Just as the bulk collection of e-mail metadata was relevant to FBI investigations . . . so is the bulk collection of telephony metadata described herein."[140]

While acknowledging that its request would result in the collection of a "substantial portion" of call detail records that "would not relate to [terrorist] operatives," the government argued that the records as a whole were nevertheless relevant because "the intelligence tool that the Government hopes to use to find [terrorist] communications — metadata analysis — requires collection and storing large volumes of the metadata to enable later analysis."[141] "All of the metadata collected is thus relevant," the government concluded, "because the success of this investigative tool depends on bulk collection."[142]

The government's application requested that during the analysis of calling records, contact chaining should be permitted to extend up to three "hops" from a seed number — instead of the two hops permitted in the Internet metadata program. In explanation for this difference, the supporting legal memorandum stated: "Going out to the third tier is useful for telephony because, unlike e-mail traffic, which includes the heavy use of 'spam,' a telephonic device does not lend itself to simultaneous contact with large numbers of individuals."[143]

Although the memorandum's discussion of the "relevance" requirement in Section 215's relied heavily on the FISC's earlier opinion approving the bulk collection of Internet metadata, the memorandum did not discuss whether that comparison was affected by differences between the telephone and Internet metadata collection programs. As noted earlier, under the Internet program records were acquired only if they travelled through certain designated communications channels that were relatively likely to contain messages of counterterrorism interest — to build a metadata archive that would be, in relative terms, "richly populated" with terrorism-related communications.[144]

---

138   2006 Mem. at 17.

139   2006 Mem. at 18 (citing *Board of Educ. v. Earls*, 536 U.S. 822, 829 (2002).

140   2006 Mem. at 17.

141   2006 Mem. at 15.

142   2006 Mem. at 15.

143   2006 Mem. at 9.

144   PR/TT Op. at 47.

The memorandum also did not discuss whether Section 215 permits the court to prospectively order a company to turn over new records as they are created, on a daily basis, for a set period of time. (The Internet metadata program was conducted under the authority of FISA's pen/trap provision, which is designed to authorize the *prospective* collection of communications metadata.) The memorandum neither identified any portion of Section 215 that authorized such a procedure nor discussed whether any language in the statute foreclosed it.

While the government's application requested that the telephone companies be ordered to provide their records to the NSA, its memorandum did not discuss the fact that Section 215 states that records obtained under its authority are to be "made available to," "obtained" by, and "received by" the FBI.[145]

The government's application also did not discuss whether any legal impediment to its application was presented by the Electronic Communications Privacy Act ("ECPA"). That act makes it unlawful for a telephone company to share records about its customers with the government, except in response to certain designated circumstances. Those enumerated circumstances do not include the issuance of an order from the FISA court under Section 215.[146]

On May 24, 2006, FISA court Judge Malcolm J. Howard signed an order approving the government's application.[147] The order was not accompanied by an opinion explaining the decision to grant the application. Judge Howard's ten-page order recited the specific findings called for by Section 215 and stated that the government's application satisfied those statutory requirements.[148] Much of the order was devoted to listing restrictions on the NSA's maintenance and use of the calling records it would receive.[149] In accordance with the conditions proposed by the government, a number of such rules were imposed. These rules were similar to, though less comprehensive than, the rules that govern the program today, and they included the requirement that Section 215 records could be

---

[145] *See* 50 U.S.C. § 1861(b)(2)(B), (d)(1), (d)(2)(B), (g)(1), (h). Similarly, while the memorandum explained the minimization procedures that *the NSA* would apply to the calling records it obtained under the proposed order, it did not discuss the statutory requirement that its application include "an enumeration of the minimization procedures adopted by the Attorney General . . . that are applicable to the retention and dissemination *by the Federal Bureau of Investigation* of any tangible things to be *made available to the Federal Bureau of Investigation* based on the order requested in such application." 50 U.S.C. § 1861(b)(2)(B) (emphasis added).

[146] *See* 18 U.S.C. §§ 2702, 2703. The government brought this issue to the FISA court's attention in late 2008.

[147] *See* Order at 10, *In re Application of the Federal Bureau of Investigation for an Order Requiring the Production of Tangible Things*, No. BR 06-05 (FISA Ct. May 24, 2006) ("2006 Order").

[148] *See* 2006 Order at 3.

[149] *See* 2006 Order at 4-10.

searched only with selections terms for which there already was "reasonable, articulable suspicion" of a connection with terrorism.[150]

The May 2006 order directed that each telephone company produce its call detail records to the NSA, "and continue production on an ongoing daily basis thereafter for the duration of th[e] order."[151]

The court's order expired approximately ninety days after issuance. At the end of that period, it was renewed for a similar amount of time. Since May 2006, the court has continuously renewed its authorization of the NSA's telephone records program approximately every ninety days.

Under the authority granted by the FISA court pursuant to Section 215, the NSA was able to collect the same telephone calling records it had previously obtained through the President's Surveillance Program. No break in collection was caused by the transition to FISA court authority.

V.   NSA Violations of FISA Court Orders and Modifications to the Program

Between 2006 and 2009, the terms of the FISA court's orders approving the NSA's calling records program remained essentially unchanged. But a series of compliance issues brought to the attention of the FISA court in 2009 resulted in some modifications to the program.

---

[150]   Under the order, calling records obtained by the NSA were to be "stored and processed on a secure private network that NSA exclusively will operate," and access to the records was to be limited by means of software to authorized analysts. 2006 Order at 5. Five years after collection by the NSA, the calling records had to be destroyed. *Id.* at 8. Echoing the rules previously imposed on the analysis of bulk Internet metadata, the order provided that the calling records could be accessed "only when NSA has identified a known telephone number for which, based on the factual and practical considerations of everyday life on which reasonable and prudent persons act, there are facts giving rise to a reasonable, articulable suspicion" that the telephone number is "associated with" specific terrorist organizations. *Id.* at 5. While the FISA court's order did not explain what it meant for a telephone number to be "associated with" a terrorist organization, it provided that a telephone number believed to be used by a U.S. person could not be regarded as associated with terrorism solely on the basis of activities that are protected by the First Amendment to the Constitution. *Id.* Searches targeting particular telephone numbers could be approved by only seven NSA officials, and the agency's Office of General Counsel was ordered to "review and approve proposed queries of archived metadata based on seed accounts numbers [sic] reasonably believed to be used by U.S. persons." *Id.* at 6-7. Any use of the calling records for analysis, the order directed, "shall be strictly tailored to identifying terrorist communications and shall occur solely according to the procedures described in the application." *Id.* at 6. The order required that every analyst's access to the archived data be automatically logged for auditing capability. It also imposed rules for the dissemination outside the NSA of information identifying a U.S. person, and required the NSA to periodically review the program, including assessing the adequacy of the management controls for the processing and dissemination of U.S. person information. *Id.* at 6-9. See Part 3 of this Report for a description of the rules that presently govern the program.

[151]   2006 Order at 4.

A. Improper Searches of Records by Automated Systems

In January 2009, representatives from the DOJ attended an NSA briefing concerning the agency's bulk telephone records program.[152] This briefing, along with subsequent communication between the DOJ and the NSA, confirmed that the NSA was operating an automated searching system that utilized the telephone records obtained under FISA court approval in a manner contrary to the court's orders.[153]

The NSA had developed and implemented a software system, called an "alert list," that automatically scanned new telephone records obtained by the agency as those new records were input into the agency's databases. The alert list system was set up to search telephone numbers that were obtained by the NSA through a number of means, including through the Section 215 orders. The alert list had been developed and implemented at a time when the NSA's collection was undertaken pursuant to the President's Surveillance Program, and thus before the FISA court's rules on the use of the records were in place.[154]

The alert list contained thousands of telephone numbers that were of interest to NSA analysts. Most of these numbers had never been approved for use in querying the Section 215 calling records, because no determination had been made that those numbers satisfied the "reasonable, articulable suspicion" or "RAS" standard. As of January 2009, fewer than 2,000 of the nearly 18,000 numbers on the alert list were RAS-approved. But when newly obtained telephone records entered the NSA's databases from any source — including from the telephone companies providing records under Section 215 — the alert list automatically searched the incoming data to see if it contained records of any telephone calls that matched numbers on the alert list. If so, the system notified analysts of the match. According to a filing later submitted to the FISA court, NSA personnel "appear to have viewed the alert list process as merely a means of identifying a particular identifier on the alert list that might warrant further scrutiny," which might then lead to a determination of whether analysis based on that number should take place. The alert list did not automatically create contact chains for the telephone numbers it identified that were not RAS-approved.[155]

Using the alert list system to search the telephone records obtained through Section 215 violated the FISA court's orders, which stated that analysts could not query those records except by searching the contacts of a selection term that had been given RAS

---

[152] Memorandum of the United States in Response to the Court's Order Dated January 28, 2009, at 5, *In re Production of Tangible Things*, No. BR 08-13 (FISA Ct. Feb. 17, 2009)("2009 Mem.").

[153] *See* 2009 Mem. at 6.

[154] 2009 Mem. at 8.

[155] 2009 Mem. at 8, 11-12.

approval.[156] It also contradicted the sworn attestations of several executive branch officials who filed declarations with the FISA court about the operation of the NSA's program.[157]

Upon discovering these problems, the DOJ promptly reported them to the FISC.[158] At the same time, the NSA made several failed attempts to implement a software fix but, unable to do so, it shut down the alert list process completely.[159]

Upon being notified about noncompliance and misrepresentations regarding the alert system, FISA court Judge Reggie B. Walton — the judge who had most recently reauthorized the NSA's program — ordered the government to file a written brief, with supporting documentation, to help the court determine what remedial or punitive steps should be taken in light of the disclosure.[160]

Responding to the FISA court's order, the government acknowledged that "the NSA's descriptions to the Court of the alert list process" were "inaccurate" and that the court's orders "did not provide the Government with authority to employ the alert list in the manner in which it did."[161] The government attributed this problem in part to the NSA's mistaken interpretation of the FISA court's orders, which applied restrictions to the NSA's "archived data." According to the government, the NSA believed these restrictions did not apply to records as they were being transmitted into the NSA's databases but before they had been formatted and "archived" for use by analysts.[162]

In sum, the government stated, the NSA's violations resulted not from an intent to mislead or disobey the court's orders, but rather from misunderstanding among the personnel involved with running the program and describing it to the FISA court about exactly how certain aspects of the program operated. As explained in a supporting declaration filed by NSA Director Keith Alexander, "it appears there was never a complete understanding among the key personnel" who reviewed the agency's reports to the court "regarding what each individual meant by the terminology used" in the reports. "Furthermore, from a technical standpoint, there was no single person who had a complete technical understanding of the [program's] system architecture."[163]

---

[156]   *See* 2009 Mem. at 16.

[157]   *See* Order Regarding Preliminary Notice of Compliance Incident Dated January 15, 2009, at 2, *In re Production of Tangible Things*, No. BR 08-13 (FISA Ct. Jan. 28, 2009) ("Jan. 2009 Order").

[158]   *See* Jan. 2009 Order at 2.

[159]   2009 Mem. at 17.

[160]   Jan. 2009 Order at 2-3.

[161]   2009 Mem. at 1-2.

[162]   *See* 2009 Mem. at 11-12, 25-26.

[163]   Declaration of Lieutenant General Keith B. Alexander, at 18-19, *In re Production of Tangible Things*, No. BR 08-13 (FISA Ct. Feb. 13, 2009).

The government argued, however, that in light of the "vital" role played by the calling records in the government's ability to find and identify terrorist agents, along with a number of extensive corrective measures the NSA was undertaking, the FISA court should not rescind its orders approving the collection of telephone records or take any other remedial action.[164]

The government also reported that the NSA reviewed all 275 intelligence reports that the agency had disseminated since 2006 based on analysis of telephone records obtained under Section 215. While thirty-one of those reports were prompted by the alert list process, the NSA did not identify any such report that resulted from the query of a telephone number that lacked RAS approval. In addition, the agency determined that in all instances where a U.S. number served as the initial "seed" number targeted for analysis since 2006 (which occurred in twenty-two of the 275 reports), the U.S. number was either already the subject of electronic surveillance approved by the FISA court or had been reviewed by the NSA's Office of General Counsel to ensure that the RAS determination for that number was not based solely on activities protected by the First Amendment. [165]

In a subsequent order, Judge Walton observed that, as illustrated in the government's response, "since the earliest days of the FISC-authorized collection of call-detail records by the NSA, the NSA has on a daily basis, accessed the BR metadata for purposes of comparing thousands of non-RAS approved telephone identifiers on its alert list against the BR metadata in order to identify any matches."[166] He further wrote that the agency's professed misinterpretation of the court's orders — viewing their restrictions as applying only to telephone records that had been "archived" in the agency's databases — "strains credulity."[167] As Judge Walton put it: "It is difficult to imagine why the Court would intend the applicability of the RAS requirement — a critical component of the procedures proposed by the government and adopted by the Court — to turn on whether or not the data being accessed has been 'archived' by the NSA in a particular database at the time of access."[168] Such an "illogical interpretation," Judge Walton continued, "renders compliance with the RAS requirement merely optional."[169]

Regardless of what factors contributed to the NSA's misrepresentations to the Court, Judge Walton wrote, "the government's failure to ensure that responsible officials

---

[164]   2009 Mem. at 22-28.

[165]   2009 Mem. at 17-18.

[166]   Order at 4-5, *In re Production of Tangible Things*, No. BR 08-13 (FISA Ct. Mar. 2, 2009) ("Mar. 2009 Order").

[167]   Mar. 2009 Order at 5.

[168]   Mar. 2009 Order at 5.

[169]   Mar. 2009 Order at 5.

adequately understood the NSA's alert list process, and to accurately report its implementation to the Court, has prevented, for more than two years, both the government and the FISC from taking steps to remedy daily violations of the minimization procedures set forth in FISC orders," which were designed to protect call detail records that "could not otherwise have been legally captured in bulk."[170]

After the alert list problems were brought to the FISA court's attention, the NSA undertook an end-to-end review of its technical and operational processes for handling telephone records obtained under Section 215.[171] That review uncovered another automated system implemented by the NSA that routinely permitted searches of the Section 215 telephone records without RAS approval.[172]

According to a filing notifying the FISC about the issue, this analytical tool "determined if a record of a telephone identifier was present in NSA databases and, if so, provided analysts with certain information regarding the calling activity associated with that identifier." When NSA analysts utilized the tool to search for particular numbers, the system would query the Section 215 database of calling records along with other NSA databases. The tool did not, however, "provide analysts with the telephone identifiers that were in contact with the telephone identifier that served as a basis for the query."[173]

In response to this new discovery, in February 2009 the NSA restricted access to its Section 215 calling records to permit only manual queries based on RAS-approved telephone numbers, preventing any automated process from accessing the records.[174]

B. Improper Searches of Records by Analysts

In 2008 and 2009, the government also brought to the attention of the FISA court a series of improper manual searches of telephone records by analysts that violated the court's orders.

During a five-day period in April 2008, the NSA determined, thirty-one NSA analysts queried the telephone records database "without being aware they were doing so."[175] Upon discovering this problem, Judge Walton later explained, "the NSA undertook a number of remedial measures, including suspending the 31 analysts' access pending additional

---

[170]   Mar. 2009 Order at 8-9.

[171]   *See* Notice of Compliance Incidents, at 1, *In re Production of Tangible Things*, No. BR 08-13 (FISA Ct. Feb. 26, 2009).

[172]   *Id.*

[173]   Notice of Compliance Incidents, *supra*, at 2-3.

[174]   Notice of Compliance Incidents, *supra*, at 3.

[175]   Mar. 2009 Order at 9 (quoting government report).

training, and modifying the NSA's tool for accessing the data so that analysts were required specifically to enable access to the BR metadata and acknowledge such access."[176]

These corrective steps did not entirely solve the problem. As the government informed the FISA court in December of that year, "one analyst had failed to install the modified access tool and, as a result, inadvertently queried the data using five identifiers for which NSA had not determined that the reasonable articulable suspicion standard was satisfied."[177]

Similar problems continued, and in late January 2009 the government informed the court that, during December and January, two NSA analysts had used 280 foreign telephone numbers to query the records without determining that the RAS standard had been satisfied.[178] As Judge Walton noted upon being informed of this latest problem, those queries apparently were conducted "despite full implementation" of the software modifications and additional training that the NSA carried out in response to previous violations.[179]

In February 2009, the NSA initiated an audit of all queries made of its Section 215 telephone records in the preceding three months. This audit identified more instances of improper analyst queries of the data: three analysts were responsible for fourteen instances of improper querying during that period. None of the improper queries resulted in any intelligence reporting and none of the identifiers used were associated with a U.S. telephone number or person. The NSA concluded that each analyst thought he or she was conducting queries of other repositories of telephone records not subject to the FISA court's orders. The government stated that software changes were made to ensure that analysts could access the Section 215 data only through one specific tool.[180]

C. FISA Court Response to NSA Violations

By March 2009, all of the violations described above had been reported to the FISA court. After surveying the violations, Judge Walton reminded the government that the FISA court had authorized the bulk collection of telephone records based upon "(1) the government's explanation, under oath, of how the collection of and access to such data are necessary to analytical methods that are vital to the national security of the United States; and (2) minimization procedures that carefully restrict access to the BR metadata and

---

[176] Mar. 2009 Order at 9-10.

[177] Mar. 2009 Order at 10.

[178] Mar. 2009 Order at 10.

[179] Mar. 2009 Order at 10.

[180] Supplemental Declaration of Lieutenant General Keith B. Alexander, at 8-9, *In re Production of Tangible Things*, No. BR 08-13 (FISA Ct. Feb. 26, 2009).

include specific oversight requirements."[181] The judge noted that given the executive branch's expertise in matters of national security, and the large scale of the collection program, "the Court must rely heavily on the government to monitor this program to ensure that it continues to be justified, in the view of those responsible for our national security, and that it is being implemented in a manner that protects the privacy interests of U.S. persons as required by applicable minimization procedures."[182] Judge Walton wrote that he "no longer" had confidence "that the government is doing its utmost to ensure that those responsible for implementation fully comply with the Court's orders."[183]

Observing that "from the inception of this FISA BR program, the NSA's data accessing technologies and practices were never adequately designed to comply with the governing minimization procedures," Judge Walton concluded that "notwithstanding the remedial measures undertaken by the government . . . more is needed to protect the privacy of U.S. person information acquired and retained pursuant to the FISC orders issued in this matter."[184] However, "given the government's repeated representations that the collection of the BR metadata is vital to national security," and in light of the court's earlier determinations that the program met the statutory requirements of Section 215, when conducted "in compliance with appropriate minimization procedures," Judge Walton decided that "it would not be prudent to order that the government's acquisition of the BR metadata cease at this time."[185]

Instead, Judge Walton prohibited NSA analysts from conducting any searches of the telephone records without obtaining prior approval from the FISA court to search a particular number.[186] Once the NSA completed its end-to-end system engineering and process reviews, he ordered, it was to file a number of documents and affidavits with the FISA court regarding the results of this review, remedial steps taken, proposed oversight procedures for any future court order, and the national security value of the telephone records program.[187]

D. Improper Dissemination of Call Records Outside the NSA

As the NSA was conducting its end-to-end review of the Section 215 program, the government reported to the FISA court another violation of its orders. As the government explained, calling records that had been analyzed by the NSA were made available to other

---

181   Mar. 2009 Order at 12 (quoting government report).

182   Mar. 2009 Order at 12.

183   Mar. 2009 Order at 12.

184   Mar. 2009 Order at 14-15, 17.

185   Mar. 2009 Order at 17.

186   Mar. 2009 Order at 18-19.

187   Mar. 2009 Order at 19-20.

intelligence agencies without taking the steps that were required before such dissemination of information about U.S. persons was permitted. This violated not only the FISA court's orders but also the generally applicable dissemination rules governing all of the NSA's activities.

In June 2009, the government notified the FISA court that the unminimized results of some queries of Section 215 telephone records — meaning the results of contact-chaining searches, including information regarding U.S. persons — had been uploaded by the NSA into a database to which other intelligence agencies had access. Providing such access, the government explained, may have resulted in the dissemination of U.S. person information in violation of the NSA's general dissemination rules and the more restrictive rules on disseminations imposed by the FISA court in its Section 215 orders.[188] The government asserted that the NSA promptly terminated the access of outside agencies to these records and investigated the matter.[189]

Judge Walton responded by ordering the government to file a weekly report listing each instance during the preceding week in which the NSA shared, in any form, information derived from the Section 215 program with anyone outside of the agency. He also directed the government to furnish a full explanation of how this violation came about in its forthcoming submissions reporting the results of its end-to-end systems review.[190]

E. FISA Court Reauthorization of the Program with More Detailed Rules

In August 2009 the government submitted to the FISA court documents reporting the results of its end-to-end review and responding to the court's concerns regarding violations of its orders. These documents included a lengthy report to the court, a declaration from NSA Director Keith Alexander concerning incidents of NSA noncompliance with the court's orders, a declaration from General Alexander concerning the value of the NSA's bulk telephone records program, an affidavit from FBI Director Robert Mueller concerning the value of the program, and an NSA review of the program's operation.

Collectively, these documents sought to explain previous instances of NSA noncompliance with the FISA court's orders, identify new areas in which the agency's practices had not been fully or accurately described to the court, describe remedial steps taken to correct those deficiencies, articulate the value of the program in combating terrorism, and propose a set of expanded rules and restrictions for the continuation of the program.

---

[188]   Order at 5, *In re Application of the Federal Bureau of Investigation for an Order Requiring the Production of Tangible Things*, No. BR 09-06 (FISA Ct. June 22, 2009) ("June 2009 Order").

[189]   June 2009 Order at 6.

[190]   June 2009 Order at 7-8.

As the program came up for renewal by the FISA court the following month, the government requested permission to resume analyzing calling records based on the NSA's own determinations that the RAS standard was satisfied — rather than by seeking prior permission of the FISA court, as the agency had been required to do for the previous six months. The government's application proposed a more detailed set of conditions restricting the NSA's handling and use of telephone records obtained under Section 215, in keeping with the results of the investigations carried out over the previous months. In early September 2009, Judge Walton granted the government's application, restoring the bulk telephone records program to its original footing with the addition of these more detailed conditions. The resulting primary order closely resembles the orders that have since been issued by the FISA court up to the present day.[191]

VI.   Operation of the Program Between 2009 and the Present

Since 2009, there have been no major changes in the operation of the Section 215 program. Between late 2009 and late 2013, the government submitted notices to the FISA court reporting ten different types of violations of the court's orders. Nearly all of the incidents in question involved isolated violations that the NSA took steps to remedy and prevent in the future. Two incidents involved more widespread, though inadvertent, violations of the rules governing the Section 215 program.

The isolated incidents reported to the FISA court comprised the following violations: (1) The NSA inadvertently received a tiny amount of cell site location information from a provider on one occasion (the data was accessible only to technical personnel and was never available to intelligence analysts); (2) An analyst performed a query on a selection term whose RAS approval had expired earlier that month (the agency responded with technical modifications to prevent such incidents); (3) A RAS determination was made based on what was later discovered to be incorrect information (the resulting query results were destroyed, and no intelligence reports were issued based on the query); (4) On several occasions analysts shared the results of queries via email with NSA personnel who were not authorized to receive such information (the agency responded with new procedures for email distribution); (5) An analyst sent an email message containing information derived from the Section 215 data to the wrong person, due to a typographical error in the email address (the recipient reportedly deleted the message without reading it, recognizing the error); (6) Information about U.S. persons was on three occasions disseminated outside the NSA before any official made the determinations that are required for such disseminations (officials later concluded that the

---

191   *See* Primary Order, *In re Application of the Federal Bureau of Investigation for an Order Requiring the Production of Tangible Things*, No. BR 09-13 (FISA Ct. Sept. 3, 2009).

standards for dissemination were satisfied in each case); (7) The government filed nine reports with the FISA court that lacked certain information required to be in such reports (the missing information involved no wrongdoing or noncompliance, and it subsequently was furnished to the court); (8) The government filed a compliance report with the FISA court on a Monday, instead of on the deadline the previous Friday.

The two other noncompliance incidents were more far-reaching, although both represented inadvertent violations. In one incident, NSA technical personnel discovered a technical server with nearly 3,000 files containing call detail records that were more than five years old, but that had not been destroyed in accordance with the applicable retention rules. These files were among those used in connection with a migration of call detail records to a new system. Because a single file may contain more than one call detail record, and because the files were promptly destroyed by agency technical personnel, the NSA could not provide an estimate regarding the volume of calling records that were retained beyond the five-year limit. The technical server in question was not available to intelligence analysts.

In the other incident, the NSA discovered that it had unintentionally received a large quantity of customer credit card numbers from a provider. These related to cases in which a customer used a credit card to pay for a phone call. This problem, which involved cases in which customers used credit cards to pay for phone calls, resulted from a software change implemented by the provider without notice to the NSA. In response to the discovery, the NSA masked the credit card data so that it would not be viewable for intelligence analysis. It also asked providers to give advance notice of changes that might affect the data transmitted to the NSA. The agency later eliminated the credit card data from its analytic stores, although the data remained in the agency's non-analytic online stores and in back-up tapes. Despite repeated efforts to attempt a technical fix, six months later the agency was still receiving a significant amount of credit card information from the provider. As a result of additional efforts, this was reduced to fewer than five credit card numbers per month, and the provider continued to work to eliminate such production entirely.

In June 2013, the British newspaper *The Guardian* began publishing a series of articles regarding the Section 215 program and other secret NSA activities, based on unauthorized disclosures of classified documents by NSA contractor Edward Snowden. In the months following these disclosures, the executive branch declassified certain information about the telephone records program, and intelligence officials testified about it before Congress. In August 2013, the Obama Administration released a white paper setting forth the Administration's legal position on the statutory and constitutional legitimacy of the program.[192] Later that month, FISA court Judge Claire V. Eagan issued the first FISA court opinion that explained the court's rationale for approving the program.[193] On October 11, 2013, the FISA court again renewed the program, and Judge Mary A. McLaughlin issued a memorandum adopting and expanding on Judge Eagan's reasoning.[194] The FISA court reauthorized the Section 215 program most recently on January 3, 2014.

---

[192]   *See* Administration White Paper, Bulk Collection of Telephony Metadata under Section 215 of the USA PATRIOT Act (Aug. 9, 2013).

[193]   *See* Amended Memorandum Opinion, *In re Application of the Federal Bureau of Investigation for an Order Requiring the Production of Tangible Things*, No. BR 13-109 (FISA Ct. Aug. 29, 2013).

[194]   Memorandum, *In re Application of the Federal Bureau of Investigation for an Order Requiring the Production of Tangible Things*, No. BR 13-158 (FISA Ct. Oct. 11, 2013).

Part 5:
STATUTORY ANALYSIS

I.   Overview

Since 2006, the government has argued before the FISA court that Section 215 of the Patriot Act provides a legal basis for the NSA's bulk telephone records program. The FISA court has agreed and has authorized the program. In the wake of public disclosure of the program in June 2013, the government has further defended its statutory legitimacy in litigation and in a publicly issued white paper. Having independently examined this statutory question, the Board disagrees with the conclusions of the government and the FISA court. The Board believes that the following analysis is the most comprehensive analysis to date of Section 215 as it relates to the NSA's bulk telephone records program. We find that there are multiple and cumulative reasons for concluding that Section 215 does not authorize the NSA's ongoing daily collection of telephone calling records concerning virtually every American.

To be clear, the Board believes that this program has been operated in good faith to vigorously pursue the government's counterterrorism mission and appreciates the government's efforts to bring the program under the oversight of the FISA court. However, the Board concludes that Section 215 does not provide an adequate legal basis to support this program. Because the program is not statutorily authorized, it must be ended.

Section 215 is designed to enable the FBI to acquire records that a business has in its possession, as part of an FBI investigation, when those records are relevant to the investigation. Yet the operation of the NSA's bulk telephone records program bears almost no resemblance to that description.

First, the telephone records acquired under this program have no connection to any specific FBI investigation at the time the government obtains them. Instead, they are collected in advance to be searched later for records that do have such a connection. Second, because the records are collected in bulk — potentially encompassing all telephone calling records across the nation — they cannot be regarded as "relevant" to any FBI investigation without redefining that word in a manner that is circular, unlimited in scope, and out of step with precedent from analogous legal contexts involving the production of records. Third, instead of compelling telephone companies to turn over records already in their possession, the program operates by placing those companies under a continuing obligation to furnish newly generated calling records on a daily basis. This is an approach lacking foundation in the statute and one that is inconsistent with FISA as a whole, because it circumvents another provision that governs (and limits) the prospective collection of the same type of information. Fourth, the statute permits only the FBI to obtain items for use in its own investigations. It does not authorize the NSA to collect anything.

In addition, the Board concludes that the NSA's program violates the Electronic Communications Privacy Act. That statute prohibits telephone companies from sharing customer records with the government except in response to specific enumerated circumstances — which do not include orders issued under Section 215.

Finally, the Board does not believe that these flaws are overcome because Congress twice delayed the expiration of Section 215 during the operation of the program without amending the statute. The "reenactment doctrine," under which Congress is presumed to have adopted settled administrative or judicial interpretations of a statute, does not trump the plain meaning of a law, and it cannot save an administrative or judicial interpretation that contradicts the statute itself. Moreover, the circumstances presented here differ in pivotal ways from any in which the reenactment doctrine has ever been applied. Applying the doctrine here would undermine the public's ability to know what the law is and hold their elected representatives accountable for their legislative choices.

II.   Connection Between Calling Records and Specific FBI Investigations

In order for business records or other tangible things to be acquired through Section 215, the government must provide a statement of facts showing reasonable grounds to believe that they are "relevant to an authorized investigation (other than a threat assessment)" to obtain foreign intelligence information or to protect against international terrorism or clandestine intelligence activities.[195]

Before examining whether the massive quantity of telephone records acquired under Section 215 can plausibly be regarded as relevant to the government's counterterrorism efforts, given that nearly all of them are not connected to terrorism in any way, the latter part of the statutory formulation "relevant to *an authorized investigation*" merits independent consideration. Regardless of how expansively the word "relevant" may be construed, the statute demands some nexus between the records sought and a specific investigation.

Notably, Section 215 requires that records sought be relevant to "an" authorized investigation. Elsewhere, the statute similarly describes the records that can be obtained

---

[195]   50 U.S.C. § 1861(b)(2)(A) ("Each application under this section . . . shall include . . . a statement of facts showing that there are reasonable grounds to believe that the tangible things sought are relevant to an authorized investigation (other than a threat assessment) conducted in accordance with subsection (a)(2) to obtain foreign intelligence information not concerning a United States person or to protect against international terrorism or clandestine intelligence activities[.]").

under its auspices as those sought "for an investigation."[196] The use of the singular noun in these passages signals an expectation that the records are being sought for use in a specific, identified investigation. This interpretation is reinforced by the requirement that the FISA court make specific findings about the investigation for which the records are sought — that it is supported by a factual predicate, conducted according to guidelines approved by the Attorney General, and not based solely upon activities protected by the First Amendment when conducted of a U.S. person.[197]

The government's applications to the FISA court seeking renewal of the NSA's program do not link the applications to a single counterterrorism investigation. Instead, the applications list multiple terrorist organizations, assert that the FBI is investigating all of them, and declare that the telephone records being sought are relevant to each of those investigations. The FISA court orders granting the government's applications all contain a finding that there are reasonable grounds to believe that the records sought are relevant to authorized "investigations."[198] The orders further conclude that these investigations satisfy the three criteria listed above.[199] The FISA court has stated that the purpose of the government's applications "is to obtain foreign intelligence information in support of . . . individual authorized investigations to protect against international terrorism and concerning various international terrorist organizations."[200]

The government's approach, in short, has been to declare that the calling records being sought are relevant to *all* of the investigations cited in its applications. This approach, at minimum, is in deep tension with the statutory requirement that items obtained through a Section 215 order be sought for "an investigation," not for the purpose of enhancing the government's counterterrorism capabilities generally. Declaring that the calling records are relevant to every counterterrorism investigation cited by the government is little

---

[196]   50 U.S.C. § 1861(a)(1).

[197]   By referring to an "authorized" investigation, "other than a threat assessment," 50 U.S.C. § 1861(b)(2)(A), Section 215 excludes those FBI investigatory activities that "do not require a particular factual predicate" — limiting its reach to approved investigations that have been initiated "on the basis of any 'allegation or information' indicative of possible criminal activity or threats to the national security." FBI Domestic Investigations and Operations Guide §§ 5.1, 6.2 (Oct. 15, 2011). The investigation for which the records are sought also must be "conducted under guidelines approved by the Attorney General under Executive Order 12333 (or a successor order)," and must "not be conducted of a United States person solely upon the basis of activities protected by the first amendment to the Constitution of the United States." 50 U.S.C. § 1861(a)(2).

[198]   *See* Primary Order at 2, *In re Application of the Federal Bureau of Investigation for an Order Requiring the Production of Tangible Things*, No. BR 13-158 (Oct. 11, 2013) ("Primary Order").

[199]   *See* Primary Order at 2.

[200]   Amended Memorandum Opinion at 4, *In re Application of the Federal Bureau of Investigation for an Order Requiring the Production of Tangible Things*, No. BR 13-109 (FISA Ct. Aug. 29, 2013) ("Amended Memorandum Opinion").

different, in practical terms, from simply declaring that they are relevant to counterterrorism in general.

That is particularly so when the number of calling records sought is not limited by reference to the facts of any specific investigation. At its core, the approach boils down to the proposition that essentially all telephone records are relevant to essentially all international terrorism investigations. The Board does not believe that this approach comports with a fair reading of the statute.

Moreover, this approach undermines the value of an important statutory limitation on the government's collection of records under Section 215. The statute provides that records cannot be obtained for a "threat assessment," meaning those FBI investigatory activities that "do not require a particular factual predicate."[201] By excluding threat assessments from the types of investigations that can justify an order, Congress directed that Section 215 not be used to facilitate the broad and comparatively untethered investigatory probing that is characteristic of such assessments. But by collecting the nation's calling records *en masse*, under an expansive theory of their relevance to multiple investigations, the NSA's program undercuts one of the functions of the "threat assessment" exclusion: ensuring that records are not acquired by the government without some reason to suspect a connection between those records and a specific, predicated terrorism investigation. While the rules governing the program limit the *use* of telephone records to searches that are prompted by a specific investigation, the relevance requirement in Section 215 restricts the *acquisition* of records by the government.

III.   Relevance

The government has argued, and the FISA court has agreed, that essentially the entire nation's calling records are "relevant" to every counterterrorism investigation cited in the government's applications to the court. This position is untenable. Moreover, the interpretation of Section 215 adopted by the FISA court is dangerously overbroad, leading to the implication that virtually all information may be relevant to counterterrorism and therefore subject to collection by the government.

Since the public disclosure of the NSA's program, two related rationales have been offered in support of the government's interpretation of the word "relevant" under Section

---

[201]   FBI Domestic Investigations and Operations Guide §§ 5.1, 6.2 (Oct. 15, 2011). Although threat assessments do not require a factual predicate, they may not be based on "arbitrary or groundless speculation" or "solely on the exercise of First Amendment protected activities or on the race, ethnicity, national origin or religion of the subject." *Id.* § 5.1. *See also* The Attorney General's Guidelines for Domestic FBI Operations, § II (Sept. 29, 2008) (distinguishing between assessments and predicated investigations).

215. One is found in a FISA court opinion from August 2013, which reflects the interpretation presented to the court since 2006 in the government's applications.[202] The other, related, rationale is found in a publicly issued administration white paper and in filings submitted to other courts by the government in response to legal challenges to the program.[203] We address these two rationales in turn.

A. "Necessity"

While recognizing that the NSA collects telephone records indiscriminately under its Section 215 program — potentially acquiring the entire nation's daily calling records — the FISA court has concluded that all of those records are relevant to the government's counterterrorism investigations. The court's reasoning: collecting telephone records in bulk is necessary to enable a particular analytic tool that the government wishes to employ in its investigations. Because this tool involves searching all calling records in order to identify those that are related to terrorism, all calling records are relevant to the government's investigations.

In the FISA court's words, its finding of relevance "most crucially depended on the conclusion that bulk collection is *necessary* for NSA to employ tools that are likely to generate useful investigative leads to help identify and track terrorist operatives."[204] As with an earlier NSA program that collected Internet metadata in bulk, the court determined that "bulk collections such as these are necessary to identify the much smaller number of [international terrorist] communications," and the court explained that "it is this showing of necessity that led the Court to find that that the entire mass of collected metadata is relevant to investigating [international terrorist groups] and affiliated persons."[205] Because "the subset of terrorist communications is ultimately contained within the whole of the metadata produced, but can only be found after the production is aggregated and then queried using identifiers determined to be associated with identified international terrorist organizations, the whole production is relevant to the ongoing investigation out of necessity."[206] Therefore, according to the FISA court, "[a]ll of the metadata collected is thus

---

[202]   *See* Amended Memorandum Opinion, *In re Application of the Federal Bureau of Investigation for an Order Requiring the Production of Tangible Things*, No. BR 13-109 (FISA Ct. Aug. 29, 2013).

[203]   *See* Administration White Paper, Bulk Collection of Telephony Metadata under Section 215 of the USA PATRIOT Act, at 8-15 (Aug. 9, 2013); Defendants' Memorandum of Law in Support of Motion to Dismiss the Complaint, at 20-29, *ACLU v. Clapper*, No. 13-3994 (S.D.N.Y. Aug. 26, 2013).

[204]   Amended Memorandum Opinion at 20 (quoting Memorandum Opinion, No. PR/TT [*redacted*] (FISA Ct. 2010)); *see id.* at 21 ("This case is no different.").

[205]   Amended Memorandum Opinion at 20 (quoting Memorandum Opinion, No. PR/TT [*redacted*] (FISA Ct. 2010) (internal quotation marks omitted; brackets in Amended Memorandum Opinion)).

[206]   Amended Memorandum Opinion at 22.

relevant, because the success of this investigative tool depends on bulk collection."[207] A recent decision from the Southern District of New York adopted the same reasoning, stating that "aggregated telephony metadata is relevant because it allows the [NSA's] querying technique to be comprehensive."[208]

In the Board's view, this interpretation of the statute is circular and deprives the word "relevant" of any interpretive value. All records become relevant to an investigation, under this reasoning, because the government has developed an investigative tool that functions by collecting all records to enable later searching. The implication of this reasoning is that if the government develops an effective means of searching through *everything* in order to find *something*, then *everything* becomes relevant to its investigations. The word "relevant" becomes limited only by the government's technological capacity to ingest information and sift through it efficiently.

If Section 215's relevance requirement is to serve any meaningful function, however, relevance cannot be premised on the government's desire to use a tool whose very operation depends on collecting information without limit. We believe that a tool designed to capture *all* records of a particular type is simply incompatible with a statute requiring reasonable grounds to believe that "the tangible things sought are relevant to an authorized investigation."[209]

We find such a result not only inconsistent with the text of Section 215 but dangerously overbroad. While terrorists use telephone communications to facilitate their plans, they also write emails, open bank accounts, use debit and credit cards, send money orders, rent vehicles, book hotel rooms, sign leases, borrow library books, and visit websites, among other things. Having information about *all* such transactions, as conducted by every person in the United States, would aid the government's counterterrorism efforts so long as the government developed a technological means of sorting through the mass of data to find clues about suspected operatives. This elastic definition of relevance not only proves too much, but also supplies a license for nearly unlimited governmental acquisition of other kinds of transactional information.

This rationale also is inconsistent with Section 215's requirement that the government provide "a statement of facts" showing that there are "reasonable grounds to

---

[207]   Amended Memorandum Opinion at 21 (quoting Mem. of Law in Support of App. for Certain Tangible Things for Investigations to Protect Against International Terrorism, at 15, No. BR 06-05 (May 23, 2006)).

[208]   Memorandum & Order at 35, *ACLU v. Clapper*, No. 13-3994 (S.D.N.Y. Dec. 27, 2013). As the government has put it, the entire nation's telephone calling records are relevant to the FBI's counterterrorism investigations because "NSA's analytic tools require the collection and storage of a large volume of metadata" and its querying process "is not feasible unless NSA analysts have access to telephony metadata in bulk." Administration White Paper at 13.

[209]   50 U.S.C. § 1861(b)(2)(A).

believe" that items sought are relevant to an investigation.[210] Such language calls upon the government to supply a fact-bound explanation of why the particular group of records it seeks may have some bearing on one of its investigations. But because the NSA's program depends on collecting virtually all telephone records, only two facts are cited by the government in support of its applications: that terrorists communicate by telephone, and that it is necessary to collect records in bulk to find the connections that can be uncovered by NSA analysis.[211]

Neither of these facts shows why a particular group of telephone records may be relevant to an investigation, because the government has not limited its request to any particular group at all — only to a particular *type* of record (telephone calling records). But the *type* of records that can be acquired under Section 215 is defined elsewhere in the statute.[212] Unless the relevance requirement imposes an additional restriction beyond those provisions, it serves no real function at all. Thus we disagree that "all telephony metadata is a relevant category of information" that the government may request under Section 215.[213] Because if the category "all telephony metadata" is acceptable, why not "all metadata"? Or simply "all data"? That is the future that can be expected if the government's interpretation of Section 215 prevails.

B. Analogous Contexts

Noting that the word "relevant" is undefined in Section 215, the FISA court believed that it must be given its "ordinary meaning."[214] In contrast, the government has argued in a white paper and in litigation that the concept of relevance "has developed a particularized legal meaning in the context of the production of documents and other things in conjunction with official investigations and legal proceedings."[215] The government argues that Congress "legislated against that legal backdrop in enacting Section 215 and thus

---

[210]   50 U.S.C. § 1861(b)(2)(A).

[211]   As the FISA court put it: "The fact that international terrorist operatives are using telephone communications, and that it is necessary to obtain the bulk collection of a telephone company's metadata to determine those connections between known and unknown international terrorist operatives as part of authorized investigations, is sufficient to meet the low statutory hurdle set out in Section 215 to obtain a production of records." Amended Memorandum Opinion at 22-23.

[212]   Specifically, the statute authorizes production of "any tangible things (including books, records, papers, documents, and other items)" that "can be obtained with a subpoena duces tecum issued by a court of the United States in aid of a grand jury investigation or with any other order issued by a court of the United States directing the production of records or tangible things." 50 U.S.C. § 1861(a)(1), (c)(2)(D).

[213]   Memorandum & Order, *ACLU v. Clapper, supra*, at 37.

[214]   Amended Memorandum Opinion at 18 (citing *Taniguchi v. Ken Pacific Saipan, Ltd.*, 132 S. Ct. 1997, 2002 (2012)).

[215]   Administration White Paper at 9.

'presumably kn[e]w and adopt[ed] the cluster of ideas that were attached to [the] word in the body of learning from which it was taken.'"[216]

Accordingly, the government has cited decisions involving civil discovery, grand jury subpoenas, and administrative subpoenas, arguing that in these analogous contexts courts recognize that "the relevance standard permits requests for the production of entire repositories of records, even when any particular record is unlikely to directly bear on the matter being investigated, because searching the entire repository is the only feasible means to locate the critical documents."[217] More broadly, the government views this case law as illustrating that "the relevance standard permits discovery of large volumes of information in circumstances where the requester seeks to identify much smaller amounts of information within the data that directly bears on the matter."[218] A recent decision of the Southern District of New York cited some of these decisions for the same purpose.[219]

We agree that the word "relevant" in Section 215 should be interpreted in light of precedent from analogous legal contexts involving the production of documents. But a close look at the decisions cited by the government, and others concerning the standards of relevance governing discovery and subpoenas, refutes the idea that the NSA's bulk collection of telephone records would be regarded as satisfying the relevance standard in any of those contexts.

The first problem is that, as the government acknowledges, "the cases that have been decided in these contexts do not involve collection of data on the scale at issue in the telephony metadata collection program."[220] But the second and more fundamental problem is that these cases do not employ an analytical concept of "relevance" that matches the one being offered in support of the NSA's program. Simply put, there is no precedent for the notion that the government may collect a massive trove of records, of which virtually none can be expected to be pertinent to its investigation, merely because it has developed a technological tool that it believes will enable it to locate an infinitesimal fraction of pertinent records within that trove. Superficial similarities to that notion in the case law cited by the government dissolve upon further inspection.

It certainly is true that in the civil, grand jury, and administrative subpoena contexts, parties requesting materials may seek broad categories of documents, among which many of the individual records produced may prove unrelated. Such categories of materials can

---

[216]   Administration White Paper at 9 (quoting *FAA v. Cooper*, 132 S. Ct. 1441, 1449 (2012)).

[217]   Administration White Paper at 10.

[218]   Administration White Paper at 10.

[219]   Memorandum & Order, *ACLU v. Clapper*, at 37.

[220]   Administration White Paper at 11.

be regarded as "relevant" if obtaining them aids a party's fact-finding efforts, even if not all of the records are expected to be directly pertinent. Civil litigants, grand juries, and administrative agencies, when pursuing the "discovery of evidence" or acting in their "investigative function," need not be "limited [by] forecasts of the probable result of the investigation."[221] The case law also shows that the sheer volume of a discovery request is not alone grounds for a finding of irrelevance — at least in the scenarios confronted so far by the courts, which have involved dramatically fewer materials.

These broad propositions are not sufficient to justify the NSA's bulk collection of records under Section 215. In every decision cited by the government, the category of records sought has been limited in *some* way by reference to the facts of the specific investigation at hand. There is always some qualitative reason to suspect that the particular group of items requested has some special significance to the investigation, making the items in that category "relevant" even if many of them turn out to be immaterial. For instance, suspecting a doctor of health care fraud, the government may broadly subpoena that doctor's records for evidence of wrongdoing. Or suspecting that an employer is discriminating against women, plaintiffs may obtain a wide range of human resource records to analyze for patterns of discrimination. The scope of the request is always defined and limited by the specific facts of the investigation.

Not so for the NSA's bulk telephone records program, where the government seeks virtually all telephone calling records based on the premise that terrorists use telephones. The only limiting principle is that the government's request is confined to a particular *type* of record: telephone calling records. As to that type of record, however, the government seeks access to virtually everything. Such a concept simply is not found in the case law that, as the government acknowledges, Congress presumably incorporated into Section 215's definition of "relevant."

Simply put, analogous precedent does not support anything like the principle that necessity equals relevance, or that a body of records can be deemed relevant when virtually all of them are known to be unrelated to the purpose for which they are sought. Regardless of the broad scope courts have afforded the relevance standard with respect to discovery and government subpoenas, there is always a qualitative limiting principle that connects the range of documents sought to the facts of the investigation at hand, thus placing a check on the power to acquire information. Relevance limitations are a shield that protects against overreaching, not a sword that enables it.

Below, we discuss in detail the case law from which we draw these conclusions. In doing so, we separate decisions from the civil, criminal, and administrative contexts, to

---

[221] *Oklahoma Press Pub. Co. v. Walling*, 327 U.S. 186, 216 (1946) (quoting *Blair v. United States*, 250 U.S. 273, 282 (1919)).

better explain how particular holdings fit into the standards that govern each production or discovery regime.

1. Relevance in Civil Discovery

The relevance requirement in civil discovery is rooted in Rule 26 of the Federal Rules of Civil Procedure, which permits parties to obtain discovery "regarding any nonprivileged matter that is relevant to any party's claim or defense" and authorizes courts to "order discovery of any matter relevant to the subject matter involved in the action."[222] "Relevant information," under Rule 26, "need not be admissible at the trial if the discovery appears reasonably calculated to lead to the discovery of admissible evidence."[223]

The phrase "relevant to the subject matter involved in the action" has been "construed broadly to encompass any matter that bears on, or that reasonably could lead to other matter that could bear on, any issue that is or may be in the case."[224] Thus, the scope of civil discovery under the Federal Rules "is traditionally quite broad," and the test "is whether the line of interrogation is reasonably calculated to lead to the discovery of admissible evidence."[225] These standards also reflect the reality that a party cannot know in advance the content of all the materials it seeks. To some inevitable extent, therefore, "pretrial discovery is a fishing expedition and one can't know what one has caught until one fishes."[226]

Nevertheless, "discovery, like all matters of procedure, has ultimate and necessary boundaries."[227] As one court has put it, "practical considerations dictate that the parties should not be permitted to roam in shadow zones of relevancy and to explore matter which does not presently appear germane on the theory that it might conceivably become so."[228] And the broad scope of relevance "should not be misapplied" to permit overbearing requests.[229] The "boundaries defining information that is relevant to the subject matter

---

[222]   FED. R. CIV. P. 26(b)(1).

[223]   FED. R. CIV. P. 26(b)(1).

[224]   *Oppenheimer Fund, Inc. v. Sanders*, 437 U.S. 340, 351 (1978) (citing *Hickman v. Taylor*, 329 U.S. 495, 501 (1947)).

[225]   *Lewis v. ACB Bus. Servs., Inc.*, 135 F.3d 389, 402 (6th Cir. 1998) (quotation marks omitted) (citing, *inter alia, Oppenheimer Fund, Inc.*, 437 U.S. at 351); *accord Daval Steel Products v. M/V Fakredine*, 951 F.2d 1357, 1367 (2d Cir. 1991) ("This obviously broad rule is liberally construed."); *Nat'l Serv. Indus., Inc. v. Vafla Corp.*, 694 F.2d 246, 250 (11th Cir. 1982) ("This phrase is to be construed broadly."); *Santiago v. Fenton*, 891 F.2d 373, 379 (1st Cir. 1989) ("As a general matter, parties are entitled to broad discovery.").

[226]   *Nw. Mem'l Hosp. v. Ashcroft*, 362 F.3d 923, 931 (7th Cir. 2004).

[227]   *Oppenheimer Fund, Inc.*, 437 U.S. at 351 (quoting *Hickman*, 329 U.S. at 507); *see id.* at 354 (finding discovery request to be beyond "the scope of legitimate discovery").

[228]   *In re Sur. Ass'n of Am.*, 388 F.2d 412, 414 (2d Cir. 1967) (citation & quotation marks omitted).

[229]   *Hofer v. Mack Trucks, Inc.*, 981 F.2d 377, 380 (8th Cir. 1992).

involved in the action are necessarily vague," however, "and it is practically impossible to state a general rule by which they can be drawn[.]'"[230]

The absence of clearly defined boundaries means that resolving disputes over relevance in civil discovery typically calls for an examination of analogous cases. To that end, the government has cited several decisions addressing the scope of civil discovery that, in its view, support the expansive concept of relevance embodied in the FISA court's approval of the NSA's telephone records program.[231] Some of these decisions simply are not germane, and none are sufficient to support that expansive definition.

The plaintiffs in *Goshawk Dedicated Ltd. v. Am. Viatical Servs., LLC*, two insurance companies, sought discovery from the defendant of "an underwriting database" maintained by the defendant that contained detailed actuarial data used by the defendant "in purchasing life insurance policies, in procuring insurance from Plaintiffs, and in analyzing whether its actuarial data was accurate."[232] The defendant objected "that the database contains a significant amount of actuarial data not relevant to this litigation" — apparently meaning data that was not utilized in obtaining insurance from the plaintiffs. The defendant also contended "that the 'methodologies, policies, and practices' of its life expectancy evaluations are protected trade secrets and thus should not be subject to discovery."[233]

The court rejected the defendant's arguments as follows: "The problem with AVS's contention is that its methodologies, policies, and practices of conducting life expectancy evaluations are themselves at the center of this litigation." Stating that AVS's legitimate confidentiality concerns were addressed through a confidentiality order, the court concluded that the database sought "is highly relevant to the claims and defenses in this litigation" and that "AVS has not come forth with a valid legal basis for resisting its disclosure."[234]

The entire discussion in *Goshawk* is only three paragraphs long, and the court did not explicitly weigh in on whether, as the defendant maintained, the database truly "contain[ed] a significant amount of actuarial data not relevant to th[e] litigation." But the court's brief discussion suggests that it rejected the very notion that data relating to

---

[230] *Food Lion, Inc. v. United Food & Commercial Workers Int'l Union, AFL-CIO-CLC*, 103 F.3d 1007, 1012 (D.C. Cir. 1997) (quoting 8 WRIGHT, MILLER & MARCUS, FEDERAL PRACTICE AND PROCEDURE: CIVIL 2D § 2008, at 105-06 (1994)).

[231] *See* Administration White Paper at 9-11.

[232] *Goshawk Dedicated Ltd. v. Am. Viatical Servs., LLC*, No. 05-2343, 2007 WL 3492762, at *1 (N.D. Ga. Nov. 5, 2007).

[233] *Id.*

[234] *Id.*

transactions with other insurers was immaterial. Such data revealed the defendant's "methodologies, policies, and practices of conducting life expectancy evaluations," which were "at the center" of the litigation.[235]

In other words, the court in *Goshawk* did not conclude that "searching the entire repository [was] the only feasible means to locate the critical documents."[236] It did not endorse the assertion that that the database "contained a significant amount of irrelevant data"[237] but order production nevertheless. Rather, the court appears to have concluded that *all* of the documents were critical, rejecting the premise that data pertaining to other insurers was irrelevant.

Another case cited by the government, *Chen-Oster v. Goldman, Sachs & Co.*, is even less on-point.[238] In this gender-discrimination Title VII case, where former employees brought a putative class action against Goldman Sachs, the plaintiffs sought a discovery order requiring Goldman Sachs to extract certain human resources information from four separate and differently structured databases. The information was alleged to be "necessary for any statistical analysis of Goldman Sachs' employment practices" at both the class-certification and merits stages.[239] Goldman Sachs objected on proportionality grounds under Rule 26(b)(2)(C), citing the immense number of hours it would take to extract the requested information from its databases.[240]

The passage in this decision relied on by the government, which is not its holding, occurs during a discussion of less costly alternatives to the plaintiffs' request. The court first floated the possibility of ordering Goldman Sachs to extract and analyze small samples from the database, but concluded that it lacked the expertise to unilaterally impose any particular technique on the parties.[241] "The other alternative — and one that the plaintiffs advocate — would require Goldman Sachs to produce in digital form all of the information contained in each of the databases. Goldman Sachs acknowledges that, at least in the short run, such a 'data dump' would impose less of a burden on it than a more targeted production."[242] In the passage highlighted by the government, the court noted that "[t]here is no legal impediment to ordering production in that form," but for pragmatic reasons the

---

235   *Id.*

236   Administration White Paper at 10.

237   Administration White Paper at 10 n.7.

238   *Chen-Oster v. Goldman, Sachs & Co.*, 285 F.R.D. 294 (S.D.N.Y. 2012).

239   *Id.* at 297.

240   *Id.* at 303-04.

241   *Id.* at 304.

242   *Id.* at 305.

court declined to order Goldman Sachs to proceed in this way.[243] Instead, the court granted the plaintiffs' original request and ordered Goldman Sachs to extract the requested information from the databases.[244]

All that *Chen-Oster* provides, therefore, is a passing nod to the idea that civil plaintiffs can obtain compelled disclosure of an entire database from a defendant. And the plaintiffs in that case intended to analyze *all* of the information in those four databases, arguing that it was "relevant *in the aggregate* to perform the applicable analyses to show patterns of statistically significant shortfalls or effects of challenged policies."[245]

Chen-Oster cites two decisions in support of its observation that there was "no legal impediment" to ordering disclosure of a database. One is *Goshawk*, described above. The other is *High Point SARL v. Sprint Nextel Corp.*[246]

In *High Point*, a patent infringement case, one of the plaintiff's interrogatories asked Sprint to identify information about certain technical components within its cellular telephone network. In response, Sprint produced a spreadsheet drawn from its so-called "ATLAS" system, "the tool used by Sprint to comply with the internal control requirements of the Sarbanes–Oxley Act, as they relate to inventory and installed equipment."[247] Sprint later produced a supplement to this spreadsheet, but the plaintiff notified Sprint that it thought this supplement was incomplete. Sprint then produced yet another supplemental spreadsheet. The plaintiff, High Point, told the court that it was "skeptical of how Sprint queried its ATLAS database given that each supplemental spreadsheet contained substantial new information." To address these concerns, High Point requested that Sprint be ordered to produce "the whole ATLAS database from which the report was generated."[248]

Sprint objected "that the ATLAS database in its entirety includes tremendous quantities of irrelevant information." Rejecting this argument, the court explained that "High Point has raised sufficient questions regarding whether Sprint's production of the spreadsheets generated from the ATLAS database includes all responsive information," and that "Sprint's only objection to this proposal appears to be that production of the database

---

[243]   *Id.*

[244]   *Id.*

[245]   *Id.* at 304 (emphasis in original); *see id.* at 305 (agreeing that "[t]he information in the databases is central to the plaintiffs' claims of gender discrimination in compensation, promotion, and evaluation").

[246]   *High Point SARL v. Sprint Nextel Corp.*, No. 09-2269, 2011 WL 4526770 (D. Kan. Sept. 28, 2011).

[247]   *High Point SARL*, 2011 WL 4526770, at *12.

[248]   *Id.*

would include large quantities of irrelevant information." But "[t]his is not a persuasive argument against producing the ATLAS database."[249]

In other words, the court in *High Point* ordered production of the entire database, irrelevant information and all, in response to specific facts undermining confidence that Sprint was querying the database in a manner that would retrieve all of the relevant information requested by its adversary. Only in that context did the court find disclosure of the entire database to be appropriate. Rather than constituting a statement on the scope of relevance, this opinion represents a court exercising its discretionary power to ensure fairness between adversaries and completeness of their mutual disclosures. Moreover, obtaining a database that includes "large quantities of irrelevant information" is different from obtaining one that consists nearly entirely of irrelevant information — much less all such databases.

In another case cited by the government, *Medtronic Sofamor Danek, Inc. v. Michelson*, "the parties [did] not seriously dispute the relevance of the electronic data at issue."[250] The question was who would be required to shoulder the considerable burden and cost of converting discoverable electronic data held by the plaintiff into a usable format.[251] The decision implicitly accepts that a party may request a "large volume of data" from the other party in discovery, and that such requests may return irrelevant materials along with those that prove to be relevant: it notes that the materials sought are relevant because they "may contain discoverable material, although neither party can estimate how much."[252] Thus, the decision illustrates the basic proposition that civil litigants may request large numbers of records in discovery with the intention of sifting through them for those that support their case. But there is no suggestion that the likely proportion of relevant to irrelevant material in that case even approached that in the NSA's Section 215 program. Indeed, the parties "could not estimate" how much discoverable material was within the request. In contrast, the government knows in advance that virtually everything produced in response to the FISA court's orders will be irrelevant.

The last case cited by the government, *In re Adelphia Commc'ns Corp.* has nothing to do with the permissible breadth of discovery or the meaning of the word "relevance."[253] There, the party seeking discovery wanted production of *fewer* documents, not more, and the court noted that it "does not endorse a method of document production that merely

---

249   *Id.*

250   *Medtronic Sofamor Danek, Inc. v. Michelson*, 229 F.R.D. 550, 553 (W.D. Tenn. 2003).

251   *Id.* at 552-53.

252   *Id.* at 553.

253   *See In re Adelphia Commc'ns Corp.*, 338 B.R. 546 (Bankr. S.D.N.Y. 2005),

gives the requesting party access to a 'document dump,' with an instruction to the party to 'go fish.'"[254]

In sum, it is clear that the "relevance" standard in civil discovery permits litigants to seek large batches of material even though *some* or even many of those materials may prove irrelevant. But the case law does not sanction requesting an entire class of records, without limit or any specific connection to the matter at hand, and with knowledge that only an infinitesimal portion of those records conceivably are pertinent.

2. Relevance and Grand Jury Subpoenas

The government has extraordinarily broad power to subpoena documents when investigating possible criminal activity with a grand jury. "The function of the grand jury is to inquire into *all information that might possibly bear on its investigation* until it has identified an offense or has satisfied itself that none has occurred. As a necessary consequence of its investigatory function, the grand jury paints with a broad brush."[255] Accordingly, a grand jury investigation "is not fully carried out until *every available clue has been run down* and all witnesses examined in every proper way to find if a crime has been committed."[256] The scope of its inquiry "is not to be limited narrowly by questions of propriety or forecasts of the probable result of the investigation, or by doubts whether any particular individual will be found properly subject to an accusation of crime."[257] When a subpoena is challenged on relevancy grounds, therefore, "the motion to quash must be denied unless the district court determines that there is no reasonable possibility that the category of materials the Government seeks will produce information relevant to the general subject of the grand jury's investigation."[258] After all, "the decision as to what offense will be charged is routinely not made until after the grand jury has concluded its investigation," and "[o]ne simply cannot know in advance whether information sought

---

254   *Id.* at 551. In *Adelphia*, a bankruptcy trust conducting discovery against certain defendants objected when the defendants proposed to comply by "making their warehoused document archive available for inspection" by the trust — an archive containing "approximately 20,000 large bankers boxes of business records as well as over 600 boxes of business records deemed relevant to the various investigations underway." The trust argued that Rule 34 does not allow production of requested materials "in the midst of a large quantity of un-requested, non-responsive materials." *Id.* at 549. Instead, the trust argued that the defendants, rather than the trust, "should be forced to cull through the boxes and produce responsive documents." *Id.* at 553. The court sided with the defendants, but on the condition that "any archived documents produced must be thoroughly indexed, the boxes accurately labeled and the depository kept in good order." *Id.* at 551. A "document dump," with instructions to "go fish," was "emphatically not the situation presented to the Court in this matter," where the defendants' archive was "an orderly facility with neatly stacked rows of boxes organized by department and labeled as to content[.]" *Id.*

255   *United States v. R. Enterprises, Inc.*, 498 U.S. 292, 297 (1991) (emphasis added).

256   *Id.* (quoting *Branzburg v. Hayes*, 408 U.S. 665, 701 (1972) (emphasis added).

257   *Branzburg*, 408 U.S. at 688 (quoting *Blair*, 250 U.S. at 282).

258   *R. Enterprises, Inc.*, 498 U.S. at 301.

during the investigation will be relevant and admissible in a prosecution for a particular offense."[259]

"The investigatory powers of the grand jury are nevertheless not unlimited. Grand juries are not licensed to engage in arbitrary fishing expeditions, nor may they select targets of investigation out of malice or an intent to harass."[260] While a grand jury need not restrict its inquiry to admissible evidence, the Fourth Amendment "provides protection against a grand jury subpoena duces tecum too sweeping in its terms 'to be regarded as reasonable.'"[261] And where a grand jury subpoena implicates the freedom of speech or association, some courts have required the government to demonstrate "a compelling interest in and a sufficient nexus between the information sought and the subject matter of its investigation."[262] "In sum, the fact that grand juries must have broad investigative powers does not resolve all questions of the permissible breadth and requisite specificity of a subpoena duces tecum."[263]

To determine what might be the outer limits of a grand jury subpoena, we have examined both the cases cited by the government and others. There has never been a grand jury subpoena as broad as the FISA court's Section 215 orders. And contrary to the government's suggestion, the case law does not hold that the breadth of a grand jury subpoena is unlimited, but rather that a subpoena must be designed to address the circumstances of a specific investigation.

One decision, *In re Grand Jury Proceedings*, merely explains that district courts assessing the relevance of subpoenaed materials should not proceed "document-by-

---

[259]   *Id.* at 300; *see United States v. Triumph Capital Grp., Inc.*, 544 F.3d 149, 168 (2d Cir. 2008) ("[S]ubpoenas *duces tecum* are often drawn broadly, sweeping up both documents that may prove decisive and documents that turn out not to be. This practice is designed to make it unlikely that a relevant document will escape the grand jury's notice."); 3 WAYNE R. LaFAVE ET AL., CRIMINAL PROCEDURE, § 8.8(b) (3d. ed.) (explaining that "the nature of the criminal activity [the grand jury] seeks to investigate often requires consideration of a substantial amount of information that will prove in the end to be irrelevant"); 1 SARA SUN BEALE ET AL., GRAND JURY LAW AND PRACTICE § 6:21 (2d ed.) (noting that relevancy objections "are almost universally overruled").

[260]   *R. Enterprises, Inc.*, 498 U.S. at 299 (internal citations omitted); *see In re Grand Jury Proceedings*, 616 F.3d 1186, 1203 (10th Cir. 2010) (explaining that "fishing is permissible so long as it is not an *arbitrary* fishing expedition" (emphasis in original)); *Gher v. Dist. Court In & For Adams Cnty.*, 516 P.2d 643, 644 (Colo. 1973) (quashing grand jury subpoena where district attorney attempted to use it as means of developing facts relating to municipal dispute that did not involve "any possible violation of criminal laws").

[261]   *United States v. Dionisio*, 410 U.S. 1, 11 (1973) (quoting *Hale v. Henkel*, 201 U.S. 43, 76 (1906)).

[262]   *In re Grand Jury Subpoenas Duces Tecum*, 78 F.3d 1307, 1312 (8th Cir. 1996) (citing *In re Grand Jury Proceeding*, 842 F.2d 1229 (11th Cir. 1988), & *Glass v. Heyd*, 457 F.2d 562 (5th Cir. 1972)); *accord Bursey v. United States*, 466 F.2d 1059, 1083 (9th Cir. 1972)).

[263]   *In re Grand Jury Subpoena: Subpoena Duces Tecum*, 829 F.2d 1291, 1297 (4th Cir. 1987); *see Dionisio*, 410 U.S. at 11 ("This is not to say that a grand jury subpoena is some talisman that dissolves all constitutional protections.").

document," but should instead evaluate whether each "broad category" of requested materials could contain possibly relevant documents. The former approach would "unduly disrupt the grand jury's broad investigatory powers" and force the government "to justify the relevancy of hundreds or thousands (or more) of individual documents, which it has not yet even seen[.]" Often the government "is not in a position to establish the relevancy with respect to specific documents," because "it may not know the precise content of the requested documents" and "it may not know precisely what information is or is not relevant at the grand jury investigative stage."[264] Accepting the "incidental" production of irrelevant documents, when measured by the hundreds or thousands, does not support the legitimacy of the Section 215 calling records program, in which the NSA potentially collects billions of records per day with full knowledge that virtually all of them are irrelevant.[265]

The broadest grand jury subpoena that the government cites is *In re Grand Jury Proceedings: Subpoenas Duces Tecum.*[266] In that case, the Eighth Circuit upheld grand jury subpoenas for the records of all wire money transfers exceeding $1,000 sent during a two-year period from a Western Union office at the Royalle Inn in Kansas City, Missouri.

In rejecting the claim that the subpoenas were overbroad, the court stressed that only a single Western Union office was involved, and the "type of documents sought [was] precisely limited to those recording transactions of one thousand dollars or more occurring within a relatively short period of time."[267] As the decision explained, specific facts known to investigators pointed to the Royalle Inn office as a focal point for illegitimate, drug-related money transfers.[268]

---

264 *In re Grand Jury Proceedings*, 616 F.3d 1186, 1200-03 (10th Cir. 2010); *see also Triumph Capital Group, Inc.*, 544 F.3d at 168 ("Grand jury subpoenas *duces tecum* are customarily employed to gather information and make it available to the investigative team of agents and prosecutors so that it can be digested and sifted for pertinent matter. Before the subpoenas are issued, the government often does not have at its disposal enough information to determine precisely what information will be relevant.").

265 *In re Grand Jury Proceedings*, 616 F.3d at 1204-05.

266 *In re Grand Jury Proceedings: Subpoenas Duces Tecum*, 827 F.2d 301 (8th Cir. 1987).

267 *Id.* at 304. The court also relied on the presumption of regularity that attaches to grand jury subpoenas, and that "one challenging a grand jury subpoena has the burden of showing irregularity." *Id.* at 304. This presumption distinguishes the grand jury context from Section 215, where the government bears an initial burden of providing a statement of facts showing reasonable grounds to believe that the items it seeks are relevant. *See* 50 U.S.C. § 1861(b)(2)(A).

268 *See id.* at 302 ("In particular, the agent's affidavit stated that he had learned 'from numerous sources that drug dealers are using Western Union to transfer funds from Kansas City to various locations including Florida, California, and out of the country.' Further, the affidavit states that the agent had received information from the Kansas City, Missouri, Police Department that its Drug Enforcement Unit had discovered completed Western Union Money Transfer Applications during a search of 'dope houses' in the inner city. Jamaican nationals apparently operated these houses, and the applications revealed that funds were transmitted to the Miami area and Jamaica, both 'well known centers of narcotics trafficking.' The funds involved were wired from the Royalle Inn.").

The court emphasized that it was "upholding the subpoenas only as against the fourth amendment and Federal Communications Act challenges" brought by Western Union, pointedly mentioning that nothing would bar the trial court, upon proper motion, from "limiting the subpoenas to matters having a greater degree of general relevance to the subject matter of the investigation."[269] Noting that the government already knew what types of documents it was seeking ("records of wire transfers by numerous individuals to various points around the country"), the Eighth Circuit even suggested that the trial court "may therefore wish to consider the extent to which the government would be able to identify in advance those patterns or characteristics that would raise suspicion. These might include wire transfers to or from individual suspects, transfers to certain locales known to be sources of high volumes of illegal drugs, or other particular patterns designed to focus on illegal activity without taking in an unnecessary amount of irrelevant material."[270] Such an inquiry, the court said, "is appropriate to protect against unduly encroaching upon the expectations of innocent customers that their financial records will be kept confidential."[271]

The Western Union case does not support the expansive theory of relevance advanced in favor of the NSA's calling records program. Even where the government's request was limited to transactions over $1,000, during a limited period of time, in a single office that had a demonstrable connection to specific unlawful activity, the court still was concerned about the potentially unreasonable scope of the subpoenas and inadequate showing of relevance, and it offered suggestions on how to narrow even those subpoenas. The aspects of the subpoenas that the Eighth Circuit found troubling are multiplied exponentially under the NSA's calling records program, which collects the entire nation's calling records, for an indefinite period of time (renewed every ninety days since May 2006), based only on the fact that terrorists use telephones.

3. Relevance and Administrative Subpoenas

The closest analogue to the power conferred by Section 215 is the administrative subpoena. Indeed, Congress crafted Section 215 as a substitute for the administrative subpoena authority sought by the Administration after the 9/11 attacks.[272]

An administrative agency may conduct an investigation even though it lacks probable cause to believe that any particular statute is being violated. Like a grand jury, it can "investigate merely on suspicion that the law is being violated, or even just because it

---

269   *Id.* at 305.

270   *Id.* at 305-06.

271   *Id.* at 306.

272   *See* H.R. Rep. No. 107-236(I), at 61 (2001).

wants assurance that it is not."[273] The relevance requirement for administrative subpoenas derives from the statutes authorizing such subpoenas, inherent limits on the powers of administrative agencies, and the reasonableness requirement of the Fourth Amendment.[274] "Although 'a governmental investigation . . . may be of such a sweeping nature and so unrelated to the matter properly under inquiry as to exceed the investigatory power, it is sufficient if the inquiry is within the authority of the agency, the demand is not too indefinite and the information sought is reasonably relevant.'"[275]

Therefore, "to be valid, an administrative subpoena must seek information that is 'reasonably relevant' to the 'general purposes of the agency's investigation.'"[276] As with grand jury subpoenas, the materials sought "need only be relevant to the *investigation* — the boundary of which may be defined quite generally."[277] This relevance determination "cannot be reduced to formula; for relevancy and adequacy or excess in the breadth of the subpoena are matters variable in relation to the nature, purposes and scope of the inquiry."[278] Courts generally "defer to the agency's appraisal of relevancy,"[279] and some have said that, to be outside the bounds of a subpoena, information sought must be "plainly incompetent or irrelevant to any lawful purpose" of the agency.[280]

---

[273]   *United States v. Constr. Products Research, Inc.*, 73 F.3d 464, 470 (2d Cir. 1996) (quoting *United States v. Morton Salt Co.*, 338 U.S. 632, 642-43 (1950)); *see United States v. Powell*, 379 U.S. 48, 57 (1964); *Oklahoma Press Publishing Co.*, 327 U.S. at 201.

[274]   In *United States v. Powell*, which addressed the scope of the IRS Commissioner's subpoena power, the Supreme Court first articulated a standard that has since been applied to administrative subpoenas generally: the Commissioner was required to "show that the investigation will be conducted pursuant to a legitimate purpose, that the inquiry *may be relevant to the purpose*, that the information sought is not already within the Commissioner's possession, and that the administrative steps required by the Code have been followed." *Powell*, 379 U.S. at 57-58 (emphasis added); *see SEC v. Jerry T. O'Brien, Inc.*, 467 U.S. 735, 741-42 (1984) (characterizing these four requirements as "the general standards governing judicial enforcement of administrative subpoenas"); *Constr. Products Research, Inc.*, 73 F.3d at 471 (applying standards to evaluate reasonableness of Nuclear Regulatory Commission subpoena).

[275]   *United States v. Gurley*, 384 F.3d 316, 321 (6th Cir. 2004) (quoting *Morton Salt Co.*, 338 U.S. at 652 (internal citation omitted)).

[276]   *In re Sealed Case (Admin. Subpoena)*, 42 F.3d 1412, 1419 (D.C. Cir. 1994) (quoting *Linde Thomson Langworthy Kohn & Van Dyke, P.C. v. Resolution Trust Corp.*, 5 F.3d 1508, 1516 (D.C. Cir. 1993)); *accord In re McVane*, 44 F.3d 1127, 1135 (2d Cir. 1995); *NLRB v. Line*, 50 F.3d 311, 314 (5th Cir. 1995).

[277]   *FTC v. Invention Submission Corp.*, 965 F.2d 1086, 1090 (D.C. Cir. 1992) (emphasis in original).

[278]   *Oklahoma Press Pub. Co.*, 327 U.S. at 208-09; *see, e.g., FTC v. Turner*, 609 F.2d 743, 745 (5th Cir. 1980) ("The relevance of an F.T.C. subpoena request is measured against the purpose and scope of its investigation.").

[279]   *In re Sealed Case*, 42 F.3d at 1419; *see RNR Enterprises, Inc. v. SEC*, 122 F.3d 93, 97 (2d Cir. 1997) ("We defer to the agency's appraisal of relevancy, which must be accepted so long as it is not obviously wrong.").

[280]   *Constr. Products Research, Inc.*, 73 F.3d at 472 (quoting *Endicott Johnson*, 317 U.S. at 509).

Courts must "be careful," however, not to make relevance requirements "a nullity."[281] It is not a valid purpose of a subpoena, for instance, to investigate "other wrongdoing, as yet unknown," because such a broad mandate "makes it impossible . . . to determine whether the information demanded is 'reasonably relevant.'"[282] And while the standards governing the permissible scope of administrative subpoenas are broad, they are not as expansive as the government suggests.[283]

Because the relevance standard governing administrative subpoenas "cannot be reduced to formula" and varies along with "the nature, purposes and scope" of an investigation, here too recourse must be had to precedent involving analogous factual scenarios.[284] And here, once again, the case law fails to buttress the legitimacy of the NSA's telephone records program.

---

[281]   *EEOC v. Shell Oil Co.*, 466 U.S. 54, 69 (1984); *see id.* at 72 (rejecting argument that "would render nugatory the statutory limitation of the Commission's investigative authority to materials 'relevant' to a charge").

[282]   *In re Sealed Case*, 42 F.3d at 1418.

[283]   The government has suggested that the relevance standard in the administrative subpoena context "affords an agency 'access to virtually any material that might cast light on the allegations' at issue in an investigation." Administration White Paper at 9 (quoting *Shell Oil Co.*, 466 U.S. at 68-69). But the passage quoted from *Shell Oil* was addressed to subpoenas issue by the Equal Employment Opportunity Commission ("EEOC"), which fundamentally differ from most administrative subpoenas, because they confer access to materials only in connection with a specific charge of a violation that already has been filed. *See Shell Oil Co.*, 466 U.S. at 64 ("[T]he EEOC's investigative authority is tied to charges filed with the Commission; unlike other federal agencies that possess plenary authority to demand to see records relevant to matters within their jurisdiction, the EEOC is entitled to access only to evidence 'relevant to the charge under investigation.'" (quoting 42 U.S.C. § 2000e-8(a))). Other administrative subpoena statutes, similar to Section 215, permit discovery of materials relevant to *investigations*, which may not yet have coalesced around specific allegations or particular individuals. Thus, the broad standard articulated in *Shell Oil* — "virtually any material that might cast light on the allegations" — is from an anomalous context where the subpoena's breadth is circumscribed by its link to specific charges already filed. *See EEOC v. Randstad*, 685 F.3d 433, 448 (4th Cir. 2012) ("Once a charge has placed the Commission on notice *that a particular employer is (or may be) violating Title VII or the ADA in a particular way*, the Commission may access 'virtually any material that might cast light on the allegations against the employer.'" (quoting *Shell Oil Co.*, 466 U.S. at 68-69) (emphasis added)).

    Similarly, the government has quoted a phrase from *United States v. Arthur Young & Co.*, 465 U.S. 805, 814 (1984), indicating that the IRS Secretary may obtain items "of even *potential* relevance to an ongoing investigation.'" Administration White Paper at 10. But the Court in *Arthur Young* was merely explaining that "an IRS summons is not to be judged by the relevance standards used in deciding whether to admit evidence in federal court," and it used the adjective "potential" to acknowledge that the IRS "can hardly be expected to know whether such data will in fact be relevant until it is procured and scrutinized." The agency, therefore, "should not be required to establish that the documents it seeks are actually relevant in any technical, evidentiary sense." *Arthur Young & Co.*, 465 U.S. at 814. The Court's use of the phrase "potential relevance" here merely reaffirms the principles described earlier — that the government cannot always know in advance whether material is truly pertinent. It does not negate the more demanding requirement that "the information sought is *reasonably* relevant." *California Bankers Ass'n v. Shultz*, 416 U.S. 21, 67 (1974) (quoting *Morton Salt Co.*, 338 U.S. at 652-53 (emphasis added)).

[284]   *Oklahoma Press Pub. Co.*, 327 U.S. at 209.

For example, the government quotes passages from *Carrillo Huettel, LLP v. SEC* that appear to echo the NSA's rationale for obtaining bulk calling records. On closer examination, the similarity does not bear out. In *Carrillo*, the SEC subpoenaed the bank records of one law firm, requesting all of its trust account information over a two-year period. The request covered financial records not just for the firm's forty-two clients already identified by the SEC as possibly implicated in the securities investigation, but the records for "all its clients," of whom "100 or more" had not yet been identified or tied in any way to the investigation. Despite Carillo's argument "that the subpoena will result in the production of financial records of many clients that are irrelevant to the investigation at issue," the court enforced the subpoena.[285]

Two circumstances distinguish *Carillo*. First, the SEC was investigating not only the law firm's clients but the firm itself — that is, the subpoena was issued to the target of the SEC's investigation, unlike the situation with respect to the telephone companies covered by the NSA's program. The SEC had "obtained evidence" that Carillo not only represented the entities and individuals being investigated but "may also be actively involved in the alleged violations."[286] And this was the context in which the SEC argued that it "cannot effectively trace money through accounts without having records of all transactions," and that these records "may reveal concealed connections between unidentified entities and persons and those identified in the investigation thus far."[287] The government's request was limited to a category of records — those of the Carillo firm — that it had a cognizable reason to suspect as a whole.

The second difference is in the proportion of relevant to irrelevant materials expected to be produced. Of the law firm's roughly 150 clients, nearly a third had already been directly tied to the investigation. On the basis of these facts, the court determined that, "[o]n balance," the subpoena satisfied the relevancy requirement: "Although not *every* responsive document produced . . . may be relevant," the court reasoned, "there is reason to believe that the records *overall* contain information relevant to the investigation."[288] This conclusion was simply an application of the principle that a subpoenas duces tecum can be valid even if it may return some irrelevant materials — not that it can be valid where virtually *all* of the requested materials will be irrelevant.

In another case, *In re Subpoena Duces Tecum*, the government successfully compelled a doctor suspected of health care fraud to produce more than 15,000 patient files, "consisting of between 750,000 and 1.25 million pages of material," in spite of the

---

285   *Carrillo Huettel, LLP v. SEC*, No. 11-65, 2011 WL 601369, at *1-2 (S.D. Cal. Feb. 11, 2011).

286   *Id.* at *1; *see id.* at *2 ("The SEC contends that Carrillo's own conduct is at issue.").

287   *Id.*

288   *Id.* (emphasis added).

doctor's relevancy objection. The court explained that the "sheer volume of documents" could not be the sole criterion of reasonableness, and noted that the doctor had rejected the government's offer of accommodation under which he could maintain many of the files, subject to the U.S. Attorney expressing a need to review them.[289] The court also noted the government's argument "that it would be 'an oddity of jurisprudence' if a physician with a high-volume, government-subsidized practice could avoid complying with such subpoenas, whereas a physician with a lower volume and therefore with a narrower potential scope of fraud would have to comply," while observing that "to define the reasonableness of a subpoena based on the volume of items identified for production would be to require the government to ascertain, before issuing a subpoena, the extent of any wrongdoing. But ascertaining the extent of wrongdoing is itself a primary purpose for the issuance of the subpoena."[290]

Like *Carillo*, this decision shows that volume alone does not doom a subpoena's validity, and that some amount of over-collection is an inevitable byproduct of government investigations. But as in *Carillo*, the subpoena sought the records of an entity that was itself under investigation, and its broad reach reflected the government's desire to investigate this entity's conduct vis-à-vis the third parties to whom the records pertained. In both cases, the government's request was defined, and limited, by the facts of the investigation at hand. And in both cases the government had an articulable reason to suspect that the category of records it sought, so defined, would include a significant proportion of records pertinent to the investigation. These cases might support collecting all of a telephone company's calling records if, for instance, the company was suspected of fraudulently overbilling its customers — not because some of those customers might later turn out to be associated with an unrelated crime.

In sum, precedent involving relevance in the administrative subpoena context simply teaches the same lessons evident in the grand jury and civil discovery contexts, lessons that do not support the unbounded definition of relevance embodied in the FISA court's approval of the Section 215 program.[291]

---

[289]   *In re Subpoena Duces Tecum*, 228 F.3d 341, 345, 350-51 (4th Cir. 2000).

[290]   *Id.* at 350-51.

[291]   The government also has cited two decisions for the proposition that "[f]ederal agencies exercise broad subpoena powers or other authorities to collect and analyze large data sets in order to identify information that directly pertains to the particular subject of an investigation." Administration White Paper at 10 (citing *F.T.C. v. Invention Submission Corp.*, 965 F.2d at 1090, and *Associated Container Transp. (Australia) Ltd. v. United States*, 705 F.2d 53, 58 (2d Cir. 1983)). That broad proposition, and the cases cited, do not involve anything like the NSA's telephone records program — in which all records of a particular type are collected indiscriminately and preemptively in order to facilitate later searches of an infinitesimal fraction of those records. Similarly, the government has invoked decisions involving warrants that permit computer hard drives to be copied and later searched for incriminating evidence, *see id.* at 10-11, but these cases, involving seizures based on a finding of probable cause, have little bearing on the meaning of "relevance."

4. Expanding Relevance Beyond its Normal Legal Meaning

As illustrated above, precedent from other legal contexts involving the production of records does not support a concept of relevance like the one proffered by the government in support of the NSA's bulk calling records program. To be sure, the case law regarding civil discovery, grand jury subpoenas, and administrative subpoenas shows that relevance is interpreted broadly, and that incidental production of unrelated materials is accepted as essential to enable fulsome investigative efforts. Standards of relevance thus permit parties and the government to engage in a degree of fishing, so long as it is not arbitrary or in bad faith. But the case law makes equally clear that the definition of relevance is not boundless. And no case that we have found supports the interpretation of relevance embodied in the NSA's program.

Tacitly acknowledging that case law from analogous contexts is not adequate to support its position, the government suggests that Section 215 calls for "an even more flexible standard" of relevance.[292] But none of the government's arguments, in our view, supports a definition of "relevant" as broad as the one the government proffers.

First, had Congress wished to inscribe a standard of relevance in Section 215 even less exacting than those developed in analogous legal contexts, it could have done so. But contemporary statements from legislators, highlighted by the government itself, evince an intent to match Section 215 to the standards used in those contexts.[293] The reference to grand jury subpoenas added to the statute in 2006 was meant to reassure those with concerns about the scope of Section 215 that the statute was consistent with practice in other fields.[294]

Second, the fact that Section 215 requires only "reasonable grounds to believe" that records sought are relevant to an "investigation," as the government emphasizes, does not call for a different standard of relevance than the one used in all other contexts.[295] By demanding only "reasonable grounds to believe," rather than certainty, that items sought are relevant to an investigation, the statute ensures that Section 215 is consistent with the analogous civil and criminal contexts — where the requester need not show that every item sought *actually* is relevant in an evidentiary sense, but merely that the items

---

[292]   *See* Administration White Paper at 11-13.

[293]   *See* Defendants' Memorandum of Law, *ACLU v. Clapper*, at 23 (citing 152 Cong. Rec. S1598, 1606 (Mar. 2, 2006) (statement of Sen. Kyl) ("We all know the term 'relevance.' It is a term that every court uses .... The relevance standard is exactly the standard employed for the issuance of discovery orders in civil litigation, grand jury subpoenas in a criminal investigation, and for each and every one of the 335 different administrative subpoenas currently authorized by the United States Code.").

[294]   *See* 50 U.S.C. § 1861(c)(2)(D).

[295]   *See* 50 U.S.C. § 1861(b)(2)(A).

reasonably may be. The statute's reference to a reasonable *belief* about the items requested shows that it contemplates the same scenario faced in the subpoena and discovery arenas: the government seeks a category of items that it reasonably suspects, but cannot be sure, includes material pertinent to its investigation. That scenario, and the legal standards that govern it, still require some factual correlation between the category of documents defined by the government and the circumstances of the investigation for which they are sought. Indeed, Section 215's requirement of a "statement of facts" supporting the government's belief underscores the importance of that context-specific inquiry.

Thus, even if the qualifier "reasonable grounds to believe" imposes a lower burden of proof on the government than if the statute simply authorized production of "relevant" documents, Section 215 still embodies the assumption that specific facts will link the government's investigation to the particular group of records it seeks. That assumption is incompatible with a continuously renewed request for the daily acquisition of all records of a particular type.

Third, the unique characteristics of national security investigations do not warrant interpreting "relevance" expansively enough to support the NSA's program. The government argues, and we agree, that the scope of relevance varies based on the nature of the investigation to which it is applied.[296] Accordingly, the government cites the "remarkable breadth" of the national security investigations with which Section 215 is concerned, as contrasted with ordinary criminal matters, and emphasizes that these investigations "often focus on *preventing* threats to national security from causing harm, not on the retrospective determination of liability or guilt for prior activities."[297]

These valid distinctions, in our view, simply mean that the government will be able to make qualitative showings of relevance more often in national security investigations than in others. Because the government is investigating a broader scope of actors, over a longer period of time, across a wider geographic range, and before any specific offense has been committed, more information can be expected to be legitimately relevant to its efforts. Such considerations do not call for the wholesale elimination of relevance as a meaningful check on the government's acquisition of items.

Finally, the heightened importance of counterterrorism investigations, as compared with typical law enforcement matters, does not alter the equation. Items either are relevant to an investigation or they are not — the significance of that investigation is a separate matter. No matter how critical national security investigations are, therefore, *some* articulable principle must connect the items sought to those investigations, or else the

---

[296]   *See* Administration White Paper at 11.

[297]   Administration White Paper at 12.

word "relevant" is robbed of meaning. Congress added a relevance requirement to Section 215 in 2006 knowing full well that the statute governs national security investigations. It cannot, therefore, have meant for the importance of such investigations to efface that requirement entirely. [298]

In sum, we find the government's interpretation of the word "relevant" in Section 215 to be unsupported by legal precedent and a subversion of the statute's manifest intent to place *some* restriction, albeit a generous and flexible one, on the scope of the items that can be acquired under its auspices.[299]

IV.   Prospective Orders for Daily Disclosure of New Telephone Records

Every FISA court order renewing the bulk telephone records program puts telephone companies under a continuing obligation, over a period of ninety days, to provide the NSA with their newly generated calling records on a daily basis. In other words, when telephone companies receive an order from the FISA court, they are not directed to turn over whatever calling records they have in their possession at the time. Instead, every day for the next ninety days after receiving the order, they must furnish the NSA with the new calling records generated that day by their customers.

This arrangement differs from the normal practice that characterizes discovery between parties and the production of records in response to a subpoena. Typically, persons who receive a subpoena or court order must hand over documents already in their possession by a given date. They are not required to supply newly generated documents on a regular basis for a set period of time. Nor is this arrangement akin to the rolling production schedules sometimes approved by courts for the disclosure of records.[300] Rolling schedules merely dictate when documents that are already in existence must be made available to the opposing party, allowing the disclosures to be spread over a period of

---

[298]   Congress amended Section 215 to clarify that there must be reasonable grounds to believe that records obtained under the statute are "relevant to" an investigation, not merely sought "for" an investigation; it further required "a statement of facts" supporting that belief. *See* 50 U.S.C. § 1861(b)(2)(A). It inserted the concept of "relevance" into the statute not to broaden it, but to reassure those with concerns that the statute was tethered to concepts well known in other areas.

[299]   In analyzing the concept of relevance under Section 215, both the government and the FISA court have also cited the oversight mechanisms inscribed in the statute and devised for the bulk telephone records program that are not found in the analogous contexts of criminal or administrative subpoenas. *See* Administration White Paper at 13; Amended Memorandum Opinion at 23. We do not see how these oversight mechanisms bear on whether items are relevant to an authorized investigation.

[300]   *See, e.g., Global Client Solutions, LLC v. Executive Risk Indem., Inc.*, No. 13-0035, 2013 WL 4482992, at *1 (N.D. Okla. Aug. 19, 2013); *Prism Technologies, LLC v. Research in Motion, Ltd.*, No. 08-0537, 2010 WL 1254940, at *2 (D. Neb. Mar. 24, 2010); *In re September 11 Litig.*, 236 F.R.D. 164, 167 (S.D.N.Y. 2006).

time. That concession to the limits of human resources fundamentally differs from establishing an ongoing daily obligation to furnish new materials as they are created.

The government has offered a statutory defense of this practice.[301] But we conclude that it contravenes Section 215 for three reasons. First, the statute does not purport to authorize such orders, and case law involving the production of records in analogous contexts indicates that such authority cannot be inferred from statutory silence. Second, the text of Section 215 strongly suggests that it contemplates only the acquisition of items that already are in existence at the time the court issues an order. Third, interpreting Section 215 to permit the prospective collection of *telephone records* renders superfluous another provision of FISA that directly authorizes such collection — circumventing the limitations associated with that other provision and violating the interpretive principle that one provision in a statute should not be construed to make another superfluous.

For the reasons explained below, therefore, we believe that the language of Section 215 cannot support the government's interpretation on this matter. In our view, acceptance of that interpretation plays a key role in transforming the function of Section 215 — from a means of gathering business records for intelligence investigations (in a manner similar to the use of subpoenas in other types of investigations) into an ongoing surveillance tool.

A. Absence of Express or Implied Authorization

No language in Section 215 purports to authorize the FISA court to issue orders requiring the ongoing daily production of records not yet in existence. The government does not contend that any such language exists. Instead, it emphasizes the lack of an explicit prohibition against such orders and argues that the prospective production of records has been deemed appropriate in analogous contexts.[302] While the government highlights case law from two contexts in support of that argument, neither supports the issuance of Section 215 orders that prospectively require the daily disclosure of new records as they are generated.

The first set of cases to which the government points arise in civil discovery, where a party has been directed by a subpoena to produce materials by a deadline, the so-called return date of the subpoena. As the government notes, "courts have held that the Federal Rules of Civil Procedure give a court the 'authority to order [the] respondent to produce materials created after the return date of the subpoena.'"[303]

---

301   *See* Administration White Paper at 16.

302   *See* Administration White Paper at 16.

303   Administration White Paper at 16 (quoting *Chevron v. Salazar*, 275 F.R.D. 437, 449 (S.D.N.Y. 2011)).

These decisions, however, do not involve the type of obligation imposed by the FISA court under Section 215 — directing a party to produce as-yet-nonexistent records on an ongoing basis for a set period of time. Instead, they involve situations in which a party was ordered by the court to *supplement* its prior disclosures after the return date of a traditional subpoena. The decisions acknowledge that under Rule 26(e) of the Federal Rules of Civil Procedure, entitled "Supplementing Disclosures and Responses," courts may order parties to supplement or correct their disclosures after the subpoena's return date.[304] And the decisions further recognize that the power "to order a respondent to supplement or correct its disclosure or response to a subpoena . . . includes the authority to order a respondent to produce materials created after the return date of the subpoena."[305] This conclusion rests on "the plain language" of Rule 26(e).[306] At the time of a supplementary court order issued under Rule 26(e), therefore, the documents ordered to be produced already exist. They merely did not exist on the original date that disclosures were due.

All that these decisions illustrate, in other words, is that the civil rules contain a specific provision authorizing courts to order parties to *supplement or correct* their existing discovery responses, even after the return date of a subpoena. This does not imply that a valid subpoena may, in the first instance, require the ongoing daily production of newly generated records for the duration of a specified period. And therefore these decisions provide no basis for inferring that Section 215 implicitly authorizes the FISA court to impose such an obligation.

Second, the government discerns support for its position in decisions holding that a provision in the Stored Communications Act ("SCA") permits orders for the prospective disclosure of records.[307] These decisions involve the prospective disclosure of a particular type of telephone metadata — cell site location information. But the courts that have approved prospective orders for cell site location information have done so through a so-called "hybrid theory" that invokes "the combined authority of the Pen Register Statute and the Stored Communications Act."[308] Under this hybrid theory, the Pen Register and Trap

---

[304]   *See* FED. R. CIV. P. 26(e)(1)(B) ("A party who has made a disclosure under Rule 26(a) — or who has responded to an interrogatory, request for production, or request for admission — must supplement or correct its disclosure or response . . . as ordered by the court.").

[305]   *Chevron*, 275 F.R.D. at 449 (citing *United States v. IBM Corp.*, 83 F.R.D. 92, 96 (S.D.N.Y. 1979) (internal quotation marks omitted)).

[306]   *IBM Corp.*, 83 F.R.D. at 96.

[307]   *See* Administration White Paper at 16 (citing *In re Application of the United States for an Order Authorizing the Use of Two Pen Register & Trap & Trace Devices*, 632 F. Supp. 2d 202, 207 n.8 (E.D.N.Y. 2008)).

[308]   *In re Application of United States for an order relating to Target Phone 2*, 733 F. Supp. 2d 939, 941 (N.D. Ill. 2009).

and Trace Statute[309] provides the authority to install a pen register or trap and trace device that prospectively records call detail information. But because a different statute prohibits the acquisition of cell site location information "solely" under the pen register/trap and trace authority, courts must rely also "on some additional statutory authority when ordering the disclosure of prospective cell site information under the Pen Register Statute."[310] Under the hybrid theory, the SCA serves as that additional authority, as it permits the government to obtain records from telephone companies and other electronic communications service providers.[311] In accepting this hybrid theory, some courts have concluded that the language of the SCA is compatible with orders for the prospective disclosure of records as they are created.[312] It is this conclusion to which the government points in support of its Section 215 argument.

Regardless of the merits of the hybrid theory — which "the majority of courts" have rejected[313] — it does not support the government's argument regarding Section 215. To the contrary, it rebuts that argument.

First, the hybrid theory depends on the contribution of the pen register statute, which provides the affirmative authorization (and means) to collect telephone metadata prospectively. The SCA plays only the "supporting role" of allowing a particular *type* of data, cell site location information, to be included within that collection.[314] In the context of the NSA's program, however, no companion statute is being used in combination with Section

---

[309]   18 U.S.C. §§ 3121 *et seq.*

[310]   *In re Application of U.S. for an Order for Prospective Cell Site Location Info. on a Certain Cellular Tel.*, 460 F. Supp. 2d 448, 454 (S.D.N.Y. 2006).

[311]   *See id.* (explaining the hybrid theory). The premise of this theory "is that the Stored Communications Act will be used in *combination with* the Pen Register Statute[.]" *Id.* at 459 (emphasis in original).

[312]   *See, e.g., Two Pen Register & Trap & Trace Devices*, 632 F. Supp. 2d at 207 & n.8 ("Because the SCA in no way limits the ongoing disclosure of records to the Government as soon as they are created, the cell-site information the Government seeks is subject to disclosure to the Government[.]").

[313]   *In re Application of U.S. for an order relating to Target Phone 2*, 733 F. Supp. 2d 939, 940 44 & n.1 (N.D. Ill. 2009) (citing decisions); *see Two Pen Register & Trap & Trace Devices*, 632 F. Supp. 2d at 204 ("Courts are divided, with a majority denying the Government's requests."). Courts in the majority have disagreed with the precise argument on which the government here relies — that the text of the SCA is compatible with prospective disclosure orders. *See In re Application of U.S. for an Order for Prospective Cell Site Location Info. on a Certain Cellular Tel.*, 460 F. Supp. 2d 448, 459 (S.D.N.Y. 2006) ("A number of the magistrate judges to address this question have held that Section 2703, although it might cover historical cell site data, does not authorize the disclosure of such data on a 'real-time' or forward-looking basis.") (citing decisions).

[314]   *See Prospective Cell Site Location Info. on a Certain Cellular Tel.*, 460 F. Supp. 2d at 459 ("The Stored Communications Act is being asked to play only the supporting role of providing the required additional authorization for the disclosure of information already permitted by the Pen Register Statute.").

215 to provide an affirmative source of authority for the prospective collection of records.[315]

Second, merely because the SCA might be compatible with orders that prospectively require the disclosure of new records does not mean that Section 215 is compatible with such orders. Section 215 has its own unique language, which, as discussed below, suggests that it authorizes only the production of already existing records. And unlike the SCA, Section 215 is part of a broader statutory scheme under FISA that provides a framework for the prospective collection of telephone metadata when specific conditions are met; its language must be construed in that broader statutory context.[316]

In sum, the case law discussed above offers no basis for discerning implied authority under Section 215 for prospective disclosure orders. The analogies cited by the government actually show that a statutory obligation to disclose business records is not enough to require the prospective, daily disclosure of such records. Some additional authority is needed, which is lacking here.

B. Language Suggesting Incompatibility with Prospective Orders

Apart from the lack of express or implied authority in Section 215 for orders that require the disclosure of newly created records prospectively, the text of the statute suggests that such orders are not within its scope. First, Section 215 permits the FISA court to issue orders "approving *the release* of tangible things."[317] Approving an item's *release* — "the act or an instance of liberating or freeing (as from restraint)"[318] — implies removing barriers to the disclosure of something that already exists.

More tellingly, a production order under Section 215 must "include the date on which the tangible things must be provided, which shall allow a reasonable period of time within which the tangible things can be assembled and made available."[319] By referring to "the date," in the singular, "on which" the tangible things must be provided, the statute suggests that the requested materials will be turned over on a single date — not "on an

---

[315]   If statutory silence implied a grant of authority for prospective disclosure orders, then the SCA would *alone* permit the government to acquire a telephone company's new calling records every day, making the government's recourse to the hybrid theory unnecessary.

[316]   Objections to the hybrid theory have been based on considerations unique to the language of the SCA, such as the requirement that records be "stored" and the statute's definition of "electronic communication." *See Prospective Cell Site Location Info. on a Certain Cellular Tel.*, 460 F. Supp. 2d at 459; *Two Pen Register & Trap & Trace Devices*, 632 F. Supp. 2d at 207; *Prospective Cell Site Location Info. on a Certain Cellular Tel.*, 460 F. Supp. 2d at 460. The dismissal of those objections by some courts sheds no light on the (different) language of Section 215, discussed below.

[317]   50 U.S.C. § 1861(c)(1) (emphasis added).

[318]   MERRIAM WEBSTER ONLINE DICTIONARY (2013).

[319]   50 U.S.C. § 1861(c)(2)(B).

ongoing daily basis" for a period of ninety days.[320] Furthermore, the fact that the statute permits a reasonable period of time in which the items "can be assembled and made available" further signals an expectation that the items already exist, but that time may be needed to marshal them for delivery.

Notably *absent* from Section 215 is any language for situations in which the items to be disclosed have not yet been created. Where Congress has expressly authorized prospective orders, either through electronic surveillance or the use of pen registers, it has set forth limits and procedures regarding the permissible scope and duration of those orders. Such limits and procedures are conspicuously missing from Section 215, indicating that Congress did not intend Section 215 to be used in this way.

C. Incompatibility with FISA as a Whole

Even if Section 215 were compatible with orders for the prospective disclosure of items that do not yet exist, orders requiring the daily disclosure of new *telephone calling records* are inconsistent with the structure of FISA as a whole. A different portion of that statute directly authorizes the prospective collection of telephony metadata through pen registers or trap and trace devices.[321] Construing Section 215 to permit ongoing acquisition of the very same data renders FISA's pen register provision superfluous. It also allows the government to evade the limitations in that provision that govern such prospective monitoring.

Under FISA's pen register provision, the government may apply for an order authorizing the installation and use of a pen register or trap and trace device in a counterterrorism investigation.[322] Such devices capture the same dialing, routing, and addressing information that is included in the calling records obtained by the NSA under Section 215 — the date, time, and duration of calls, along with the participating telephone numbers.[323] Orders approving the use of these devices generally must be renewed after ninety days.[324]

---

[320] Primary Order at 3, *In re Application of the Federal Bureau of Investigation for an Order Requiring the Production of Tangible Things*, No. BR 13-158 (Oct. 11, 2013) ("Primary Order").

[321] *See* 50 U.S.C. § 1842.

[322] *See* 50 U.S.C. § 1842(a)(1).

[323] *See* 18 U.S.C. § 3127(3), (4). FISA's pen register provision also permits the government to request and obtain customer or subscriber information related to the telephone line or other facility to which the device is to be applied. *See* 50 U.S.C. § 1842(d)(2)(C). When the government obtains calling records under Section 215, however, it can obtain customer or subscriber information about particular numbers through several means under the Electronic Communications Privacy Act. *See* 18 U.S.C. § 2703(c).

[324] *See* 50 U.S.C. § 1842(e)(1) (establishing ninety-day limit). If a government applicant certifies that the information likely to be obtained from the device is foreign intelligence information not concerning a U.S. person, orders may last up to a year. 50 U.S.C. § 1842(e)(2).

Construing Section 215 to authorize orders directing the daily transmission of the same information for ninety-day periods renders FISA's pen register provision redundant. "The Government's reading is thus at odds with one of the most basic interpretive canons, that '[a] statute should be construed so that effect is given to all its provisions, so that no part will be inoperative or superfluous, void or insignificant[.]'"[325]

Interpreting Section 215 in this way also circumvents language in FISA's pen register statute that restricts the use of such devices to individually targeted persons, telephone lines, or facilities. Orders issued under the auspices of the pen register provision must specify the identity, if known, of "the person" who is the subject of the investigation and the identity, if known, of "the person" to whom is leased or in whose name is listed "the telephone line or other facility" to which the pen register or trap and trace device is to be applied.[326] Any order also must specify "the attributes of the communications to which the order applies," such as "the number or other identifier" for the account or phone line with which the device will be used.[327]

This language calls for a nexus between a government investigation and the particular telephone line or facility from which the government seeks to acquire telephony metadata. The government's interpretation of Section 215 renders that requirement a nullity, essentially permitting pen registers to be installed on every telephone line in the country, based on an expectation that this practice will, in the aggregate, produce information that is relevant to the government's investigations. Because Section 215 must be construed so as to be in harmony with FISA as a whole, such an interpretation is unsustainable.

V.   Acquisition of Records by the NSA

Under the Section 215 bulk telephone records program, the NSA acquires a massive number of calling records from telephone companies each day, potentially including the records of every call made across the nation. Yet Section 215 does not authorize the NSA to acquire anything at all. Instead, it permits the FBI to obtain records for use in its own investigations. If our surveillance programs are to be governed by law, this clear

---

[325]   *Corley v. United States*, 556 U.S. 303, 314 (2009) (quoting *Hibbs v. Winn*, 542 U.S. 88, 101 (2004)); *see Marx v. Gen. Revenue Corp.*, 133 S. Ct. 1166, 1178 (2013) (stating that "the canon against surplusage is strongest when an interpretation would render superfluous another part of the same statutory scheme"). Although "[t]here are times when Congress enacts provisions that are superfluous," *Corley*, 556 U.S. at 325 (Alito, J., dissenting), there is no reason to suspect that Congress intended such redundancy here.

[326]   50 U.S.C. § 1842(d)(2)(A)(i), (ii).

[327]   50 U.S.C. § 1842(d)(2)(A)(iii).

congressional determination about which federal agency should obtain these records must be followed.

Section 215 expressly allows only the FBI to acquire records and other tangible things that are relevant to its foreign intelligence and counterterrorism investigations. Its text makes unmistakably clear the connection between this limitation and the overall design of the statute. Applications to the FISA court must be made by the director of the FBI or a subordinate.[328] The records sought must be relevant to an authorized FBI investigation.[329] Records produced in response to an order are to be "made available to," "obtained" by, and "received by" the FBI.[330] The Attorney General is directed to adopt minimization procedures governing the FBI's retention and dissemination of the records it obtains pursuant to an order.[331] Before granting a Section 215 application, the FISA court must find that the application enumerates the minimization procedures that the FBI will follow in handling the records it obtains.[332]

These features of the statute are bound up with its purpose. As the government acknowledges: "Section 215 was enacted because the FBI lacked the ability, in national security investigations, to seek business records in a way similar to its ability to seek records using a grand jury subpoena in a criminal case or an administrative subpoena in civil investigations."[333] Because records sought under Section 215 must be requested by FBI officials, on the grounds that they are relevant to FBI investigations, and with promises made about the procedures that the FBI will follow in handling them, those records are to be obtained by the FBI, a point to which the statute makes reference five times.[334]

Under the bulk telephone records program, however, the FBI does not receive any records in response to the FISA court's orders. While FBI officials sign every application seeking to renew the program, the calling records produced in response to the court's orders are never "made available to the Federal Bureau of Investigation" or "received by

---

[328] 50 U.S.C. § 1861(a)(1), (a)(3).

[329] 50 U.S.C. § 1861(b)(2)(A), (c)(1).

[330] 50 U.S.C. § 1861(b)(2)(B), (d)(1), (d)(2)(B), (g)(1), (h).

[331] 50 U.S.C. § 1861(g)(1).

[332] 50 U.S.C. § 1861(b)(2)(B), (c)(1).

[333] Administration White Paper at 6 n.2. The legislative history of what ultimately became Section 215 supports the government's assertion about its purpose. See H.R. Rep. No. 107-236(I), at 61 (2001) ("The Administration had sought administrative subpoena authority without having to go to court. Instead, section 156 amends title 50 U.S.C. § 1861 by providing for an application to the FISA court for an order directing the production of tangible items such as books, records, papers, documents and other items upon certification to the court that the records sought are relevant to an ongoing foreign intelligence investigation." (emphasis removed)).

[334] See 50 U.S.C. § 1861(b)(2)(B), (d)(1), (d)(2)(B), (g)(1), (h).

the Federal Bureau of Investigation," as called for by the statute.[335] Instead, the FISA court's orders specifically direct telephone companies to "produce to NSA" their calling records — thwarting congressional intentions regarding the role each agency is to play in counterterrorism efforts that involve the collection of information within the United States about Americans.[336]

In compliance with the FISA court's orders, telephone companies that are subject to this program transmit their calling records to the NSA. The records are not delivered to the FBI and are never passed on to the FBI by the NSA. Instead, the NSA stores the records in its own databases, conducts its own analysis of them, and provides reports to various federal agencies — including but not limited to the FBI — with information about telephone communications that "the NSA concludes have counterterrorism value."[337] While these reports are based on information derived from the calling records, the records themselves stay with the NSA. Indeed, the NSA is ordered by the FISA court to "store and process" those records "in repositories within secure networks under NSA's control."[338]

What's more, the NSA is *prohibited* from sharing with the FBI information that it derives from the calling records it obtains, except under conditions outlined in the FISA court's orders.[339] Among those conditions, the NSA may share information with the FBI that contains information about U.S. persons only if designated NSA officials (not the FBI agents who are conducting the investigations to which the records are supposed to be relevant) determine that the information "is in fact related to counterterrorism information and that it is necessary to understand the counterterrorism information or assess its importance."[340] The NSA must even file monthly reports with the FISA court listing every instance during the previous month in which the NSA shared such information with any entity, including the FBI.[341]

The fact that the NSA, not the FBI, obtains the records produced causes the program to depart from the statute in another, related manner. Section 215 requires that any

---

[335]   50 U.S.C. § 1861(b)(2)(B), (h).

[336]   Primary Order at 3.

[337]   Shea Decl. ¶ 16; *see* Primary Order at 4 (referring to "any *information* the FBI receives as a result of this Order (information that is disseminated to it by NSA)") (emphasis added).

[338]   Primary Order at 4.

[339]   *See* Primary Order at 6 n.5 ("NSA personnel shall not disseminate BR metadata outside the NSA unless the dissemination is permitted by, and in accordance with, the requirements of this Order that are applicable to the NSA.").

[340]   Primary Order at 13; *see id.* at 16-17.

[341]   Primary Order at 16 ("Each report shall include a statement of the number of instances since the preceding report in which NSA has shared, in any form, results from queries of the BR metadata that contain United States person information, in any form, with *anyone* outside NSA." (emphasis added)).

records obtained through a FISA court order be handled according to "specific minimization procedures" adopted by the Attorney General to govern the "retention and dissemination by the Federal Bureau of Investigation" of the items or information it receives.[342] Before granting an application under Section 215, a FISA court judge must find that the application provides "an enumeration of the minimization procedures adopted by the Attorney General . . . that are applicable to the retention and dissemination by the Federal Bureau of Investigation of any tangible things to be made available to the Federal Bureau of Investigation based on the order requested in such application."[343]

Because the FBI does not receive anything from the telephone companies, it is impossible for the FISA court to make this finding. The court's orders therefore finesse the statutory language by stating that "the Court finds . . . [t]he application includes an enumeration of the minimization procedures *the government* proposes to follow with regard to the tangible things sought."[344] The orders then set forth detailed minimization procedures for *the NSA* to follow with regard to the calling records it obtains.[345] As a result, despite Congress' clear direction that one agency's minimization procedures must be followed (the FBI's), the current process substitutes another agency's procedures (the NSA's).

In sum, the bulk telephone records program violates the requirement that records produced in response to a Section 215 order are to be obtained by the FBI, not the NSA, and that their retention and dissemination is to be governed by rules approved specifically for the FBI's handling of those items. Those requirements are integral to the overall design of the statute, under which records can be obtained only when they are relevant to a specific FBI investigation. As the operation of this program illustrates, allowing the NSA to acquire calling records in bulk and subject them to the tools it possesses for mass data analysis significantly expands the nature and scope of the activity authorized by Section 215.

By no means are we suggesting that the NSA should not be allowed to collaborate with the FBI on its investigations. To the contrary, their partnership can be critical in linking the Signals Intelligence collected by the former with the latter's efforts to disrupt terrorist attacks. The perils of inadequate cooperation among different agencies tasked with combating terrorism is a lesson learned from 9/11. But that cooperation must be

---

[342]   50 U.S.C. § 1861(g)(1).

[343]   50 U.S.C. § 1861(b)(2)(B) (emphasis added); *see id.* § 1861(c)(1).

[344]   Primary Order at 2 (emphasis added).

[345]   *See* Primary Order at 4-16. Regarding the FBI, the FISA court's orders set rules only for "any *information* the FBI receives as a result of this Order . . . information that is disseminated to it by NSA[.]" Primary Order at 4. With respect to such information, the orders direct that "the FBI shall follow as minimization procedures the procedures set forth in *The Attorney General's Guidelines for Domestic FBI Operations* (September 29, 2008)." *Id.*

rooted in the law. We are simply asking whether this specific statute, as written, authorizes the NSA to undertake this specific counterterrorism program, as presently conducted. We conclude that the statute does not provide that authorization. Permitting the NSA to acquire domestic, international, and foreign telephone records in bulk under Section 215 allows the statute to be used for a fundamentally different — and far broader — purpose than the one indicated by its text: enabling the FBI to obtain records that are relevant to specific investigations being conducted by the Bureau.[346]

VI.   Violation of the Electronic Communications Privacy Act

In addition to concluding that the NSA's bulk telephone records program is unauthorized by Section 215, we also believe that it violates the Electronic Communications Privacy Act ("ECPA").

ECPA limits the circumstances under which a telephone company or other electronic communication service provider may divulge records about its customers.[347] Apart from certain enumerated exceptions, a provider "shall not knowingly divulge a record or other information pertaining to a subscriber to or customer of such service . . . to any governmental entity."[348] These enumerated exceptions, among others, include situations in which the government secures a warrant, obtains a court order under ECPA, or utilizes a subpoena.[349] But the statute does not authorize telephone companies to disclose customer information to the government in response to an order issued under Section 215.[350]

In late 2008, the government submitted an application to the FISA court seeking to renew the NSA's bulk telephone records program. This application was the first in which the government identified ECPA as potentially bearing on whether the FISA court properly

---

[346]   The disjunction between Section 215 and the telephone records program is further illustrated by the fact that the FBI already has the power to obtain telephone records that are relevant to its counterterrorism investigations, through so-called national security letters authorized by the Electronic Communications Privacy Act. *See* 18 U.S.C. §§ 2703(c), 2709. The Bureau makes extensive use of that power, and the purpose of Section 215, as the government has acknowledged, was to furnish the FBI with a more global subpoena-like authority that would cover the many types of records for which no subpoena authority existed.

[347]   *See* 18 U.S.C. § 2702(c). These provisions fall within a portion of ECPA called the Stored Communications Act.

[348]   18 U.S.C. § 2702(a)(3).

[349]   *See* 18 U.S.C. §§ 2702(c), 2703(c).

[350]   *See id.*

could issue orders under Section 215 directing telephone companies to disclose their calling records to the NSA.[351]

The FISA court concluded that its orders authorizing the NSA's program were consistent with ECPA. In reaching this conclusion, the court first determined that the terms of Section 215 and ECPA were in tension. Both statutes could not both be given "their full, literal effect," wrote the court, because Section 215 authorizes the production of "any tangible things," and applying the prohibitions of ECPA would limit the meaning of the word "any."[352]

The court then reasoned as follows. Observing that ECPA's prohibition on disclosures includes an exception for "national security letters" issued pursuant to 18 U.S.C. § 2709, the court stated that it would have been "anomalous" for Congress to permit this exception while making no comparable exception for Section 215 orders. This is so, the court wrote, because Section 215 requires a judge to agree with the government's assessment that items being sought are relevant to an investigation, whereas national security letters merely require the FBI to certify that the items sought are relevant. Therefore, the court concluded, ECPA should be interpreted to contain an implicit exception for orders issued under Section 215.[353] The FISA court's reasoning was adopted recently in a decision from the Southern District of New York.[354]

While we acknowledge that the matter is not free from doubt, we believe that these decisions are wrong. "[I]t is a commonplace of statutory construction that the specific governs the general," the Supreme Court has said.[355] "That is particularly true where . . . Congress has enacted a comprehensive scheme and has deliberately targeted specific problems with specific solutions."[356] It would be difficult to imagine a more appropriate place to apply that principle than here. ECPA sets forth a detailed, multi-faceted set of provisions governing privacy in stored electronic communications and in records about the customers of electronic communication service providers. This comprehensive scheme

---

[351]   *See* Supplemental Opinion at 1, *In re Production of Tangible Things*, No. BR 08-13 (FISA Ct. Dec. 12, 2008).

[352]   Supplemental Opinion at 1-2.

[353]   *See* Supplemental Opinion at 4-5.

[354]   Memorandum & Order at 26-28, *ACLU v. Clapper*, No. 13-3994 (S.D.N.Y. Dec. 27, 2013). That court also reasoned that ECPA does not present a problem because "Section 215 authorizes the Government to seek records that may be obtained with a grand jury subpoena," and "Section 215 orders are functionally equivalent to grand jury subpoenas." *Id.* at 27.

[355]   *RadLAX Gateway Hotel, LLC v. Amalgamated Bank*, 132 S. Ct. 2065, 2071 (2012) (quoting *Morales v. Trans World Airlines, Inc.*, 504 U.S. 374, 384 (1992)); *see HCSC-Laundry v. United States*, 450 U.S. 1, 6 (1981) (stating that "a specific statute . . . controls over a general provision").

[356]   *RadLAX Gateway Hotel, LLC*, 132 S. Ct. at 2071 (quoting *Varity Corp. v. Howe*, 516 U.S. 489, 519 (1996) (Thomas, J., dissenting) (quotation marks omitted).

directly targets the problem of when the government may gain access to such records and provides specific solutions, including court orders issued pursuant to 18 U.S.C. § 2703(d) and national security letters sent pursuant to 18 U.S.C. § 2709. The terms of Section 215, in contrast, could not be more general, simply referencing "any tangible things (including books, records, papers, documents, and other items)."[357]

As the FISA court acknowledged, the very statute that created Section 215, the Patriot Act, also amended ECPA "in ways that seemingly re-affirmed that communications service providers could divulge records to the government only in specified circumstances" — without including FISA court orders issued under Section 215.[358] The fact that the same statute both created Section 215 and amended ECPA, but without adding an exception to ECPA for Section 215 orders, undermines the notion that ECPA and Section 215 are in conflict, and provides an additional basis for strictly adhering to ECPA's prohibitions by not inferring unwritten exceptions to those prohibitions. It also demonstrates that another fundamental canon of statutory construction applies here — that the inclusion of some implies the exclusion of others not mentioned.[359] "Where there is an express exception, it comprises the only limitation on the operation of the statute and no other exceptions will be implied."[360] Congress did not add an exception to ECPA for Section 215 orders, even though it amended ECPA in other ways at the same time that it created Section 215. That omission should be respected.

---

[357] Before the Patriot Act substituted the phrase "any tangible things," FISA's business records statute permitted the government to obtain four specific types of records, one of which was records from a "common carrier." Since that term can include telephone companies, the statute offered somewhat more specificity in its pre–Patriot Act state, but it was still considerably more general than ECPA.

[358] Supplemental Opinion at 3. As the FISA court noted, legislative history indicates that before the passage of the Patriot Act, at least one senator was concerned that Section 215's reference to "any tangible things" would "effectively trump" federal and state privacy protections. *See* 147 CONG. REC. 19,530 (2001) (statement of Sen. Feingold). Without discussion, the Senate tabled an amendment offered by Senator Feingold that was meant to "make[] it clear that existing Federal and State statutory protections for the privacy of certain information are not diminished or superseded by section 215." *Id.* The Senate's rejection of this amendment could have signaled a desire for Section 215 to override those other statutes, as Senator Feingold feared, or it could have reflected disagreement that Section 215's language could possibly be interpreted so broadly. There are no statements shedding any light on the motivation of the senators who voted to reject the amendment. Such ambiguous legislative history does not warrant ignoring the clear statutory text of ECPA and the basic canons of statutory construction that counsel in favor of adhering to it. *See Milner v. Dep't of Navy*, 131 S. Ct. 1259, 1266 (2011) ("Those of us who make use of legislative history believe that clear evidence of congressional intent may illuminate ambiguous text. We will not take the opposite tack of allowing ambiguous legislative history to muddy clear statutory language.").

[359] Or: "*Expressio unius est exclusio alterius.*" *Leatherman v. Tarrant Cnty. Narcotics Intelligence & Coordination Unit*, 507 U.S. 163, 168 (1993).

[360] *Copeland v. Toyota Motor Sales U.S.A., Inc.*, 136 F.3d 1249, 1257 (10th Cir. 1998) (quoting NORMAN J. ZINGER, 2A SUTHERLAND'S STATUTES AND STATUTORY CONSTRUCTION § 47.11 (5th ed. 1992)).

The only apparent basis for permitting the general language of Section 215 to override the comprehensive and specific language of ECPA is a judgment about what it would have been logical for Congress to have enacted. The FISA court decided that Congress could not have intended to permit the government to obtain telephone calling records through a national security letter, which requires only an executive branch certification of relevance, while prohibiting the government from obtaining the same records through Section 215, which requires a court to agree with the government's assessment of relevance.[361]

But there very well may be legitimate reasons to have included an exception in ECPA for national security letters but not for Section 215 orders. Because Congress appears to have intended Section 215 to allow the FBI to obtain types of records it could not already obtain, it may have expected that the various national security letter statutes would continue to cover the specific categories of data to which they relate (telephone metadata in the case of ECPA), and that Section 215 would apply to any other categories of records. Moreover, whereas Section 215 demands only reasonable grounds to believe that items sought (of whatever kind) are relevant to an investigation, the national security letter statute requires a more specific certification "that the name, address, length of service, and toll billing records" being sought are relevant.[362]

More fundamentally, however, we do not believe that courts should interpret statutes like ECPA based on their assessment of what would have been sensible for Congress to enact, at least not when that interpretation overrides detailed statutory language and violates basic methods of interpreting statutes. The identification of an apparent "anomaly"[363] is not a sufficient basis for judicial revision of clear statutory text. And while "absurd results are to be avoided" in interpreting statutes,[364] the perceived oddity of permitting telephone records to be acquired through NSLs but not through Section 215 is hardly extreme enough to call for this doctrine, which is used "to override unambiguous legislation" only "rarely."[365] In other words, this is not "one of those rare

---

[361]   *See* Supplemental Opinion at 4-5.

[362]   18 U.S.C. § 2709(b)(1). Furthermore, Section 215 originally permitted records to be obtained without any assertion that they were relevant to an investigation, much less a judicial finding of relevance. The government needed merely to state in its application that the records concerned were "sought for" an authorized investigation. 50 U.S.C. § 1861(b)(2) (2002). Until 2006, therefore, when Section 215 was amended, it imposed a lower standard for obtaining records than the certification required to issue a national security letter under ECPA.

[363]   Supplemental Opinion at 5.

[364]   *United States v. Wilson*, 503 U.S. 329, 334 (1992) (citing *United States v. Turkette*, 452 U.S. 576, 580 (1981)).

[365]   *Barnhart v. Sigmon Coal Co.*, 534 U.S. 438, 441 (2002); *see* Memorandum & Order at 27 (stating that "to allow the Government to obtain telephony metadata with an NSL but not a section 215 order would lead to an absurd result").

cases where the application of the statute as written will produce a result 'demonstrably at odds with the intentions of its drafters.'"[366] Because the perceived anomaly identified by the FISA court is not "so bizarre that Congress 'could not have intended' it," therefore "the remedy lies with the law making authority, and not with the courts."[367]

Inferring an unwritten exception to ECPA based on an "anomaly" is particularly questionable when that exception is then used to permit the NSA's bulk collection of telephone records. As noted, the FISA court concluded that it would be irrational to prohibit the government from obtaining telephone records through Section 215, which requires a judge to agree that the records are relevant to an investigation, when the FBI can obtain those same records through a national security letter, which requires no prior judicial approval. But the FBI already widely obtains telephone records through national security letters, and the FISA court's ruling simply permits a second agency, the NSA, to obtain *all* telephone records. Even if an aggressive reading of Section 215 permits that result — which we believe is not the case — it clearly is not what Congress intended to achieve when it enacted Section 215.

VII.   The Reenactment Doctrine

In 2010, and again in 2011, Congress prevented Section 215 from expiring by extending its sunset date. Courts and the government have concluded that by twice extending the expiration date of Section 215, while the NSA's bulk telephone records program was ongoing, Congress implicitly adopted an interpretation of Section 215 that legitimizes the program.[368] This conclusion rests on the principle that "Congress is presumed to be aware of an administrative or judicial interpretation of a statute and to adopt that interpretation when it re-enacts a statute without change."[369] On multiple grounds, however, we believe that principle has no place here.

The "reenactment doctrine" does not trump the plain meaning of a law, but rather is one of many interpretive tools that come into play when statutory ambiguity demands an

---

[366]   *Demarest v. Manspeaker*, 498 U.S. 184, 190 (1991) (quoting *Griffin v. Oceanic Contractors, Inc.*, 458 U.S. 564, 571 (1982)).

[367]   *Demarest*, 498 U.S. at 191 (quoting *Griffin*, 458 U.S. at 575); *Griffin*, 458 U.S. at 575 (quoting *Crooks v. Harrelson*, 282 U.S. 55, 60 (1930)).

[368]   *See* Amended Memorandum Opinion at 23-28, *In re Application of the Federal Bureau of Investigation for an Order Requiring the Production of Tangible Things*, No. BR 13-109 (FISA Ct. Aug. 29, 2013); Memorandum & Order at 28-32, *ACLU v. Clapper*, No. 13-3994 (S.D.N.Y. Dec. 27, 2013); Administration White Paper at 17-19.

[369]   *Forest Grove Sch. Dist. v. T.A.*, 557 U.S. 230, 239-40 (2009) (quoting *Lorillard v. Pons*, 434 U.S. 575, 580 (1978)).

inquiry into congressional intent. Reenactment, in other words, "cannot save" an administrative or judicial interpretation that contradicts the requirements of the statute itself.[370] And for the many reasons explained above, any interpretation of Section 215 that would authorize the NSA's telephone records program is irreconcilable with the plain words of the statute, its manifest purpose, and its role within FISA as a whole.

Even if Section 215 were sufficiently ambiguous to justify an inquiry into congressional intent, the circumstances presented here are unlike any in which the reenactment doctrine has ever been applied — and the differences are pivotal. First, there was no judicial interpretation of Section 215 of which Congress could have been aware in 2010 or 2011: at that time the FISA court had never issued any opinion explaining the legal rationale for the NSA's program under Section 215, but had merely signed orders authorizing the program. Second, even if the FISA court's orders, combined with the government's applications to the court, are viewed as an "interpretation" of Section 215, members of Congress may have been prohibited from reading those orders and those applications (except for members of the intelligence and judiciary committees) by operation of committee rules. Thus, to apply the reenactment doctrine here, Senators and Congressmen must be presumed to have adopted an "interpretation" that they had no ability to read for themselves. Third, even if being apprised of the NSA's program were equivalent to being made aware of a judicial interpretation of a statute, applying the reenactment doctrine is improper where members of Congress must try to comprehend a secret legal interpretation without the aid of their staffs or outside experts and advocates. That scenario robs lawmakers of a meaningful opportunity to gauge the legitimacy and implications of the legal interpretation in question. Fourth, Congress did not reenact Section 215 at all in 2010 and 2011, but merely delayed its expiration. To our knowledge, no court has applied the reenactment doctrine under a combination of circumstances remotely like this.

Finally, even if Section 215 were ambiguous about whether it authorizes the NSA's bulk collection of telephone records, and even if the reenactment doctrine could be extended to the novel circumstances presented here, doing so would undermine the ability of the American public to know what the law is, and to hold their elected representatives accountable for their legislative choices. Applying the reenactment doctrine to legitimize the government's interpretation of Section 215, therefore, is both unsupported by legal precedent and unacceptable as a matter of democratic accountability.

In truth, what is urged here is not the traditional reenactment doctrine, but rather a new variant: where the executive branch makes classified information available to

---

[370]   *Leary v. United States*, 395 U.S. 6, 25 (1969) (quoting *Commissioner of Internal Revenue v. Acker*, 361 U.S. 87, 93 (1959).

Congress that a secret program is being conducted under the auspices of a particular statute, and where Congress subsequently delays the expiration of that statute without amending it, Congress's action renders the program legally authorized even if the words of the statute do not support it. This is a novel proposition that we do not accept.

A. Background

When Congress last amended Section 215, it provided that the statute would expire by 2010.[371] Early that year, Congress extended the statute's "sunset" date for another year, and in 2011 Congress further extended the sunset date for another four years.[372]

Before these two extensions, the intelligence and judiciary committees in the House and Senate were provided with the FISA court's initial order authorizing the NSA's bulk telephone records program and the government's initial application.[373] Those committees also were briefed by the executive branch about the program.[374]

Other members of the House and Senate were prohibited from reading the FISA court's order or the government's application. In 2009, prior to the first extension of Section 215's sunset date, the executive branch provided the intelligence committees with a five-page briefing paper on the NSA's bulk telephone and Internet metadata programs, encouraging the committees to make this document available to all members of Congress.[375] Before the second extension in 2011, the executive branch provided a similar

---

[371] *See* USA PATRIOT Improvement and Reauthorization Act of 2005, Pub. L. No. 109-177, § 102(b)(1), 120 Stat. 191, 195 (2006) ("Effective December 31, 2009, the Foreign Intelligence Surveillance Act of 1978 is amended so that sections 501, 502, and 105(c)(2) read as they read on October 25, 2001.").

[372] *See* An Act to Extend Expiring Provisions of the USA PATRIOT Improvement and Reauthorization Act of 2005 and Intelligence Reform and Terrorism Prevention Act of 2004 until February 28, 2011, Pub. L. No. 111-141, 124 Stat. 37 (Feb. 27, 2010); PATRIOT Sunsets Extension Act of 2011, Pub. L. No. 112-14, 125 Stat. 216 (May 26, 2011). Section 215 is now set to sunset on June 1, 2015.

[373] Administration White Paper at 18. Twice a year, the Attorney General is required to submit to the House and Senate intelligence and judiciary committees "a summary of significant legal interpretations" of FISA involving matters before the FISA court or its companion appellate court, the Foreign Intelligence Surveillance Court of Review, "including interpretations presented in applications or pleadings" filed with those courts. 50 U.S.C. § 1871(a)(4). This summary must be accompanied by "copies of all decisions, orders, or opinions" of the two courts "that include significant construction or interpretation" of the provisions of FISA. 50 U.S.C. § 1871(a)(5). In addition, on an annual basis the Attorney General must "inform" the House and Senate intelligence committees and the Senate judiciary committee "concerning all requests" for the production of items under Section 215. 50 U.S.C. § 1862(a).

[374] *See* Administration White Paper at 18 & n.14.

[375] *See* Letter from Assistant Attorney General Ronald Weich to the Honorable Silvestre Reyes, Chairman, House Permanent Select Committee on Intelligence, at 1 (Dec. 14, 2009) ("2009 Letter"); Report on the National Security Agency's Bulk Collection Programs Affected by USA PATRIOT Act Reauthorization (2009) ("2009 Report").

briefing paper to the intelligence committees.[376] Each time, the executive branch specified that the briefing paper was "being provided on the understanding that it will be provided only to Members of Congress (and cleared SSCI, Judiciary Committee, and leadership staff), in a secure location in the SSCI's offices, for a limited time period to be agreed upon, and consistent with the rules of the SSCI regarding review of classified information and non-disclosure agreements."[377] The letters also specified: "No photocopies may be made of the document, and any notes taken by Members may not be removed from the secure location."[378]

Before the first extension of Section 215's sunset date, the House and Senate committees made this briefing paper available to all members of Congress under the aforementioned conditions.[379] Before the second extension, in 2011, the Senate intelligence committee made this briefing paper available to all Senators, but the House intelligence committee did not make it available to all House members.[380]

The briefing paper provided to the intelligence committees does not contain any legal analysis or explanation of how the NSA's bulk telephone records program fits within the terms of Section 215. Instead the paper describes in general terms the operation of the NSA's telephone and Internet metadata collection programs, indicating that they involve obtaining "large amounts of transactional data obtained from certain telecommunications service providers in the United States."[381] The briefing paper further explains that "NSA is authorized to collect from telecommunications service providers certain business records that contain information about communications between two telephone numbers, such as the date, time, and duration of a call," and that FISA court orders "generally require production of the business records (as described above) relating to substantially all of the telephone calls handled by the companies, including both calls made between the United States and a foreign country and calls made entirely within the United States."[382] The document characterizes the program as an essential tool for combating terrorism,

---

[376]   *See* Letter from Assistant Attorney General Ronald Weich to the Honorable Dianne Feinstein and the Honorable Saxby Chambliss, Chairman and Vice Chairman, Senate Select Committee on Intelligence, at 1 (Feb. 2, 2011) ("2011 Letter"); Report on the National Security Agency's Bulk Collection Programs Affected by USA PATRIOT Act Reauthorization (2011) ("2011 Report").

[377]   2011 Letter at 1; *see* 2009 Letter at 2

[378]   2011 Letter at 1-2; *see* 2009 Letter at 2.

[379]   *See* Administration White Paper at 17-18.

[380]   *See* Administration White Paper at 18 n.13.

[381]   2011 Report at 2.

[382]   2011 Report at 3.

emphasizes the strict rules governing it, discloses that it has generated compliance issues, and includes certain details of the program that illustrate its limitations.[383]

B. Discussion

"When Congress reenacts statutory language that has been given a consistent judicial construction," the Supreme Court "often adhere[s] to that construction in interpreting the reenacted statutory language."[384] In other words, "Congress is presumed to be aware of an administrative or judicial interpretation of a statute and to adopt that interpretation when it re-enacts a statute without change."[385]

"There is an obvious trump to the reenactment argument, however, in the rule that '[w]here the law is plain, subsequent reenactment does not constitute an adoption of a previous administrative construction.'"[386] Congressional reenactment "has no interpretive effect where regulations clearly contradict [the] requirements of [a] statute,"[387] and in such cases reenactment "cannot save" the faulty interpretation.[388] Rather: "In a statutory construction case, the beginning point must be the language of the statute, and when a statute speaks with clarity to an issue judicial inquiry into the statute's meaning, in all but the most extraordinary circumstance, is finished."[389] An interpretation that "flies against the plain language of the statutory text exempts courts from any obligation to defer to

---

[383]   While the briefing paper explains that the NSA's program operates "on a very large scale" and involves "substantially all" of the calling records generated by "certain" telephone companies, it does not make explicit that the program is designed to collect the records of essentially all telephone calls. And while the document explains certain operational details about the program that confine its reach — such as the fact that "[b]efore NSA analysts may query bulk records, they must have reasonable articulable suspicion . . . that the number or e-mail address they submit is associated with" a terrorist organization" — it omits other details having the opposite implication, such as the fact that a single query permits analysts to view the full calling records of all telephone numbers that are two "hops" away from the target, which generally means thousands of numbers. 2011 Report at 3-4. Similarly, while document cites "a number of technical compliance problems and human implementation errors" reported to the FISA court, highlighting the absence of "any intentional or bad-faith violations," it does not hint at the full scope of these compliance issues, reflected in the FISA court's 2009 declaration that "from the inception of this FISA BR program, the NSA's data accessing technologies and practices were never adequately designed to comply with the governing minimization procedures." Order at 14-15, *In re Production of Tangible Things*, No. BR 08-13 (FISA Ct. Mar. 2, 2009).

[384]   *Cent. Bank of Denver, N.A. v. First Interstate Bank of Denver, N.A.*, 511 U.S. 164, 185 (1994) (citing *Keene Corp. v. United States*, 508 U.S. 200, 212-13 (1993), *Pierce v. Underwood*, 487 U.S. 552, 567 (1988), & *Lorillard v. Pons*, 434 U.S. at 580-81).

[385]   *Forest Grove Sch. Dist. v. T.A.*, 557 U.S. at 239-40 (quoting *Lorillard*, 434 U.S. at 580).

[386]   *Brown v. Gardner*, 513 U.S. 115, 121 (1994) (quoting *Demarest v. Manspeaker*, 498 U.S. 184, 190 (1991)).

[387]   *Brown*, 513 U.S. at 121 (citing *Massachusetts Trustees of Eastern Gas & Fuel Associates v. United States*, 377 U.S. 235, 241-42 (1964)).

[388]   *Leary v. United States*, 395 U.S. 6, 25 (1969) (citing *Massachusetts Trustees of Eastern Gas and Fuel Associates*, 377 U.S. at 241-42).

[389]   *Estate of Cowart v. Nicklos Drilling Co.*, 505 U.S. 469, 475 (1992) (citing *Demarest*, 498 U.S. at 190).

it,"[390] because Congress cannot "add to or expand" a statute by "impliedly" approving an interpretation that "conflicts with the statute."[391] Thus, a "poor fit" between statutory language and an administrative or judicial construction, or the "eccentricity" of such a construction in light of the statutory text, prevents the reenactment doctrine from legitimizing that construction.[392]

For the many reasons explained earlier, Section 215 is not ambiguous about whether it authorizes the NSA to collect the entire nation's telephone records on an ongoing daily basis: the only way to interpret Section 215 in that fashion is to add words to the statute that it does not contain, subtract words that it does contain, and reinterpret other words beyond recognition. Because "the text and reasonable inferences from it give a clear answer," that is "the end of the matter."[393]

Even if Section 215 were ambiguous on this question, the reenactment doctrine cannot credibly be applied to the circumstances presented here, which differ in pivotal ways from any circumstances in which the doctrine has been applied. To begin with, Congress did not actually reenact Section 215 in 2010 or 2011, but merely postponed the sunset dates on which the statute would expire.[394] More importantly, at the time of these extensions, there was no judicial interpretation of Section 215 by the FISA court of which Congress can be presumed to have been aware. Until 2013, the FISA court never issued any opinion explaining how Section 215 authorized the NSA's telephone records program. And while the government's applications to the FISA court seeking authorization for the program contained the executive branch's position on that question, members of Congress outside of the intelligence and judiciary committees were prohibited from reading those applications (or the FISA court orders granting them). At most, these Senators and Representatives had access to a five-page document describing the program in general terms, along with the opportunity for briefings by executive branch officials.

---

[390]   *Brown*, 513 U.S. at 122 (citing *Dole v. Steelworkers*, 494 U.S. 26, 42 43 (1990), and *Chevron U.S.A. Inc. v. Natural Resources Defense Council, Inc.*, 467 U.S. 837, 842 43 (1984)).

[391]   *Leary*, 395 U.S. at 25 (quoting *Commissioner of Internal Revenue v. Acker*, 361 U.S. 87, 93 (1959)); *see* William N. Eskridge, Jr., *Interpreting Legislative Inaction*, 87 MICH. L. REV. 67, 83 (1988) ("Where the prior interpretation is flatly inconsistent with relatively clear statutory language or history, the Court may abandon the *Lorillard* presumption that Congress was aware of and adopted the prior line of interpretation.").

[392]   *Brown*, 513 U.S. at 119-21.

[393]   *Brown*, 513 U.S. at 120 (quoting *Good Samaritan Hospital v. Shalala*, 508 U.S. 402, 409 (1993) (internal quotation marks omitted)).

[394]   *See* An Act to Extent Expiring Provisions of the USA PATRIOT Improvement and Reauthorization Act of 2005 and Intelligence Reform and Terrorism Prevention Act of 2004 until February 28, 2011, Pub. L. No. 111-141, 124 Stat. 37 (2010) (striking "February 28, 2010" and inserting "February 28, 2011"); PATRIOT Sunsets Extension Act of 2011, Pub. L. No. 112-14, 125 Stat. 216 (2011) (striking "May 27, 2011" and inserting "June 1, 2015").

While this document gave notice of the existence of the NSA's program, it cannot be regarded as a judicial or administrative interpretation of a statute — because it lacks any explanation of how Section 215 can be interpreted to authorize the program. (Indeed, it contains no legal analysis at all.) And even this document was never made available to the full House of Representatives before the most recent extension of Section 215's sunset date. While the briefing paper may have been intended to help lawmakers make informed policy choices, simply providing notice of an ongoing program is not the same as making Congress aware of an administrative or judicial interpretation of a statute.

Moreover, even if having access to the executive branch's briefing paper were equivalent to being aware of an administrative or judicial interpretation of a statute, the reenactment doctrine would still be out of place here. The doctrine has never been applied to secret interpretations of the law summarized in classified papers that members of Congress must comprehend without the aid of their own staffs or outside experts.[395] When legislators set about determining whether to reenact a statute, they normally are aided by the insights and advice of their staff as well as commentary by legal scholars, practitioners, journalists, advocates, and others regarding how that statute has been interpreted. Thus, before reenacting a statute that has been interpreted in a particular way, legislators have the means of becoming educated about the nature of that interpretation, its strength as a doctrinal matter, and its full ramifications as a practical matter. By contrast, when the only means through which legislators can try to understand a prior interpretation of the law is to read a short description of an operational program, prepared by executive branch officials, made available only at certain times and locations, which cannot be discussed with others except in classified briefings conducted by those same executive branch officials, legislators are denied a meaningful opportunity to gauge the legitimacy and implications of the legal interpretation in question. Under such circumstances, it is not a legitimate method of statutory construction to presume that these legislators, when reenacting the statute, intended to adopt a prior interpretation that they had no fair means of evaluating.

Finally, even if the reenactment doctrine were a valid means of discerning congressional intent under these circumstances, its application would have unacceptable consequences for the public's ability to know what the law is. When a secret court accepts a counterintuitive reading of a law — one that could not possibly be guessed by reading the

---

[395] Personal staff for members of Congress are not eligible to obtain the level of security clearance required for access to Section 215 program information. *See, e.g.*, Office of Senate Security, United States Senate Security Manual, § III.5 (Apr. 2007) ("There are three 'levels' of security clearance, which correspond with the three levels of classification: Confidential, Secret and Top Secret. *In addition, certain categories of classified information require special clearances and access approval. These special clearances and approvals are granted on a rigidly controlled need-to-know basis, and are not granted to personal staff.*" (emphasis added)). Therefore, many members of Congress — anyone who does not sit on a committee where review of classified information is common — have no staff who would have been able to assist them in reviewing the classified descriptions of the Section 215 program.

statutory language alone, and which invests the government with significant new powers — permitting congressional reenactment to enshrine that novel interpretation deprives the public of any ability to know that the law is, much less have any voice in changing it.

For these reasons, we believe that the statutory legitimacy of the NSA's bulk telephone records program must be assessed only with reference to the words of the law that purportedly authorizes it.

VIII. Conclusion

The NSA's bulk telephone records program was initiated more than four years before the government sought authorization for it under Section 215 of the Patriot Act. In light of that history, it may not be surprising that the operation of the program bears almost no relationship to the text of the statute — which is designed to confer subpoena-like authority on the FBI, not to enable nationwide bulk data collection by the NSA. As we believe the foregoing analysis has demonstrated, sanctioning the NSA's program under Section 215 requires an impermissible transformation of the statute: Where its text fails to authorize a feature of the program (such as the daily production of new telephone records), such authority must be inferred from silence. Where its text uses limiting words (such as "relevant"), those words must be redefined beyond their traditional meaning. And where its text simply cannot be reconciled with the program (such as its direction that the FBI, not the NSA, receive any items produced), those words must be ignored.

It may have been a laudable goal for the executive branch to bring this program under the supervision of the FISA court. Ultimately, however, that effort represents an unsustainable attempt to shoehorn a preexisting surveillance program into the text of a statute with which it is not compatible. Because Section 215 does not provide a sound legal basis for the NSA's bulk telephone records program, we believe the program must be ended.

Part 6:
CONSTITUTIONAL ANALYSIS

I. Overview

The NSA's bulk telephone records program potentially implicates both the First and Fourth Amendments to the United States Constitution. Yet evaluating the legitimacy of the program under those amendments presents a challenge: while constitutional analysis involves drawing inferences and conclusions from existing precedent, the scope and duration of the Section 215 telephone records program go beyond anything ever before confronted by the courts. In addition, as a result of technological development, the government now possesses capabilities to collect, store, and analyze data that were not available when key portions of the existing case law were decided. For these reasons, a mechanical application of cases decided many years ago regarding the particularized collection of limited amounts of data may miss the point. In future decisions, the courts will take account of those technological developments, as they have begun to do in other cases applying the Fourth Amendment to new technological realities. In this section, we do not try to predict the future path of constitutional doctrine. We do, however, note where existing doctrine seems an ill fit for evaluating the Section 215 telephone records program and where that doctrine may be unsustainable given the realities of modern technology. And we recommend as a policy matter that all three branches of government, in developing and assessing data collection programs, look beyond the application of cases decided in a very different environment and instead consider how to preserve the underlying constitutional principles in the face of modern communications technology and surveillance capabilities.

We first consider the Fourth Amendment, which prohibits unreasonable searches and seizures by the government. Analysis of the NSA's telephone records program under the Fourth Amendment must begin by asking whether the agency's collection of calling records qualifies as a "search" within the meaning of the Amendment. If not, as the government has argued in defense of the program, the Fourth Amendment and its restrictions do not apply to the NSA's activity.

The Supreme Court has ruled that the Fourth Amendment does not provide individuals with a right of privacy in the numbers that they dial from their telephones. More broadly, the Court has concluded, any information that a person voluntarily discloses to a business or other entity loses all Fourth Amendment protection. This rule, referred to as the "third-party doctrine," means that when government agents obtain records about a person that are held by a telephone company, bank, or other institution, that does not qualify as a search under the Constitution.

Although the Section 215 program encompasses much more information than the telephone numbers that a person dials, all of the information that the NSA collects under the program has been disclosed to telephone companies by their customers. Therefore, under the broad reading of the third-party doctrine widely adopted in the federal courts, none of the information is constitutionally protected, and the NSA may collect it without seeking a warrant or ensuring that its behavior satisfies the Fourth Amendment's standard of reasonableness.

The third-party doctrine has long been criticized as permitting undue government intrusion into personal privacy. Those criticisms have gained particular force in light of two trends stemming from modern technological developments. First, Americans increasingly must share personal information with institutions in order to conduct business and avail themselves of services that have become commonplace features of contemporary life. Second, new technology has dramatically enhanced the government's ability to collect, aggregate, and analyze immense quantities of information. Moreover, until last year, no court had considered whether there is any limit to the third-party doctrine in the context of the collection of data about essentially all individuals nationwide on an ongoing, indefinitely renewable basis.[396]

It is possible that the third-party doctrine or its scope will be judicially revised. The Supreme Court has recognized the danger that technological developments may erode Fourth Amendment privacy guarantees if constitutional law does not respond to those developments. In addition, a majority of Justices recently indicated that the rise of powerful new surveillance tools demands that not everything an individual reveals to another person is undeserving of Fourth Amendment protection.

To date, however, the Supreme Court has not modified the third-party doctrine or overruled its conclusion that the Fourth Amendment does not protect telephone dialing records. Most courts continue to follow those precedents, and government lawyers are entitled to rely on them, including in their formulation and defense of the Section 215 program.

Furthermore, a reversal or narrowing of these principles would establish only that the NSA's collection of telephone records is a "search" under the Fourth Amendment. Additional questions would then follow about whether this type of search required a warrant and whether it was reasonable within the meaning of the amendment.

---

[396] *See* Memorandum & Order, *ACLU v. Clapper*, No. 13-3994 (S.D.N.Y. Dec. 27, 2013); Memorandum Opinion, *Klayman v. Obama*, No. 13-0851 (D.D.C. Dec. 16, 2013); Amended Memorandum Opinion, *In re Application of the Federal Bureau of Investigation for an Order Requiring the Production of Tangible Things*, No. BR 13-109 (FISA Ct. Aug. 29, 2013).

Notwithstanding the agreement of most federal courts that telephony metadata lacks Fourth Amendment protection, however, the collection of telephone calling records by the government clearly implicates considerable privacy interests. Those interests, accordingly, deserve significant weight when the value of the NSA's telephone records program is balanced with its effects on privacy and civil liberties, an analysis we undertake in the next section of this Report.

We also consider in this section whether the telephone records program may impact rights under the First Amendment, which, among other safeguards, provides protection for the freedoms of speech and association. The Supreme Court has recognized that the freedom of association involves the rights of people to join together in support of their common beliefs on political, religious, cultural, economic and other matters. To the extent that the NSA's telephone records program reveals the patterns of individuals' connections and associations, this may implicate such First Amendment rights.

The Supreme Court has ruled that government programs can violate the First Amendment freedom of association even if they are not directly aimed at limiting the ability of people to join together for a common purpose. Indirect actions that have the effect of "chilling" the right of association can also infringe this constitutional right. In other words, the government can interfere with this constitutional protection by making people afraid to exercise their freedom of association.

The Supreme Court has explored the constitutional freedom of association in depth in connection with challenges to government actions that force disclosure of individuals' associations to the government. In this context, the Court has recognized that the freedom of association includes protection for the privacy of associations, so that individuals will not be afraid to join together in exercising their rights. This right to privacy of association was grounded in the need to protect people who promote controversial or dissident beliefs, and has also been recognized where revealing associations to the government could subject an individual to adverse consequences. Courts have also found that surveillance programs can have a chilling effect on the freedom of association. However, due to the doctrine of standing, the Supreme Court has never reached the question of whether a surveillance program can create a "chilling effect" sufficient to violate the First Amendment.

The First Amendment right of association is not absolute, but courts will review challenges under the "exacting scrutiny" test. Government actions that may chill associational conduct must be supported by a sufficiently important government interest, and must be designed to limit the intrusions on First Amendment rights.

Just as with the Fourth Amendment, changes in technology have altered the analysis. There has never been a program of the scope of the one being conducted under Section 215, and the government has never had at its disposal the analytic tools now available. Our analysis of the NSA telephone records program concludes that the collection of telephone metadata records for all Americans' phone calls extending over a five year time period implicates the First Amendment freedom of association. Although the program is supported by a compelling government interest in combatting terrorism, which can justify some intrusions on First Amendment rights, it is not narrowly tailored. The extraordinary breadth of this collection program creates a chilling effect on the First Amendment rights of Americans, and we factor this concern into our policy analysis later in this Report.

II.   THE FOURTH AMENDMENT

A. Protections of the Fourth Amendment against Unreasonable Searches

The Fourth Amendment to the United States Constitution prohibits unreasonable searches and seizures by the government. The Amendment reads:

> The right of the people to be secure in their persons, houses, papers, and effects, against unreasonable searches and seizures, shall not be violated, and no Warrants shall issue, but upon probable cause, supported by Oath or affirmation, and particularly describing the place to be searched, and the persons or things to be seized.

Before conducting most types of searches, government agents must obtain a warrant from a judge that describes what they plan to search, after demonstrating probable cause to believe that the search will yield evidence of a criminal offense.[397] Requiring agents to obtain a warrant before conducting a search limits the potential for abuse of their authority, the Supreme Court has explained, by requiring them to "present their estimate of probable cause for detached scrutiny by a neutral magistrate," to "observe precise limits established in advance by a specific court order," and "to notify the authorizing magistrate in detail of all that had been seized."[398]

Warrants are not required for government searches in "a few specifically established and well-delineated exceptions."[399] Even searches that fall within those

---

[397]   *See Arizona v. Gant*, 556 U.S. 332, 338 (2009) (stating that "searches conducted outside the judicial process, without prior approval by judge or magistrate, are *per se* unreasonable under the Fourth Amendment — subject only to a few specifically established and well-delineated exceptions") (quoting *Katz v. United States*, 389 U.S. 347, 357 (1967)).

[398]   *Katz*, 389 U.S. at 356.

[399]   *City of Ontario, Cal. v. Quon*, 130 S. Ct. 2619, 2630 (2010).

exceptions violate the Fourth Amendment if they are not "reasonable."[400] Whether a search is reasonable, the Supreme Court has said, "is determined by assessing, on the one hand, the degree to which it intrudes upon an individual's privacy and, on the other, the degree to which it is needed for the promotion of legitimate governmental interests."[401]

While Fourth Amendment questions are raised most frequently in criminal prosecutions, where defendants can argue that evidence against them was obtained unconstitutionally, its protections are not limited to situations where law enforcement officers are searching for evidence of a crime.[402] "The Amendment guarantees 'the privacy, dignity, and security of persons against certain arbitrary and invasive acts by officers of the Government,' without regard to whether the government actor is investigating crime or performing another function."[403] This means that the executive branch must comply with the Fourth Amendment and may not engage in unreasonable searches when performing other vital functions of the government, such as protecting the nation from terrorism.[404]

The Fourth Amendment's restrictions come into play, however, only when the government carries out a search (or seizure). Whether a particular action taken by the government qualifies as a search is sometimes a difficult question. The quintessential example of a Fourth Amendment search occurs when government agents enter someone's home to look through his or her belongings, but the Amendment covers many other types of intrusions into personal privacy.

The telephone records program carried out by the NSA under Section 215 of the Patriot Act begins with the collection of individual Americans' calling records from private telephone companies. The NSA does not obtain these records from Americans themselves by probing their mail or computers, nor does it intercept the records in transmission or use any special technical means to gather them. Instead, private telephone companies disclose the records to the NSA, as ordered by the Foreign Intelligence Surveillance Court ("FISC" or "FISA court").[405] In defense of the NSA's program, the government argues that collecting telephone calling records in this manner does not qualify as a "search" within the meaning of the Fourth Amendment.

---

[400] *See Maryland v. King*, 133 S. Ct. 1958, 1970 (2013) ("Even if a warrant is not required, a search is not beyond Fourth Amendment scrutiny; for it must be reasonable in its scope and manner of execution.").

[401] *Samson v. California*, 547 U.S. 843, 848 (2006); *accord Maryland v. King*, 133 S. Ct. at 1970.

[402] *Quon*, 130 S. Ct. at 2627.

[403] *Quon*, 130 S. Ct. at 2627 (quoting *Skinner v. Railway Labor Executives' Ass'n*, 489 U.S. 602, 613-614 (1989)).

[404] *In re Directives Pursuant to Section 105B of Foreign Intelligence Surveillance Act*, 551 F.3d 1004 (FISA Ct. Rev. 2008).

[405] See Part 3 this Report for a description of this process.

If the government is correct, the Fourth Amendment does not apply at all to the NSA's telephone records program, meaning that the program may be conducted without obtaining warrants and without meeting the constitutional standard of reasonableness. While the government has devised a strict set of rules limiting the NSA's use and dissemination of the records it collects — recognizing that many individuals feel a privacy interest in their calling records, particularly with respect to governmental access to those records — these rules place no limits on the government's initial *collection* of telephone records. The question, then, is whether the NSA's collection of these records constitutes a search under the Fourth Amendment.

B. Telephone Eavesdropping and Reasonable Expectations of Privacy

Through the middle of the last century, defining a "search" was relatively simple because the Fourth Amendment was understood to protect certain *places* and *things* — such as one's home or vehicle — from unreasonable government searches. As a result, Fourth Amendment law was linked with the concept of property.[406] When government agents physically invaded a person's home or seized personal property to gather information; that conduct was regarded as a search and was subject to the restrictions of the Fourth Amendment.[407]

In a landmark 1967 decision, however, the Supreme Court clarified that "the Fourth Amendment protects people, not places" and ruled that government investigatory conduct can qualify as a search even where agents do not interfere with an individual's private property.[408] That decision, *Katz v. United States*, involved eavesdropping on telephone conversations. FBI agents had attached a listening device to the outside of a public telephone booth that was frequently used by a criminal suspect, allowing them to hear the words that he spoke into the telephone receiver. Although the agents did not physically intrude into the suspect's home or even into the telephone booth, the Supreme Court declared their eavesdropping to be a "search" under the Fourth Amendment, explaining that what a person "seeks to preserve as private, even in an area accessible to the public, may be constitutionally protected."[409]

A person in a telephone booth, the Court said in *Katz*, "is surely entitled to assume that the words he utters into the mouthpiece will not be broadcast to the world[.]"[410]

---

[406] *See United States v. Jones*, 132 S. Ct. 945, 949 (2012); *Kyllo v. United States*, 533 U.S. 27, 31-32 (2001) (citing, *inter alia*, *Olmstead v. United States*, 277 U.S. 438, 465-66 (1928)).

[407] *See Jones*, 132 S. Ct. at 949; *id.* at 955 (Sotomayor, J., concurring).

[408] *Katz v. United States*, 389 U.S. 347, 351 (1967); *see Jones*, 132 S. Ct. at 949 (quoting *Katz*, 389 U.S. at 351).

[409] *Katz*, 389 U.S. at 351.

[410] *Katz*, 389 U.S. at 352.

Therefore, the act of "electronically listening to and recording the [suspect's] words violated the privacy upon which he justifiably relied while using the telephone booth and thus constituted a 'search and seizure' within the meaning of the Fourth Amendment."[411]

The *Katz* decision made clear that, unless an exception applied, government eavesdropping on private telephone conversations without a warrant violates the Constitution. As the Court put it a few years later: "Though physical entry of the home is the chief evil against which the wording of the Fourth Amendment is directed, its broader spirit now shields private speech from unreasonable surveillance."[412]

More broadly, *Katz* established a two-part test for determining whether government conduct qualifies as a "search" under the Fourth Amendment. This "twofold requirement," from Justice John Marshall Harlan's concurring opinion, requires "first that a person have exhibited an actual (subjective) expectation of privacy and, second, that the expectation be one that society is prepared to recognize as 'reasonable.'"[413] Justice Harlan's two-part test was soon adopted by the Court itself and ever since has been the Fourth Amendment standard. [414] Thus, "a Fourth Amendment search occurs when the government violates a subjective expectation of privacy that society recognizes as reasonable."[415]

Unlike the surveillance addressed by the Supreme Court in *Katz*, the NSA's calling records program does not allow the government to listen to the content of telephone conversations. Indeed, because calling records are transmitted to the NSA by the telephone companies only after the calls have been completed, and because the telephone companies do not record these calls, the program gives the agency no means of listening to phone conversations. The government does not argue that the NSA could eavesdrop on purely domestic telephone calls without obtaining a warrant.

Under the Supreme Court's guidance, therefore, determining whether the NSA's collection of telephone records qualifies as a search involves applying the two-part test set forth above, and asking whether individuals have a subjective expectation of privacy in their calling records that society recognizes as reasonable. Answering that two-part question, however, requires taking into account another important Fourth Amendment doctrine.

---

411   *Katz*, 389 U.S. at 353.

412   *United States v. U.S. Dist. Court for E. Dist. of Mich., S. Div.*, 407 U.S. 297, 313 (1972).

413   *Katz*, 389 U.S. at 361 (Harlan, J., concurring).

414   *Mancusi v. DeForte*, 392 U.S. 364, 368 (1968).

415   *See, e.g., Kyllo*, 533 U.S. at 33 (citing *Katz*, 389 U.S. at 361 (Harlan, J., concurring)).

C. The "Third-Party Doctrine"

Government agents have other ways of obtaining information about people besides eavesdropping on their conversations or searching their property. One method is to subpoena information about a person from a third party. In the 1976 decision *United States v. Miller*, the Supreme Court concluded that law enforcement agents, without a warrant, could use a grand jury subpoena to obtain a customer's personal financial records from a bank. The Court rejected the customer's argument that under *Katz* he had a reasonable expectation of privacy in his bank records. The Court noted that "checks are not confidential communications but negotiable instruments to be used in commercial transactions." They are "voluntarily conveyed to the banks and exposed to their employees in the ordinary course of business." A bank customer has "neither ownership nor possession" of such records, the Court said, which "are the business records of the banks."[416] A bank depositor, the Court reasoned, "takes the risk, in revealing his affairs to another, that the information will be conveyed by that person to the Government."[417]

This situation was different from the one in *Katz*, where government agents covertly recorded a suspect's conversation from the outside of a telephone booth. The suspect in *Katz* had attempted to keep his conversation private from everyone except for the other participant, and so the government, without a warrant, could learn what was said in that conversation only from the other participant. The difference in *Miller* was that the government obtained the suspect's bank records directly from the bank, which itself participated in every financial transaction catalogued in its customers' records. "All of the documents obtained," therefore, "including financial statements and deposit slips, contain[ed] only information voluntarily conveyed to the banks and exposed to their employees in the ordinary course of business."[418]

In fashioning the third-party doctrine and applying it to business records, the Court thus concluded "that the Fourth Amendment does not prohibit the obtaining of information revealed to a third party and conveyed by him to Government authorities, even if the information is revealed on the assumption that it will be used only for a limited purpose and the confidence placed in the third party will not be betrayed."[419] That principle, said the Court, holds true even where, as in *Miller*, the Bank Secrecy Act forced banks to create

---

[416]   *United States v. Miller*, 425 U.S. 435, 440, 442-43 (1976).

[417]   *Miller*, 425 U.S. at 443 (citing *United States v. White*, 401 U.S. 745, 751-52 (1971)).

[418]   *Miller*, 425 U.S. at 442.

[419]   *Miller*, 425 U.S. at 443 (citing *White*, 401 U.S. at 752, *Hoffa*, 385 U.S. at 302, and *Lopez v. United States*, 373 U.S. 427 (1963)); *see also S.E.C. v. Jerry T. O'Brien, Inc.*, 467 U.S. 735, 743 (1984).

and maintain certain records about their customers, and where a bank was later compelled by a grand jury subpoena to turn over those records to the government.[420]

D. Warrantless Collection of Telephone Records

The rule that the Fourth Amendment does not protect information that a person has voluntarily conveyed to a third party was the foundation for the 1979 Supreme Court decision *Smith v. Maryland*, in which the Court concluded that individuals have no constitutional right of privacy in the numbers that they dial from their telephones. That decision is now the lynchpin of the government's constitutional rationale underlying the NSA's telephone records program.[421]

Given the significance of the *Smith* decision, its facts bear recounting in some detail. In 1976, Michael Lee Smith robbed a woman in Baltimore, Maryland. After the robbery, he began to make threatening and obscene telephone calls to her, identifying himself as the robber, and at least once drove his car by her house to intimidate her. The police learned Smith's address from his license plate number, and asked the telephone company to install a "pen register" at its central office to record the numbers dialed from the telephone at Smith's home.[422] A pen register is a device that, at the time, was attached to a telephone line and recorded the numbers dialed from a telephone but was not capable of hearing or recording telephone conversations themselves. While the technology of pen registers has evolved since the 1970s, the Supreme Court explained then that the machines "decode outgoing telephone numbers by responding to changes in electrical voltage caused by the turning of the telephone dial (or the pressing of buttons on pushbutton telephones) and present the information in a form to be interpreted by sight rather than by hearing."[423] The machine's name derives from the fact that early models used a pen to mark dashes on a piece of paper corresponding to each pulse from a rotary spin dial.[424]

In the *Smith* case, the police did not obtain a warrant or court order before having the pen register installed at the telephone company. On the same day that the device was installed, it revealed that a call was placed to the victim's home from Smith's telephone.

---

[420]   *Miller*, 425 U.S. at 443-45.

[421]   *See, e.g.*, Administration White Paper, Bulk Collection of Telephony Metadata under Section 215 of the USA PATRIOT Act, at 19-20 (Aug. 9, 2013) (citing *Smith v. Maryland*, 442 U.S. 735 (1979)).

[422]   *Smith*, 442 U.S. at 737.

[423]   *United States v. New York Tel. Co.*, 434 U.S. 159, 167 (1977).

[424]   "A pen register is a mechanical instrument attached to a telephone line, usually at a central telephone office, which records the outgoing numbers dialed on a particular telephone. In the case of a rotary dial phone, the pen register records on a paper tape dots or dashes equal in number to electrical pulses which correspond to the telephone number dialed." *Application of U.S. in Matter of Order Authorizing Use of a Pen Register*, 538 F.2d 956, 957 (2d Cir. 1976), *rev'd sub nom. United States v. New York Tel. Co.*, 434 U.S. 159 (1977).

Based on this and other evidence, the police then secured a warrant to search his residence, where incriminating evidence was found ultimately leading to his conviction.[425] Appealing this conviction, Smith's attorneys argued in the Supreme Court that the installation of the pen register without a warrant violated his Fourth Amendment rights.

Because the pen register was installed at the telephone company's office, there was no trespass to Smith's property. Therefore, the Supreme Court explained, under the *Katz* test the question was whether Smith had a "legitimate expectation of privacy" that had been "invaded by government action."[426]

A divided Court concluded that no legitimate privacy interest had been violated by warrantless use of the pen register. The five-Justice majority emphasized that "a pen register differs significantly from the listening device employed in *Katz*, for pen registers do not acquire the *contents* of communications." In fact, "a law enforcement official could not even determine from the use of a pen register whether a communication existed."[427] As the Court explained:

> These devices do not hear sound. They disclose only the telephone numbers that have been dialed — a means of establishing communication. Neither the purport of any communication between the caller and the recipient of the call, their identities, nor whether the call was even completed is disclosed by pen registers.[428]

"Given a pen register's limited capabilities," the Court said, Smith's argument that its installation and use constituted a "search" rested upon a claim that he had a "legitimate expectation of privacy regarding the numbers he dialed on his phone."[429]

The Court rejected that claim, expressing doubt "that people in general entertain any actual expectation of privacy in the numbers they dial." All telephone users "realize that they must 'convey' phone numbers to the telephone company," the Court continued, "since it is through telephone company switching equipment that their calls are completed. All subscribers realize, moreover, that the phone company has facilities for making permanent records of the numbers they dial, for they see a list of their long-distance (toll) calls on their monthly bills."[430] In short, according to the Supreme Court, telephone customers have no actual, subjective expectation that the numbers they dial are private,

---

425   *Smith*, 442 U.S. at 737.

426   *Smith*, 442 U.S. at 740.

427   *Smith*, 442 U.S. at 741 (emphasis in original).

428   *Smith*, 442 U.S. at 741 (quoting *New York Tel. Co.*, 434 U.S. at 167).

429   *Smith*, 442 U.S. at 742 (internal quotation marks omitted).

430   *Smith*, 442 U.S. at 742.

because they "typically know that they must convey numerical information to the phone company; that the phone company has facilities for recording this information; and that the phone company does in fact record this information for a variety of legitimate business purposes."[431]

Even if Michael Lee Smith did harbor a personal, subjective expectation that the numbers he dialed were private, the Court continued, that expectation was not "one that society is prepared to recognize as 'reasonable,'" and therefore the expectation was not protected by the Fourth Amendment.[432] This was so, the Court said, because under the third-party doctrine described above "a person has no legitimate expectation of privacy in information he voluntarily turns over to third parties."[433]

Applying this principle in *Smith*, the Court concluded that the suspect, by using his telephone, "voluntarily conveyed numerical information to the telephone company and 'exposed' that information to its equipment in the ordinary course of business."[434] Just as a person who reveals information to a friend or associate assumes the risk that his confidant will share it with the government, a person making telephone calls assumes the risk that the telephone company will share with the government the numbers he has dialed.

The upshot of *Smith v. Maryland* is that under the Constitution the government does not need a warrant to use a pen register to obtain the telephone numbers that a person dials from his or her telephone. The government can intercept that information, as the police did in *Smith*, by installing a pen register to record those numbers.[435] Similarly, the courts have concluded, warrants are not constitutionally required to install and use a "trap and trace" device, which monitors the *inbound* calls made to a particular telephone, much like caller-ID service.[436] In lieu of using such devices for real-time collection, the government can issue a subpoena to the telephone company for the stored calling records of one of its customers.[437]

---

[431]   *Smith*, 442 U.S. at 743.

[432]   *Smith*, 442 U.S. at 743 (quoting *Katz*, 389 U.S. at 361).

[433]   *Smith*, 442 U.S. at 743-44.

[434]   *Smith*, 442 U.S. at 744.

[435]   In 1986, Congress adopted legislation requiring governmental entities to obtain a court order to install and use a pen register. The standard for such orders is much lower than the standard required for issuance of a warrant: a court must issue an order if the government certifies that the evidence sought is relevant to an ongoing criminal investigation. *See* 18 U.S.C. §§ 3121-3127.

[436]   *See, e.g., United States v. Reed*, 575 F.3d 900, 914 (9th Cir. 2009); *United States v. Hallmark*, 911 F.2d 399, 402 (10th Cir. 1990). The pen register statute adopted in 1986 also requires court orders for the installation and use of trap and trace devices.

[437]   *See* 18 U.S.C. §§ 2703(c)(2), 2709.

While *Smith v. Maryland* addresses law enforcement tools of a more primitive technological era — the decision declares that the equipment that processes dialed telephone numbers "is merely the modern counterpart of the operator who, in an earlier day, personally completed calls for the subscriber" — it remains the law of the land.[438] Many recent court decisions have relied on a broad reading of *Smith* to conclude, among other things, that there is no Fourth Amendment expectation of privacy in email addressing information, such as the "to" and "from" lines in an email.[439]

E. Comparing the NSA's Telephone Records Program with the Surveillance Approved in *Smith v. Maryland*

In the view of the government and the FISA court, *Smith v. Maryland* settles the question of whether the NSA's telephone records program constitutes a search under the Fourth Amendment: because people have no reasonable expectation of privacy in the numbers that they dial, collecting those numbers from a telephone company is not a "search" within the meaning of the Fourth Amendment, and therefore the Amendment simply does not apply.[440] As previously noted, *Smith v. Maryland* still stands as the law of the land, and government attorneys were entitled to rely on it as the telephony metadata program was developed and approved by the court.

However, the case does not provide a good fit for the telephone records program, particularly in light of rapid technological changes and in light of the nationwide, ongoing nature of the program. The NSA's Section 215 program gathers significantly more information about each telephone call and about far more people than did the pen register surveillance approved in *Smith* (essentially everyone in the country who uses a phone) and it has collected that data now for nearly eight years without interruption.[441] In contrast, the pen register approved in *Smith v. Maryland* compiled only a list of the numbers dialed from Michael Lee Smith's telephone. It did not show whether any of his attempted calls were actually completed — thus it did not reveal whether he engaged in any telephone conversations at all. Naturally, therefore, the device also did not indicate the duration of any conversations. Furthermore, the pen register provided no information about incoming telephone calls placed to Smith's home, only the outbound calls dialed from his telephone.

---

[438]   *Smith*, 442 U.S. at 744; *but see* Memorandum Opinion at 45, *Klayman v. Obama*, No. 13-0851 (D.D.C. Dec. 16, 2013) (concluding that *Smith v. Maryland* does not apply to the NSA telephone metadata program).

[439]   *See, e.g., United States v. Forrester*, 512 F.3d 500 (9th Cir. 2008).

[440]   *See* Administration White Paper at 19-20; Amended Memorandum Opinion at 6-9, *In re Application of the Federal Bureau of Investigation for an Order Requiring the Production of Tangible Things*, No. BR 13-109 (FISA Ct. Aug. 29, 2013); Memorandum at 4-6, *In re Application of the Federal Bureau of Investigation for an Order Requiring the Production of Tangible Things*, No. BR 13-109 (FISA Ct. Oct. 11, 2013).

[441]   The court orders authorizing the program last for only ninety days, but the concept of the program is one of indefinite collection, and since May 2006 there has never been a lapse in court approval.

The pen register was in operation for no more than two days.[442] And finally, the device recorded only the dialing information of one person: Smith himself. The police had no computerized ability to aggregate Smith's dialing records with those of other individuals and gain additional insight from that analysis.

In contrast, for each of the millions of telephone numbers covered by the NSA's Section 215 program, the agency obtains a record of all incoming and outgoing calls, the duration of those calls, and the precise time of day when they occurred. When the agency targets a telephone number for analysis, the same information for every telephone number with which the original number has had contact, and every telephone number in contact with any of those numbers. And, subject to regular program renewal by the FISA court, it collects these records every day, without interruption, and retains them for a five year time period. Sweeping up this vast swath of information, the government has explained, allows the NSA to use "sophisticated analytic tools" to "discover connections between individuals" and reveal "chains of communication" — a broader power than simply learning the telephone numbers dialed by a single targeted individual.[443]

To illustrate the greater scope of the NSA's program, the pen register discussed in *Smith* might have shown that, during the time that Michael Lee Smith's telephone was monitored, he dialed another number three times in a single day. That information could have simply evinced three failed attempts to reach the other number. The NSA's collection program, however, would show not only whether each attempted call connected but also the precise duration and time of each call. It also would reveal whether and when the other telephone number called Smith and the length and time of any such calls. Because the NSA collects records continuously and stores them for five years, it would be in a position to see how frequently those two numbers contacted each other during the preceding five years and the pattern of their contact. And because the agency would have full access to the calling records of the other telephone number as well, it could examine the activity of that other number and see, for instance, whether it ever communicated with any of the same numbers as Smith over a five-year period, or what numbers it communicated with around the time of its calls with Smith. The agency could then do the same thing for every other number that Smith had communicated with in the past five years, employing what it calls contact-chaining analysis. It could then go further and analyze the complete calling records of every number that was called by any of the numbers that ever communicated with Smith — going three "hops" from the original number.

---

[442]   *Smith*, 442 U.S. at 737.

[443]   Administration White Paper at 13-14.

The NSA's Section 215 program, therefore, is dramatically broader than the practice approved by the Supreme Court in *Smith*, which was directed at a single criminal suspect and gathered only "the numbers he dialed on his phone" during a limited period.[444]

The government argues that these differences are irrelevant under the Fourth Amendment. It argues that the third-party doctrine described earlier applies whether the government is obtaining data on one person or hundreds of millions. All of the information collected by the NSA in its calling records program is recorded by telephone companies for their own business purposes. Thus, just like the numbers that a telephone user dials, all of this information has been shared with telephone companies by their customers. As long as the third-party doctrine remains in force and assuming it applies regardless of the breadth of the data acquired, the NSA's collection of calling records is not a search under the Fourth Amendment.

F. Privacy-Based Criticisms of *Smith v. Maryland* and the Third-Party Doctrine

The third-party doctrine, which serves as the constitutional underpinning of the NSA's telephone records program, has been heavily criticized by legal scholars and others. The leading academic treatise on the Fourth Amendment calls the Supreme Court's decision in *United States v. Miller*, which concluded that there are no privacy rights in bank records, "dead wrong," asserting that its "woefully inadequate reasoning does great violence to the theory of Fourth Amendment protection the Court had developed in *Katz*."[445] The same treatise opines that the Court's rationale in *Smith v. Maryland*, which applied the doctrine to telephone calling records, "makes a mockery of the Fourth Amendment."[446] Even some defenders of the doctrine express the view that the Supreme Court "has never offered a clear argument in its favor."[447] A number of state supreme courts have rejected the doctrine with respect to the privacy guarantees of their own constitutions, even where those constitutions mimic the language of the Fourth Amendment.[448] A number of such courts have explicitly disagreed with *Smith v. Maryland*'s

---

[444] *Smith*, 442 U.S. at 742.

[445] 1 WAYNE R. LaFAVE, SEARCH AND SEIZURE: A TREATISE ON THE FOURTH AMENDMENT §§ 2.7(b), (c) (5th ed.).

[446] *Id.*

[447] Orin S. Kerr, *The Case for the Third-Party Doctrine*, 107 MICH. L. REV. 561, 564 (2009) ("The closest the Court has come to justifying the doctrine has been its occasional assertion that people who disclose communications to a third party 'assume the risk' that their information will end up in the hands of the police. But assumption of risk is a result rather than a rationale: A person must assume a risk only when the Constitution does not protect it. Exactly why the Constitution does not protect information disclosed to third parties has been left unexplained.").

[448] As of 2006, eleven states had rejected the federal third-party doctrine and ten others had given some reason to believe that they might reject it. *See* Stephen E. Henderson, *Learning from All Fifty States: How to Apply the Fourth Amendment and Its State Analogs to Protect Third Party Information from Unreasonable Search*, 55 CATH. U. L. REV. 373, 376 (2006).

reasoning and have concluded that the use of pen registers or the collection of telephone calling records implicates protected privacy interests.[449] A number of federal magistrates and judges have rejected the doctrine as applied to cell site information transmitted or stored in connection with cell phone calls.[450]

Many criticisms of the third-party doctrine were first voiced by Supreme Court Justices who vigorously dissented from the decisions that established it. One such critique is that the doctrine is premised on an unrealistic view of privacy expectations. In *Smith*, for example, Justice Potter Stewart argued in dissent that the "central question" was whether a person making telephone calls from his home is entitled to assume that the numbers he dials, like the words he speaks, "'will not be broadcast to the world.'"[451] In Justice Stewart's view, "[w]hat the telephone company does or might do with those numbers is no more relevant to this inquiry than it would be in a case involving the conversation itself."[452] Although the numbers dialed from a telephone are "more prosaic than the conversation," he wrote, "I doubt there are any who would be happy to have broadcast to the world a list of the local or long distance numbers they have called. This is not because such a list might in some sense be incriminating, but because it easily could reveal the identities of the persons and the places called, and thus reveal the most intimate details of a person's life."[453]

Justice Thurgood Marshall, joined by Justice William Brennan, similarly observed in his own *Smith* dissent: "Just as one who enters a public telephone booth is 'entitled to assume that the words he utters into the mouthpiece will not be broadcast to the world,' so too, he should be entitled to assume that the numbers he dials in the privacy of his home will be recorded, if at all, solely for the phone company's business purposes."[454] The legitimacy of privacy expectations, in Justice Marshall's view, depended "not on the risks an individual can be presumed to accept when imparting information to third parties, but on the risks he should be forced to assume in a free and open society."[455] The use of pen registers, he continued, was an "extensive intrusion" into privacy, because of "the vital role

---

[449]   *See, e.g., Commonwealth v. Melilli*, 555 A.2d 1254, 1258 59 (Pa. 1989); *Shaktman v. State*, 553 So.2d 148, 149 51 (Fla. 1989); *State v. Thompson*, 760 P.2d 1162, 1164 67 (Idaho 1988); *State v. Gunwall*, 720 P.2d 808, 814 16 (Wash. 1986); *People v. Sporleder*, 666 P.2d 135, 140 42 (Colo. 1983); *State v. Hunt*, 450 A.2d 952, 954 57 (N.J. 1982).

[450]   *See* Testimony of Magistrate Judge Stephen W. Smith before the Subcommittee on the Constitution, Civil Rights and Civil liberties of the House Judiciary Committee, Hearing on ECPA reform and the Revolution in location based Technologies and Service (June 24, 2010).

[451]   *Smith*, 442 U.S. at 747 (Stewart, J., dissenting) (quoting *Katz*, 389 U.S. at 352).

[452]   *Smith*, 442 U.S. at 747 (Stewart, J., dissenting).

[453]   *Smith*, 442 U.S. at 748 (Stewart, J., dissenting).

[454]   *Smith*, 442 U.S. at 752 (Marshall, J., dissenting) (quoting *Katz*, 389 U.S. at 352).

[455]   *Smith*, 442 U.S. at 750 (Marshall, J., dissenting).

telephonic communication plays in our personal and professional relationships."[456] The prospect of unregulated governmental monitoring of calling records, Justice Marshall wrote, would "undoubtedly prove disturbing even to those with nothing illicit to hide":

> Many individuals, including members of unpopular political organizations or journalists with confidential sources, may legitimately wish to avoid disclosure of their personal contacts. Permitting governmental access to telephone records on less than probable cause may thus impede certain forms of political affiliation and journalistic endeavor that are the hallmark of a truly free society.[457]

A related critique of the third-party doctrine is that it reflects an all-or-nothing approach to privacy, under which a person's entitlement to keep information secret is entirely vitiated whenever he or she shares that information with anyone, "even if the information is revealed on the assumption that it will be used only for a limited purpose and the confidence placed in the third party will not be betrayed" (as the Supreme Court put it in *Miller*).[458] The result of this approach is that a person who shares information with a telephone company, bank, Internet service provider, credit card company, hospital, library, pharmacy, or any other institution — even on the understanding that the information will be kept confidential — forfeits any Fourth Amendment right to prevent the government from obtaining that information from the institution with which it was shared.

In *Smith*, Justice Marshall took issue with this all-or-nothing approach: "Privacy is not a discrete commodity, possessed absolutely or not at all. Those who disclose certain facts to a bank or phone company for a limited business purpose need not assume that this information will be released to other persons for other purposes."[459] Regarding bank records, for instance, he wrote: "The fact that one has disclosed private papers to the bank, for a limited purpose, within the context of a confidential customer-bank relationship, does not mean that one has waived all right to the privacy of the papers."[460] Likewise, merely because people know "that a phone company monitors calls for internal reasons, it does not follow that they expect this information to be made available to the public in general or the government in particular."[461]

---

[456]   *Smith*, 442 U.S. at 751 (Marshall, J., dissenting).

[457]   *Smith*, 442 U.S. at 751 (Marshall, J., dissenting) (internal citations omitted).

[458]   *Miller*, 425 U.S. at 443.

[459]   *Smith*, 442 U.S. at 749 (Marshall, J., dissenting).

[460]   *California Bankers Ass'n v. Shultz*, 416 U.S. 21, 95-96 (1974) (Marshall, J., dissenting).

[461]   *Smith*, 442 U.S. at 749 (Marshall, J., dissenting). The fact that a bank or telephone company is itself a participant in its customers' transactions, according to Justice Marshall, "is irrelevant to the question of

The implications of this all-or-nothing approach to privacy have grown since the 1970s, as Americans increasingly must share personal information with companies in order to avail themselves of services and products that have become typical features of modern living. Another major criticism of the third-party doctrine, which has gained increased salience in light of these developments, challenges the notion that a customer of such companies, simply by "revealing his affairs to another," truly chooses to risk "that the information will be conveyed by that person to the Government."[462] This criticism rejects the idea that conducting business that is essential to contemporary life represents a voluntary decision to lay bare the details of one's habits to governmental scrutiny.

"For all practical purposes," Justice Brennan observed in his *Miller* dissent, "the disclosure by individuals or business firms of their financial affairs to a bank is not entirely volitional, since it is impossible to participate in the economic life of contemporary society without maintaining a bank account."[463] Justice Marshall, dissenting in *Smith*, expanded on this point:

> Implicit in the concept of assumption of risk is some notion of choice. At least in the third-party consensual surveillance cases, which first incorporated risk analysis into Fourth Amendment doctrine, the defendant presumably had exercised some discretion in deciding who should enjoy his confidential communications. By contrast here, unless a person is prepared to forgo use of what for many has become a personal or professional necessity, he cannot help but accept the risk of surveillance. It is idle to speak of "assuming" risks in contexts where, as a practical matter, individuals have no realistic alternative.[464]

There are cases in which the Supreme Court has rejected the notion that there is no privacy interest in what is disclosed to a third party.[465] The third-party doctrine was recently questioned at the Supreme Court by Justice Sonia Sotomayor, who wrote in *United States v. Jones* that the assumption-of-risk approach "is ill suited to the digital age, in which

---

whether a Government search or seizure is involved." *California Bankers Ass'n*, 416 U.S. at 95 (Marshall, J., dissenting).

[462]   *Miller*, 425 U.S. at 443 (citing *White*, 401 U.S. at 751-52); *see Smith*, 442 U.S. at 744.

[463]   *Miller*, 425 U.S. at 451 (Brennan, J., dissenting) (quoting *Burrows v. Superior Court*, 529 P.2d 590, 596 (Cal. 1974)); *see id.* ("In the course of such dealings, a depositor reveals many aspects of his personal affairs, opinions, habits and associations. Indeed, the totality of bank records provides a virtual current biography.").

[464]   *Smith*, 442 U.S. at 749-50 (Marshall, J., dissenting) (internal citations omitted).

[465]   *See* Stephen E. Henderson, *The Timely Demise of the Fourth Amendment Third Party Doctrine*, 96 IOWA L. REV. BULL. 39, 41-43 (2011). *See also Department of Justice v. Reporters Committee for Freedom of the Press*, 489 U.S. 749 (1989) (in FOIA case, finding a privacy interest in the FBI's compilation of police rap sheets, even though the events summarized in the rap sheets had previously been disclosed to the public, noting: "In an organized society, there are few facts that are not at one time or another divulged to another.").

people reveal a great deal of information about themselves to third parties in the course of carrying out mundane tasks," including "the phone numbers that they dial or text," "the URLs that they visit and the e-mail addresses with which they correspond," and "the books, groceries, and medications they purchase."[466] As this comment suggests, the lack of any meaningful option to withhold personal information from third-party institutions is even greater today than it was at the time of *Smith v. Maryland*, because of intervening developments in communications and commerce.

G. Fourth Amendment Implications of Technological Advancements

The societal developments noted above, abetted by changes in technology, have increased the range of information available to government investigators without a warrant. Meanwhile, the same technological advances fueling this trend have markedly heightened the government's capacity to collect, aggregate, and analyze immense quantities of information — a development amply demonstrated by the NSA's telephone records program. The Supreme Court has acknowledged that new technology has the potential to erode Fourth Amendment protections,[467] and that it can also alter societal conceptions about the legitimacy of certain privacy expectations.[468] Given these considerations, the Supreme Court's decision in *Smith v. Maryland* may not forever settle the question of whether individuals have a reasonable expectation of privacy in their telephone calling records, especially in the context of bulk and indefinite collection.

The potential for enhanced surveillance technology to undermine privacy guarantees was already evident in the 1970s when the third-party doctrine was being developed by the Supreme Court — leading some Justices to warn in dissents that unless constitutional jurisprudence were to evolve in response to such developments, the liberty secured by the Fourth Amendment would irredeemably wither.

In *United States v. Miller*, for instance, Justice Brennan in his dissenting opinion noted that Fourth Amendment doctrine had long condemned "violent searches and invasions of an individual's right to the privacy of his dwelling," yet "[t]he imposition upon privacy, although perhaps not so dramatic, may be equally devastating when other methods are employed."

---

[466]   *Jones*, 132 S. Ct. at 957 (Sotomayor, J., concurring).

[467]   *See Kyllo*, 533 U.S. at 33-34.

[468]   *See Quon*, 130 S. Ct. at 2629-30 ("Rapid changes in the dynamics of communication and information transmission are evident not just in the technology itself but in what society accepts as proper behavior. . . . [T]he Court would have difficulty predicting how employees' privacy expectations will be shaped by those changes or the degree to which society will be prepared to recognize those expectations as reasonable.").

Development of photocopying machines, electronic computers and other sophisticated instruments have accelerated the ability of government to intrude into areas which a person normally chooses to exclude from prying eyes and inquisitive minds. Consequently judicial interpretations of the reach of the constitutional protection of individual privacy must keep pace with the perils created by these new devices.[469]

A failure of constitutional law to respond to developing technology, Justice Marshall similarly observed in a dissent, would functionally diminish the Amendment's protections against the very sort of evils that it was designed to shield against: "Our Fourth Amendment jurisprudence should not be so wooden as to ignore the fact that through micro-filming and other techniques of this electronic age, illegal searches and seizures can take place without the brute force characteristic of the general warrants which raised the ire of the Founding Fathers."[470]

More recently, the Supreme Court has acknowledged that it "would be foolish to contend that the degree of privacy secured to citizens by the Fourth Amendment has been entirely unaffected by the advance of technology."[471] The Court recognized that it must sometimes confront the question of "what limits there are upon this power of technology to shrink the realm of guaranteed privacy."[472] In a case involving a thermal-imaging device aimed at a private home from a public street, which revealed details about the interior of the home that previously could have been known only by physical entry, the Court declared use of the device to be a "search," rejecting a rigid interpretation of the Fourth Amendment that "would leave the homeowner at the mercy of advancing technology."[473]

Such technological advancement during the past thirty years, particularly in the storage, transmission, and manipulation of digital information, has allowed the NSA to institute a program of amassing and analyzing telephone records that is exponentially more far-reaching than the pen register surveillance addressed by the Supreme Court in

---

[469]   *Miller*, 425 U.S. at 451-52 (Brennan, J., dissenting) (quoting *Burrows*, 529 P.2d at 593-96).

[470]   *California Bankers Ass'n*, 416 U.S. at 95 (Marshall, J., dissenting) (citing *Entick v. Carrington*, 19 How. St. Tr. 1029 (1765), and *Stanford v. Texas*, 379 U.S. 476, 483-84 (1965)); *see also Smith*, 442 U.S. at 746 (Stewart, J., dissenting) (echoing observation that "the broad and unsuspected governmental incursions into conversational privacy which electronic surveillance entails necessitate the application of Fourth Amendment safeguards" (quoting *United States v. U.S. Dist. Court for E. Dist. of Mich., S. Div.*, 407 U.S. at 313)).

[471]   *Kyllo*, 533 U.S. at 33-34.

[472]   *Kyllo*, 533 U.S. at 34.

[473]   *Kyllo*, 533 U.S. at 35, 40.

1979. At the same time, the ubiquity of mobile phone technology has increasingly placed telephone-based connections at the center of human interaction.[474]

Given the unprecedented breadth of the NSA's collection of telephone records under Section 215 of the Patriot Act, coupled with the agency's enhanced ability to sift through those records and map out an individual's communications network, and in light of changes in Americans' habits caused by modern technology, it is possible that the contemporary Supreme Court — if called upon to evaluate the NSA's program under the Fourth Amendment — would not consider *Smith v. Maryland* to have resolved the question.

Reaching the conclusion that a Fourth Amendment interest was implicated by bulk, ongoing calling record collection would require the Court to scale back the third-party doctrine, a step the Court has not taken. But a recent decision, involving Global-Positioning-System ("GPS") monitoring, indicates that a majority of Justices believes that the rise of novel technological tools for the collection, aggregation, and analysis of large quantities of information demands judicial recognition that not everything an individual exposes to the public loses Fourth Amendment protection.

In *United States v. Jones*, the Supreme Court ruled that placing a GPS device on a Jeep driven by a criminal suspect, and then using the device to track the Jeep's movements continuously for four weeks, was a "search" under the Constitution. The Court's majority opinion based this conclusion on traditional, trespass-related Fourth Amendment principles: by installing a GPS device on the Jeep, the Court wrote, the government "physically occupied private property for the purpose of obtaining information," and the Court had "no doubt" that "such a physical intrusion would have been considered a 'search' within the meaning of the Fourth Amendment when it was adopted."[475]

By focusing on the physical placement of a GPS device on the vehicle, the opinion left unresolved whether its driver reasonably could expect privacy in its whereabouts — a matter that he exposed to others by driving on public streets. "It may be that achieving the same result through electronic means, without an accompanying trespass, is an unconstitutional invasion of privacy," the majority said, "but the present case does not require us to answer that question."[476]

---

[474]   *See In re Orders Authorizing Use of Pen Registers & Trap & Trace Devices*, 515 F. Supp. 2d 325, 328 (E.D.N.Y. 2007) ("Telephone use has expanded rapidly since the constitutionality of pen registers was examined in 1979. Today, Americans regularly use their telephones not just to dial a phone number, but to manage bank accounts, refill prescriptions, check movie times, and so on.").

[475]   *Jones*, 132 S. Ct. at 949. As Justice Sotomayor's concurring opinion put it: "The Government usurped Jones' property for the purpose of conducting surveillance on him, thereby invading privacy interests long afforded, and undoubtedly entitled to, Fourth Amendment protection." *Id.* at 954 (Sotomayor, J., concurring).

[476]   *Jones*, 132 S. Ct. at 954.

Justice Samuel Alito, joined by three other justices, agreed with the majority's result, but not its reasoning, which he wrote "largely disregards what is really important . . . the *use* of a GPS for the purpose of long-term tracking."[477] He would instead have applied the two-part *Katz* test to the GPS surveillance, asking whether monitoring the suspect's vehicle continuously for four weeks "involved a degree of intrusion that a reasonable person would not have anticipated."[478] Answering that question, he concluded that "longer term GPS monitoring in investigations of most offenses impinges on expectations of privacy," because in such cases "society's expectation has been that law enforcement agents and others would not — and indeed, in the main, simply could not — secretly monitor and catalogue every single movement of an individual's car for a very long period."[479]

Similar concerns are reflected in the concurring opinion written by Justice Sotomayor, who provided the fifth vote for the majority opinion. Agreeing with Justice Alito "that, at the very least, longer term GPS monitoring in investigations of most offenses impinges on expectations of privacy," Justice Sotomayor wrote that, even with respect to short-term monitoring, the ability of modern technology to generate "a precise, comprehensive record of a person's public movements that reflects a wealth of detail about her familial, political, professional, religious, and sexual associations" has Fourth Amendment implications deserving of special attention.[480] That is particularly so, she wrote, because the government "can store such records and efficiently mine them for information years into the future."[481] Thus, in assessing the constitutionality of such technology with respect to GPS tracking, Justice Sotomayor wrote that the proper question is "whether people reasonably expect that their movements will be recorded and aggregated in a manner that enables the Government to ascertain, more or less at will, their political and religious beliefs, sexual habits, and so on."[482]

The observations of Justices Alito and Sotomayor echo the rationale of the Court of Appeals decision in *Jones*, which rested on the insight that knowing the whole of a person's activity is different from knowing only parts of it, "because that whole reveals more — sometimes a great deal more — than does the sum of its parts."[483] Prolonged surveillance, the appellate court wrote, "reveals types of information not revealed by short-term

---

477   *Jones*, 132 S. Ct. at 961 (Alito, J., concurring in the judgment) (emphasis in original).

478   *Jones*, 132 S. Ct. at 964 (Alito, J., concurring in the judgment).

479   *Jones*, 132 S. Ct. at 964 (Alito, J., concurring in the judgment).

480   *Jones*, 132 S. Ct. at 955 (Sotomayor, J., concurring).

481   *Jones*, 132 S. Ct. at 956 (Sotomayor, J., concurring).

482   *Jones*, 132 S. Ct. at 956 (Sotomayor, J., concurring).

483   *United States v. Maynard*, 615 F.3d 544, 558 (D.C. Cir. 2010), *aff'd on other grounds sub nom. United States v. Jones*, 132 S. Ct. 945 (2012). The circuit court invoked the term "mosaic theory" to describe this phenomena.

surveillance," and these types of information "can each reveal more about a person than does any individual trip viewed in isolation."[484]

> Repeated visits to a church, a gym, a bar, or a bookie tell a story not told by any single visit, as does one's not visiting any of these places over the course of a month. The sequence of a person's movements can reveal still more; a single trip to a gynecologist's office tells little about a woman, but that trip followed a few weeks later by a visit to a baby supply store tells a different story.[485]

"A person who knows all of another's travels," the court continued, "can deduce whether he is a weekly church goer, a heavy drinker, a regular at the gym, an unfaithful husband, an outpatient receiving medical treatment, an associate of particular individuals or political groups — and not just one such fact about a person, but all such facts."[486]

If this approach were applied to the NSA's collection of telephone records under Section 215, it might lead to the conclusion that customers' disclosure of calling information to a telephone company — to enable the completion and billing of individual calls — is different from relinquishing the totality of their calling histories over a five-year period for digitally facilitated analysis. Just as the sum of one's movements in a vehicle over a four-week period tells a different story than a smattering of individual trips, the comprehensive record of a person's entire telephone communication history over five years reveals much more than the log of a day's worth of calls.

We stress that there is no indication that the government has used the telephone records collected under Section 215 to trace religious or political affiliations or deduce other sensitive matters. But in *Jones*, the government likewise was not using the location data to deduce who was a weekly churchgoer, a heavy drinker or an unfaithful husband, yet five Justices agreed nevertheless that the long-term collection of location data constituted a search under the Fourth Amendment.

Justice Sotomayor's *Jones* concurrence explicitly drew a connection between her analysis of GPS monitoring and *Smith v. Maryland* and other decisions applying the third-party doctrine. [487] Her concurrence suggested that "it may be necessary to reconsider the

---

484   *Maynard*, 615 F.3d at 562.

485   *Maynard*, 615 F.3d at 562.

486   *Maynard*, 615 F.3d at 562.

487   In defense of warrantless GPS monitoring, the government's brief had relied on *Smith v. Maryland*, arguing that disclosure of one's location to the public is like the disclosures of calling information to a telephone company. *See* Brief for the United States at 20-21, 23-24, 31-33, *United States v. Jones*, No. 10-1259 (U.S. Aug. 2011).

premise that an individual has no reasonable expectation of privacy in information voluntarily disclosed to third parties."[488] She elaborated:

> This approach is ill suited to the digital age, in which people reveal a great deal of information about themselves to third parties in the course of carrying out mundane tasks. People disclose the phone numbers that they dial or text to their cellular providers; the URLs that they visit and the e-mail addresses with which they correspond to their Internet service providers; and the books, groceries, and medications they purchase to online retailers.[489]

As the disclosure of such information to third parties becomes more and more unavoidable, Justice Sotomayor observed, American society may or may not develop concomitant expectations of privacy in the confidentiality of this information vis-à-vis the government. But such expectations "can attain constitutionally protected status only if our Fourth Amendment jurisprudence ceases to treat secrecy as a prerequisite for privacy."[490] Echoing and citing Justice Marshall's dissenting opinion in *Smith v. Maryland*, Justice Sotomayor concluded: "I would not assume that all information voluntarily disclosed to some member of the public for a limited purpose is, for that reason alone, disentitled to Fourth Amendment protection."[491]

H. Relevance of the Third-party Doctrine to the NSA Telephone Records Program

Beyond generalized criticisms of the third-party doctrine, the more pertinent question may be whether the doctrine can be stretched to exempt from Fourth Amendment scrutiny a program as broad and long-running as the Section 215 telephone metadata program. That program goes far beyond anything that has ever before been upheld under the doctrine. As suggested by the observations of Justices Alito and Sotomayor in *United States v. Jones*, collectively representing the views of five Justices, the Supreme Court might find that the third-party doctrine, regardless of its validity as applied to traditional pen/trap devices and particularized subpoenas, does not apply to the compelled disclosure of data on a scope as broad and persistent as the NSA's telephone records program. One district court has recently stated an argument for limiting the third-party doctrine in a case challenging the constitutionality of the NSA telephone records program. In *Klayman v. Obama*, Judge Richard Leon analyzed in detail the changes in technology since *Smith* was

---

488   *Jones*, 132 S. Ct. at 957 (Sotomayor, J., concurring).

489   *Jones*, 132 S. Ct. at 957 (Sotomayor, J., concurring).

490   *Jones*, 132 S. Ct. at 957 (Sotomayor, J., concurring).

491   *Jones*, 132 S. Ct. at 957 (Sotomayor, J., concurring) (citing *Smith*, 442 U.S. at 749 (Marshall, J., dissenting)).

decided in 1979 and compared the capabilities of the pen register at issue in *Smith* to the scope of the NSA telephone records program. He concluded that "present-day circumstances" are "so thoroughly unlike those considered by the Supreme Court thirty-four years ago" that *Smith* should not apply to analysis of the telephone records program.[492]

However, the decision in *Klayman v. Obama,* which the government has appealed, represents the opinion of a single district court judge. Illustrating the deep split among courts over the breadth of the third-party doctrine, a different district court has upheld the 215 program on the basis of *Smith v. Maryland.*[493] Until the Supreme Court rules otherwise, *Smith v. Maryland* and the third-party doctrine remain in force today. Government lawyers are entitled to rely on them when appraising the constitutionality of a given action.

I. Implications of Regarding the Metadata Program as a "Search"

If the Supreme Court reversed or narrowed *Smith,* for example, by holding that certain bulk collections of data were covered by the Fourth Amendment, this would establish only that the NSA's collection of telephone records pursuant to Section 215 of the Patriot Act is a "search" under the Fourth Amendment. The next question would be whether this search — carried out to prevent international terrorism, not to prosecute ordinary crimes after they have been committed — requires a warrant. The Supreme Court has left open the question of whether there is a "foreign intelligence exception" to the Fourth Amendment's warrant requirement that permits the executive branch to engage in warrantless surveillance "with respect to the activities of foreign powers, within or without this country."[494] A number of lower courts have concluded that such an exception exists "when the object of the search or the surveillance is a foreign power, its agent or collaborators."[495]

---

[492]   Memorandum Opinion at 45, *Klayman v. Obama,* No. 13-0851 (D.D.C. Dec. 16, 2013).

[493]   *See* Memorandum & Order at 38-44, *ACLU v. Clapper,* No. 13-3994 (S.D.N.Y. Dec. 27, 2013).

[494]   *United States v. U.S. Dist. Court for E. Dist. of Mich., S. Div.,* 407 U.S. at 308. When the Court ruled in *Katz* that warrantless government eavesdropping on telephone conversations violates the Constitution, it was careful to note that "a situation involving the national security" might call for a different result, and that in such situations "safeguards other than prior authorization by a magistrate" might satisfy the Fourth Amendment's reasonableness requirement. *Katz,* 389 U.S. at 358 n.23. A few years later, the Court concluded that there is no exception to the Fourth Amendment's warrant requirement for *domestic* national security surveillance that does not involve foreign powers. *United States v. U.S. Dist. Court for E. Dist. of Mich., S. Div.,* 407 U.S. at 324. The legitimacy of warrantless foreign intelligence surveillance has never been resolved by the Court, *see In re Directives Pursuant to Section 105B of Foreign Intelligence Surveillance Act,* 551 F.3d 1004, 1010 (FISA Ct. Rev. 2008), in part because the passage of FISA in the late 1970s established a statutory framework for such surveillance that was followed by the executive branch until the events of September 11, 2001.

[495]   *United States v. Truong Dinh Hung,* 629 F.2d 908, 915 (4th Cir. 1980); *accord United States v. Butenko,* 494 F.2d 593 (3rd Cir. 1974); *United States v. Brown,* 484 F.2d 418 (5th Cir. 1973). In more recent years, the

If no warrant is required for the government to collect telephone records in pursuit of foreign intelligence, a further decision would have to be made about whether the NSA's collection of these records under Section 215 is constitutionally "reasonable," which would involve balancing the governmental interests at stake with the program's intrusion into privacy.[496]

J. "Just Because We Can Do Something Doesn't Mean We Necessarily Should"[497]

To hold, as most courts have, that telephony metadata enjoys no privacy protection under the Fourth Amendment does not mean that such data is without privacy implications. Telephone calling records, especially when assembled in bulk, clearly implicate privacy interests as a matter of public policy. The significance of those privacy implications is magnified in the digital era. Although the government may rely on *Smith v. Maryland* and the third-party doctrine when formulating legal arguments, whether it should, as matter of sound public policy, make use of the fullest extent of its authority under current Fourth Amendment doctrine is a different question. The comprehensive scope of the 215 program is enabled by technology that did not exist when the Supreme Court decided *Smith v. Maryland*. While reaping the benefit of such technological prowess, the NSA's program relies on a legal doctrine formulated before the privacy implications of such technology could be factored into the Court's Fourth Amendment calculus. This legal doctrine, moreover, was fashioned at a time when American life did not involve sharing confidential information with as wide a range of institutions as it does today, and before telephone-based communication was as pervasive a feature of life.

It should be remembered that the *Katz* standard for evaluating the application of the Fourth Amendment was not always the standard. For almost forty years, from 1928, in *Olmstead v. United States*, reinforced by *Goldman v. United States*, in 1942, the Fourth Amendment trigger was physical penetration. The development of electronic surveillance technology, allowing the government to listen to and record telephone booth conversations electronically, led the Supreme Court to revise its approach to the Fourth Amendment. Now, forty-seven years after *Katz*, with dramatic changes in technology, including the

---

Foreign Intelligence Surveillance Court of Review has found such an exception for surveillance "directed at a foreign power or an agent of a foreign power reasonably believed to be located outside the United States." *In re Directives Pursuant to Section 105B of Foreign Intelligence Surveillance Act*, 551 F.3d at 1011.

[496]   In *Klayman v. Obama,* the court concluded that, in light of "serious doubts about the efficacy of the metadata collection program" and the program's infringement on "'that degree of privacy' that the Founders enshrined in the Fourth Amendment," the "plaintiffs have a substantial likelihood of showing that their privacy interests outweigh the Government's interest in collecting and analyzing bulk telephony metadata and therefore the NSA's bulk collection program is indeed an unreasonable search under the Fourth Amendment." Memorandum Opinion at 62-64, *Klayman v. Obama,* No. 13-0851 (D.D.C. Dec. 16, 2013).

[497]   Press Conference by the President (Dec. 20, 2013), *available at* http://www.whitehouse.gov/the-press-office/2013/12/20/press-conference-president.

ability to record calling data for almost every citizen on an ongoing basis, may be the occasion for the Supreme Court to, once again, expand on the Fourth Amendment to protect citizens' calling patterns. These Fourth Amendment questions are currently being litigated in several cases pending in federal court which may ultimately find their way to the Supreme Court. We explore the policy questions in the next section of this Report, where we weigh the privacy interests implicated by the Section 215 program against the national security benefits it provides.

III.   FIRST AMENDMENT

The First Amendment to the United States Constitution protects several fundamental rights including the freedoms of speech and association. The Amendment reads:

> Congress shall make no law respecting an establishment of religion, or prohibiting the free exercise thereof; or abridging the freedom of speech, or of the press; or the right of the people peaceably to assemble, and to petition the Government for a redress of grievances.

Although the amendment's text does not explicitly refer to a freedom of association, the Supreme Court has long held that the First Amendment freedom of speech encompasses the "freedom to associate with others for the common advancement of political beliefs and ideas."[498]

A. Freedom of Association Entails Privacy of Association

The Court first described the freedom of association as a critical constitutionally protected right in *NAACP v. Alabama* in 1958. In that case, the NAACP challenged a state court order requiring it to disclose its membership lists. The NAACP objected that revealing the identities of its members would impair the rights of these individuals to engage in "lawful association in support of their common beliefs." In finding that this claim deserved constitutional protection, the Supreme Court stated: "Effective advocacy of both public and private points of view, particularly controversial ones, is undeniably enhanced by group association, as this Court has more than once recognized by remarking upon the close nexus between the freedoms of speech and assembly."[499] In subsequent years, the Supreme

---

498   *Kusper v. Pontikes*, 414 U.S. 51, 56-57 (1973).

499   *NAACP v. Alabama*, 357 U.S. 449, 460 (1958) (internal citations omitted). The Court rejected the State of Florida's assertion that it was entitled to the membership lists in order to assess whether the NAACP was doing business in the state without properly registering.

Court made clear that this freedom of association is grounded in the First Amendment.[500] The freedom of association is thus protected as "an indispensable means of preserving" the First Amendment right of freedom of speech and other individual liberties.[501] It protects not only actual speech, but also the associations among people, especially when they come together to advance common beliefs such as those on political, religious, cultural or economic matters.[502]

Government action may impinge on such First Amendment rights even if it is not directly aimed at limiting freedom of speech or association. The Supreme Court has recognized that the First Amendment "rights of free speech and association .... are protected not only against heavy-handed frontal attack, but also from being stifled by more subtle governmental interference."[503] In particular, disclosure of associations among individuals, and of connections between individuals and advocacy groups, can have a chilling effect on the exercise of associational rights that impinges on these constitutional freedoms. In originally outlining the freedom of association in *NAACP v. Alabama,* the Court explained that individuals should be free not only to join together in advocacy but also to do so without fear that their associations will be revealed, noting that:

> It is hardly a novel perception that compelled disclosure of affiliation with groups engaged in advocacy may constitute as effective a restraint on freedom of association as the forms of governmental action in the cases above were thought likely to produce upon the particular constitutional rights there involved. This Court has recognized the vital relationship between freedom to associate and privacy in one's associations.[504]

The Court continued by noting that this safeguard was particularly important "where a group espouses dissident beliefs."[505] Thus, the constitutional guarantee of

---

[500]   *See Buckley v. Valeo,* 424 U.S. 1, 15 (1976) (noting that after *NAACP v. Alabama,* "[s]ubsequent decisions have made clear that the First and Fourteenth Amendments guarantee freedom to associate with others for the common advancement of political beliefs and ideas") (internal quotation marks omitted).

[501]   *Roberts v. U.S. Jaycees,* 468 U.S. 609, 618 (1984).

[502]   *See NAACP v. Alabama,* 357 U.S. at 460-61.

[503]   *Gibson v. Florida Legislative Investigation Committee,* 372 U.S. 539, 544 (1963) (internal citations and quotation marks omitted) (finding disclosure requirement chilled freedom of association); *see also NAACP v. Alabama,* 357 U.S. at 461 ("In the domain of these indispensable liberties, whether of speech, press, or association ... abridgement of such rights, even though unintended, may inevitably follow from varied forms of governmental action."). An *indirect* intrusion on First Amendment rights, such as that caused by disclosure requirements, can still have a serious chilling effect on associational rights and be subject to exacting scrutiny as described below.

[504]   *NAACP v. Alabama,* 357 U.S. at 462.

[505]   *NAACP v. Alabama,* 357 U.S. at 462.

associational rights under the First Amendment "encompasses protection of privacy of association in organizations."[506]

The protection for privacy of association stems from recognition that individuals who support controversial causes may be subject to harassment or intimidation if their connections with organizations promoting these causes are disclosed.[507] The Court has also acknowledged the need to protect privacy where revealing associations to the government could subject an individual to detrimental government action. For example, the Court struck down a requirement that public school teachers identify all the organizations in which they were members, noting that "the pressure upon a teacher to avoid any ties which might displease those who control his professional destiny would be constant and heavy."[508]

Since first recognizing this right to privacy in one's associations, the Court has found in numerous cases that rules requiring disclosure of affiliations violated the First Amendment because they had a chilling effect that undermined the freedom of association.[509] However, the Court has held that a disclosure requirement can be consistent with the First Amendment where it is closely tied to a compelling state interest.[510]

Accordingly, the right to associate privately is not absolute, nor are all government actions that reveal connections among individuals constitutionally suspect. The test to be applied in assessing whether the government action violates the First Amendment depends

---

[506]   *Gibson*, 372 U.S. at 544.

[507]   Early cases recognized the pressures on NAACP supporters in the civil rights era. *See NAACP v. Alabama*, 357 U.S. at 462; *Gibson v. Florida Legislative Investigation Committee*, 372 U.S. at 556-57 (finding that privacy of association is "all the more essential here, where the challenged privacy is that of persons espousing beliefs already unpopular with their neighbors"). Later cases recognized the same dynamic in the case of minor political parties such as the Socialist Workers Party. *See Brown v. Socialist Workers '74 Campaign Comm.*, 459 U.S. 87 (1982).

[508]   *Shelton v. Tucker*, 364 U.S. 479, 486 (1960).

[509]   *See, e.g., Brown*, 459 U.S. at 88 (holding Ohio law requiring disclosure of political party's campaign contributors and recipients of campaign disbursements violated First Amendment freedom of association); *Baird v. State Bar of Arizona*, 401 U.S. 1 (1971) (holding that the "First Amendment's protection of association" prohibits states from inquiring about individuals' membership in Communist Party in connection with applications for law licenses); *Gibson*, 372 U.S. at 558 (prohibiting state from compelling organization to reveal which of its members also appeared on a list of suspected members of the Communist party); *see also Buckley v. American Constitutional Law Foundation, Inc.*, 525 U.S. 182, 204 (1999) (holding that rules requiring disclosure of identities of individuals who paid to circulate ballot initiatives violated First Amendment).

[510]   *See John Doe No. 1*, 130 S. Ct. 2811 (2010) (upholding state public records requirement that to initiate any citizen referendum, proponents must file petition disclosing names of signers, where most referenda involved uncontroversial matters and state had important interest in preserving integrity of electoral process).

on the strength of the chilling effect. Government actions that may significantly chill the exercise of this right by forcing disclosure of individuals' associations to the government are subject to "exacting scrutiny."[511] This is a high standard, but it is not an impossible test. As the Supreme Court explained in *John Doe No. 1 v. Reed,* this "standard requires a substantial relation between the disclosure requirement and a sufficiently important governmental interest. To withstand this scrutiny, the strength of the governmental interest must reflect the seriousness of the actual burden on First Amendment rights."[512]

Thus, where there is a significant chilling effect, a court must assess the importance of the government's interest alongside the degree to which its action interferes with the freedom of association. In balancing these two considerations, the court will also evaluate whether the government may be able to achieve its purposes through means that are less intrusive on constitutionally protected liberties: "If the State has open to it a less drastic way of satisfying its legitimate interests, it may not choose a legislative scheme that broadly stifles the exercise of fundamental personal liberties."[513] In *John Doe No. 1,* the Court considered a Public Records Act requirement that to initiate any citizen referendum, proponents must file a petition disclosing the names of signers. The Court found that the disclosure requirement was closely tied to the state's important interest in preserving the integrity of the electoral process, and held that this interest was sufficient to justify the chilling effect of this disclosure requirement.[514]

The Supreme Court stressed the element of overbreadth in holding that a conviction for failing to turn over the NAACP membership list to a legislative committee investigating the Communist Party's activities violated the First Amendment. The Court stressed that the state should demonstrate a nexus between the illegal conduct it is investigating and the organization whose members it seeks to identify. While noting that it did not deny "the existence of the underlying legislative right to investigate . . . subversive activities by Communists or anyone else," the Court instructed that "groups which themselves are neither engaged in subversive or other illegal or improper activities nor demonstrated to have any substantial connections with such activities are to be protected in their rights of free and private association."[515]

---

[511]   *John Doe No. 1,* 130 S. Ct. at 2818.

[512]   *John Doe No. 1,* 130 S. Ct. at 2818 (internal citations and quotation marks omitted); *see also Buckley v. Valeo,* 424 U.S at 25 (stating that even a "significant interference with protected rights of political association may be sustained if the State demonstrates a sufficiently important interest and employs means closely drawn to avoid unnecessary abridgment of associational freedoms") (internal citations omitted).

[513]   *Kusper,* 414 U.S. at 58-59 (finding Illinois statute restricting voting in primaries infringes upon the right of free political association protected by the First and Fourteenth Amendments).

[514]   *John Doe No. 1,* 130 S. Ct. at 2819.

[515]   *Gibson v. Florida Legislative Investigation Committee,* 372 U.S. at 557-58.

A less stringent test applies if a court finds that the chilling effect of the government action is not significant. In the context of a minor political party's attempt to open its primary election to all voters contrary to the existing state voting system, the Supreme Court stated that while "severe burdens on associational rights" are subject to "strict scrutiny," a much lower standard of review applies when "regulations impose lesser burdens."[516] Where the burden on the freedom of association is minimal, the state's "important regulatory interests will usually be enough to justify reasonable, nondiscriminatory restrictions."[517] Thus, the rigor of the Court's inquiry will depend on the degree to which the government action is found to burden associational rights.

B. The NSA's Telephone Records Program Implicates the First Amendment

Although the NSA's telephone records program does not include an overt disclosure requirement of the type evaluated in such cases as *NAACP v. Alabama*, its operation similarly results in the compulsory disclosure of information about individuals' associations to the government. Like the government's collection of membership lists, its bulk collection of telephone records makes that information available for government analysis and can create a chilling effect on those whose records are being collected. As discussed in the next part of this Report, telephone metadata can be highly revealing of the patterns of individuals' connections and associations, including the frequency of all contacts among individuals and organizations. The networks revealed will necessarily include individuals' connections with advocacy groups and others whose political, social, religious, or cultural missions the individuals support — the type of associations at the core of the Constitution's protection for freedom of association.

The Supreme Court has acknowledged that government surveillance programs can implicate First Amendment rights in addition to Fourth Amendment rights.[518] Most

---

[516]   *Clingman v. Beaver*, 544 U.S. 581, 586-87 (2005). The case involved a state primary election system that only permitted the Libertarian Party of Oklahoma to open its primary to its own members and registered independents. The Court found that the state's refusal to permit registered members of other political parties to vote in the Libertarian Party's primary did not limit the party's capacity to communicate with the public and its members or to recruit new members. The Court therefore found that the rule only "minimally" burdened the party's freedom of association. *Id.* at 587-90.

[517]   *Id.* at 586-87.

[518]   *United States v. U.S. Dist. Court for E. Dist. of Mich., S. Div.*, 407 U.S. at 313 ("National security cases, moreover, often reflect a convergence of First and Fourth Amendment values not present in cases of 'ordinary' crime. Though the investigative duty of the executive may be stronger in such cases, so also is there greater jeopardy to constitutionally protected speech.") Some courts of appeals have concluded that government surveillance that complies with Fourth Amendment standards will also survive scrutiny under the First Amendment. *See, e.g., Reporters Committee for Freedom of the Press v. American Telephone and Telegraph Company*, 593 F.2d 1030, 1058 (D.C. Cir. 1978) (holding telephone companies' release of toll call records to law enforcement did not violate First or Fourth Amendment); *Gordon v. Warren Consol. Bd. Of Educ.*, 706 F.2d 778, 781 n.3 (6th Cir. 1983) (holding surveillance by undercover officer did not violate First or Fourth Amendments).

recently, Justice Sonia Sotomayor noted in her concurring opinion in *United States v. Jones* that "[a]wareness that the Government may be watching chills associational and expressive freedoms."[519] However, in the cases decided so far, the Court has not reached the underlying question of whether the First Amendment has been violated, because the Court has found that the individuals challenging the surveillance program are not legally entitled to do so because they are unable to show that they are directly affected by the monitoring.

In *Laird v. Tatum*, for instance, the Supreme Court considered a challenge to an Army program that gathered information on "public activities that were thought to have at least some potential for civil disorder" in order to enable contingency planning for how the government should respond in the event of such disorder.[520] The Court found that the individuals who filed the lawsuit were not legally entitled to challenge the government program, because they could only point to their "knowledge that a governmental agency was engaged" in a "data-gathering" plan and their fear that "in the future" they might suffer from some detrimental action as a result.[521] Most recently, the Supreme Court held in *Clapper v. Amnesty International USA* that attorneys and advocacy groups could not challenge the FISA Amendments Act in court because they could not show that they themselves were imminently likely to be subject to surveillance.[522] The Court did not reach the question of whether the surveillance under that program would have a sufficient chilling effect to implicate First Amendment rights.[523]

Some federal courts of appeals have considered cases in which there was not a standing issue and have more explicitly recognized the impact of government surveillance

---

[519] *Jones*, 132 S. Ct. at 956 (Sotomayor, J., concurring).

[520] *Laird v. Tatum*, 408 U.S. 1, 6 (1972).

[521] *Laird*, 408 U.S. at 10-11. The Court held that the plaintiffs lacked legal standing to bring their challenge.

[522] *Clapper v. Amnesty International USA*, 133 S. Ct. 1138 (2013). The question of whether an individual is entitled to bring such a legal challenge is separate from the question of whether a surveillance program actually infringes First Amendment rights. The chilling effect that a surveillance program may impose on speech and association may implicate the First Amendment and yet still not be sufficient to support an individual's right to file a lawsuit. As the U.S. Court of Appeals for the District of Columbia Circuit has explained: "The harm of 'chilling effect' is to be distinguished from the immediate threat of concrete, harmful action. The former consists of present deterrence from First Amendment conduct because of the difficulty of determining the application of a regulatory provision to that conduct, and will not by itself support standing. The latter — imminence of concrete, harmful action such as threatened arrest for specifically contemplated First Amendment activity — does support standing." *United Presbyterian Church in the U.S.A. v. Reagan*, 738 F.2d 1375, 1380 (D.C. Cir. 1984) (finding individuals lacked standing to challenge Executive Order 12333, which sets forth the framework for U.S. intelligence gathering).

[523] The Court noted in passing that previous cases "had held that constitutional violations may arise from the chilling effect of regulations that fall short of a direct prohibition against the exercise of First Amendment rights," but found that the attorneys and organizations lacked legal standing to bring the lawsuit since they did could not show "specific present objective harm or a threat of specific future harm." *Clapper v. Amnesty International USA*, 113 S. Ct. at 1151-53 (internal quotation marks and citations omitted).

upon First Amendment rights. For example, in a case challenging FBI electronic surveillance of an organization's headquarters, one court noted that the fear of electronic surveillance could chill "free and robust exercise of the First Amendment rights of speech and association,"[524] citing in particular the harmful impact of permitting the government to review the names and addresses of the many individuals who called the organization.[525] Similarly, another appeals court found that individuals were entitled to challenge a surveillance program of the City of Albuquerque Police Department where the individuals alleged that they were the targets of police surveillance, that the city maintained files on their activities, and that this caused a chilling effect on their First Amendment rights.[526]

Furthermore, Congress has recognized that collection of information under Section 215 can implicate the free exercise of speech and associational activities. In reauthorizing Section 215 in 2006, Congress added safeguards for government applications seeking records that directly implicate particular constitutional protections; specifically, Congress required that applications for 215 orders seeking such records be signed by high level officials and provided that this authority may not be delegated to lower level personnel.[527] That requirement covers applications seeking records that are especially sensitive from the standpoint of the First Amendment right to free speech and association, such as library circulation records and patron lists and book sales records and customer lists. [528]

By indefinitely collecting information about all Americans' telephone calls, the NSA's telephone records program clearly implicates the First Amendment freedoms of speech and association. The connections revealed by the extensive database of telephone records gathered under the program will necessarily include relationships established among

---

[524]   *Zweibon v. Mitchell*, 516 F.2d 594, 633 (D.C. Cir. 1975) (holding warrant required for surveillance of organization even though conducted for foreign intelligence, and finding that "prior judicial review [of warrant process] can serve to safeguard both First and Fourth Amendment rights"). This case involved surveillance for foreign intelligence purposes and predates passage of the Foreign Intelligence Surveillance Act. However, its analysis of the First Amendment interests at stake is still relevant to our inquiry.

[525]   *Id.* at 634-35.

[526]   *Riggs v. City of Albuquerque*, 916 F.2d 582 (10th Cir. 1990) (reversing district court's dismissal for lack of standing in case challenging surveillance program as unconstitutional). The federal courts of appeals have also considered a variety of cases in which individuals alleged that government surveillance had chilled their First Amendment rights and the courts found a lack of standing to bring such claims. *See, e.g., ACLU v. NSA*, 493 F.3d 644 (6th Cir. 2007) (dismissing constitutional challenge to Terrorist Surveillance Program for lack of standing).

[527]   *See* 50 U.S.C § 1861(a)(3).

[528]   The amendment to Section 215 also provided special treatment for records of firearms sales that are sensitive under the Second Amendment. *See* 50 U.S.C § 1861(a)(3). In addition, Section 215 requires that if the government seeks to collect information about a U.S. person, the application for a 215 order may not be sought "solely upon the basis of activities protected by the first amendment to the Constitution." 50 U.S.C. § 1861(a)(1). While this latter requirement pertains to the evidence used to justify a Section 215 collection rather than the information obtained through an order, it nonetheless shows a recognition that collection of information about individuals can impact their freedom to engage in First Amendment activities.

individuals and groups for political, religious, and other expressive purposes. Compelled disclosure to the government of information revealing these associations can have a chilling effect on the exercise of First Amendment rights.

Any First Amendment inquiry must next ask whether the chilling effect of the program is significant or only minimal, since this will determine the applicable legal standard for review. If the chilling effect is found to be minimal, then the program is not subject to stringent review. If, however, the burden is found to be significant, then the "exacting scrutiny" test applies, and the question becomes whether the government possesses "a sufficiently important interest and employs means closely drawn to avoid unnecessary abridgment of associational freedoms."[529]

As we explain in the next section of this Report, the NSA's bulk collection of telephone records can be expected to exert a substantial chilling effect on the activities of journalists, protestors, whistleblowers, political activists, and ordinary individuals. This effect stems from the government's collection of telephony metadata and the knowledge that the government has access to millions of individuals' records — regardless of whether the individuals have any suspected connection to terrorist activity. More particularized methods of government access to data do not create the same broad impact, because individuals can expect that their records will not be collected unless they are connected to a specific criminal or terrorism investigation. We think the likely deterrence of these associational activities by the 215 bulk collection program rises to the level of a "significant interference" with the protected rights of political association, and thus the exacting scrutiny test should apply.

Combatting terrorism is a compelling government interest that may justify intrusions on First Amendment rights.[530] However, we find it doubtful that the NSA's program satisfies the requirement that the program be drawn narrowly to minimize the intrusion on associational rights.[531] As with the legislative investigation at issue in *Gibson*

---

[529]   *Buckley*, 424 U.S. at 25.

[530]   *See Holder v. Humanitarian Law Project*, 130 S. Ct. 2705, 2730-31 (2010) (finding government's compelling interest in counterterrorism overcame First Amendment speech and association interests of organization seeking to teach peaceful tactics to designated terrorist groups).

[531]   *See Buckley*, 424 U.S. at 25; *Gibson*, 372 U.S. at 557-58 (in First Amendment challenge to law enforcement investigation by state legislature seeking disclosure of NAACP's membership list, emphasizing that the state should demonstrate a nexus between the illegal conduct it is investigating and the organization whose members it seeks to identify, finding this nexus lacking, and instructed that "groups which themselves are neither engaged in subversive or other illegal or improper activities nor demonstrated to have any substantial connections with such activities are to be protected in their rights of free and private association").

discussed above, the NSA program gathers information about individuals who have no demonstrated connection to illegal activities.

However, as with the Fourth Amendment questions described above, we note that the right of association questions are likely to be assessed in litigation that is already proceeding in the courts. However, we can say clearly that the 215 program implicates First Amendment rights — rights that must be considered in any policy assessment of the program. In the next section of this Report, we explore from a *policy* perspective the nature and strength of the chilling effect created by the telephone records program. We examine, as a matter of policy, whether the national security benefits provided by the calling records program outweigh its implications for privacy and civil liberties. In that assessment we consider the program's effectiveness and balance its value against its intrusions on privacy as well as on speech and association.

Part 7:
POLICY ANALYSIS AND RECOMMENDATIONS REGARDING
THE NSA SECTION 215 PROGRAM

I.   Introduction

Even where measures taken to protect the nation from terrorism comply with the law and the Constitution, the question remains: do they strike the proper balance between security and liberty, between the need to safeguard the nation and to uphold the freedoms that define it? The 9/11 Commission, which first recommended the creation of our Board, expressed a firm belief that striking the proper balance is attainable and essential. As the Commission said in its report:

> We must find ways of reconciling security with liberty, since the success of one helps protect the other. The choice between security and liberty is a false choice, as nothing is more likely to endanger American's liberties than the success of a terrorist attack at home. Our history has shown us that insecurity threatens liberty. Yet, if our liberties are curtailed, we lose the values that we are struggling to defend.[532]

Consistent with the importance of reconciling security and liberty, the Board's statutory role includes the duty to "analyze and review actions the executive branch takes to protect the Nation from terrorism, ensuring that the need for such actions is balanced with the need to protect privacy and civil liberties."[533]

Below, we set forth the capabilities that the NSA's bulk collection of telephone records offers in the government's effort to safeguard the nation from terrorism. We then discuss the extent to which the program has contributed in a demonstrable way to that effort. Next, we explore the threats to privacy and civil liberties entailed by such a wide-scale assembly of communications records by the government. Finally, we provide our assessment of how the value of the NSA's program weighs against its implications for privacy and civil liberties and our assessment of how security and liberty concerns can best be reconciled with respect to this program.

---

[532]   9/11 Commission Report at 395; *see also* 42 U.S.C. § 2000ee(b)(3) (quoting 9/11 Commission Report).

[533]   42 U.S.C. § 2000ee(c)(1).

II. The Terrorism Threat and the Challenges of Combating It

The threat of terrorism faced today by the United States is real. While the core group of Al Qaeda that planned the 9/11 attacks from Afghanistan largely has been decimated by military action, recent years have seen the rise of new al Qaeda affiliates in other nations plotting operations against the United States and Europe. President Obama described the emergence of these groups in a speech last May on the dangers currently posed by international terrorism: "From Yemen to Iraq, from Somalia to North Africa, the threat today is more diffuse, with Al Qaeda's affiliates in the Arabian Peninsula — AQAP — the most active in plotting against our homeland."[534] Most of these affiliates presently are focused on executing attacks in their own regions, but such attacks can claim U.S. lives in addition to wreaking devastation on residents of the nations where they occur. Moreover, failed attacks against the United States, such as the attempted 2009 Christmas Day airplane bombing and the attempted 2010 Times Square bombing, serve as a reminder that foreign terrorist organizations continue to pose a danger to residents of this nation.

Political upheavals in the Middle East, meanwhile, threaten to create opportunities for safe havens where new terrorist affiliates can plan attacks. At the same time, the United States has seen evidence that radicalized individuals inside this country with connections to foreign extremists can carry out horrifying acts of violence, as appears to have been the case with the shooting at Fort Hood in Texas and the bombing of the Boston Marathon.[535]

Thus, while al Qaeda's core group has not carried out a successful attack on U.S. soil since 2001 and is less capable of doing so, and while the violence now being attempted by emergent terrorist affiliates has not yet approached the scope of the 9/11 attacks, the danger posed to the United States by international terrorism is by no means over.[536]

Communications are essential to the facilitation of a terrorist attack against the United States, but awareness of those same communications can permit the United States to discover and thwart the attack. A key challenge — and a key opportunity — facing those who are tasked with preventing terrorism is that would-be terrorists utilize the same communications networks as the rest of the world. Identifying the communications of individuals plotting terrorism within those networks, without intruding on the communications of law-abiding individuals, is a formidable task. This challenge is compounded by the fact that terrorists, aware that attempts are being made to uncover

---

[534]   Remarks by the President at the National Defense University, Fort McNair, Washington, D.C. (May 23, 2013), *available at* http://www.whitehouse.gov/the-press-office/2013/05/23/remarks-president-national-defense-university.

[535]   *See id.*

[536]   *See id.*

their communications, may employ a range of measures to evade those efforts and keep their plans secret.

III.   Capabilities Provided by the NSA's Bulk Collection of Telephone Records

Because communication by telephone is useful, if not indispensable, in the coordination of terrorist efforts, would-be terrorists can be expected to employ this method of communication in planning and carrying out their violent attacks. Records of telephone calls therefore can serve as a trail helping counterterrorism investigators piece together the networks of terrorist groups and the patterns of their communications. Ultimately, such analysis can support the intelligence community's efforts to identify and locate individuals planning terrorist attacks and to discover and disrupt those attacks before they come to fruition.

The NSA's wholesale collection of the nation's telephone records, under the authority granted by the FISA court pursuant to Section 215, is but one method of gathering and analyzing telephone records for counterterrorism purposes. As described below, this method offers certain logistical advantages that may not be available through other means of gathering calling records. The broad scale of this collection, however, even when combined with strict rules on the use of the records obtained, carries serious implications for privacy and civil liberties.

A. Alternative Means of Collecting Telephone Records

Apart from the NSA's bulk collection program, the government has several means at its disposal to obtain telephone calling records for use in counterterrorism or criminal investigations.

Under the Electronic Communications Privacy Act ("ECPA"), which governs communications records, a governmental entity can use an administrative, grand jury or trial subpoena to require a telephone company to provide calling records to the government.[537] The government can also use a judicial warrant or court order issued under ECPA or the Federal Rules of Criminal Procedure to compel disclosure of calling records,[538] though it primarily relies on subpoenas.

When utilizing a grand jury subpoena, the government is entitled to whatever records it seeks unless there is "no reasonable possibility" that its request "will produce information relevant to the general subject of the grand jury's investigation."[539] Under a

---

[537]   *See* 18 U.S.C. § 2703(c)(2).

[538]   *See* 18 U.S.C. § 2703(c)(1)(B); FED. R. CRIM. P. 41.

[539]   *United States v. R. Enterprises, Inc.*, 498 U.S. 292, 301 (1991).

provision of ECPA dealing with counterterrorism and counterintelligence investigations, the government also can issue a national security letter ("NSL") to a telephone company directing it to provide calling records to the government.[540] These NSLs, which are a form of administrative subpoena, do not require permission from a court. To issue an NSL, a government official must certify in writing to the company that the records being sought are "relevant to an authorized investigation to protect against international terrorism or clandestine intelligence activities."[541]

In order to obtain telephone records using either subpoenas or NSLs, the government must specify the phone numbers or other identifiers for which it is seeking records and it must reasonably believe that those records have some connection to a criminal or counterterrorism investigation. The government cannot use these authorities preemptively to collect records concerning numbers that it has no reason to believe are connected to such an investigation, with the intent of looking at them later when it develops some particularized suspicion.

Court orders, subpoenas, and NSLs can all entail a delay between the point at which the government becomes suspicious about a particular number and the point at which it obtains the calling records of that number. Even though judicial approval is not required when the government issues a subpoena or NSL, it takes some time for governmental personnel to assure themselves that the proper conditions for the use of the subpoena or NSL have been met, obtain the necessary supervisory approval, deliver the request to the telephone company, and receive the records back from the company. The government does have means available, however, to streamline this process and eliminate delays. It has been reported, for instance, that one telephone company has placed its employees in offices of the Drug Enforcement Agency with access to the company's call records database, to disclose records pursuant to administrative subpoenas.[542] Under a similar arrangement, from April 2003 through January 2008, employees of certain communications providers were located at the FBI's Communications Assistance Unit, where they accessed call records databases in response to NSLs.[543] The on-site providers' employees would deliver

---

[540]   *See* 18 U.S.C. § 2709(a), (b).

[541]   18 U.S.C. § 2709(b)(1). If the investigation is of a U.S. person, it cannot be conducted solely on the basis of activities protected by the First Amendment to the Constitution. *Id.*

[542]   *See* Scott Shane and Colin Moynihan, Drug Agents Use Vast Phone Trove, Eclipsing N.S.A.'s, The New York Times (Sept. 1, 2013) ("The government pays AT&T to place its employees in drug-fighting units around the country. Those employees sit alongside Drug Enforcement Administration agents and local detectives and supply them with the phone data from as far back as 1987.").

[543]   *See* A Review of the Federal Bureau of Investigation's Use of Exigent Letters and Other Informal Requests for Telephone Records, Oversight Review Division, Office of the Inspector General, at 24 (January 2010), *available at* http://www.justice.gov/oig/reports/FBI/index.htm.

records to the FBI in an electronic format compatible with FBI databases, using compact disks and email.[544]

Normally, obtaining records with a subpoena or NSL only provides the government with the telephone contacts of the original number about which information is sought. However, at least in the past, NSLs and grand jury subpoenas have requested of at least one telephone company, which had this capacity, a "community of interest" for specified telephone numbers — going beyond the direct contacts of the target number.[545] It could therefore be possible for the government to seek contacts out to two hops in the contact chain through such alternate tools, although an individual request would only cover a single provider's records.

When using court orders, subpoenas, or NSLs, the government is able to obtain only those records that the telephone company has retained on file. Data retention practices vary among providers. Telephone service providers currently are required by regulation to maintain records of the calls made by each telephone number only for eighteen months.[546] Even during that limited period, some providers switch the format in which calling records are stored from digital formats — which enable quick searching and analysis — to less accessible formats such as back-up tapes. On the other hand, it has been reported that one provider's database includes calls dating back twenty-six years.[547]

B. Logistical Advantages of Collecting Telephone Records in Bulk

Under Section 215, the NSA does not limit its collection of telephone records to those with a suspected terrorism connection. Instead, orders of the FISA court permit the agency to collect potentially all of the calling records generated by United States telephone companies on a daily basis. Those records are maintained for five years in the NSA's databases. When the agency develops a "reasonable articulable suspicion" that a particular telephone number is associated with terrorism, the agency may view and analyze the complete calling records of that number, along with the complete calling records of all the numbers it has been in contact with, and the complete calling records of all the numbers that those numbers have been in contact with.[548]

---

[544]   *Id.* at 52.

[545]   *Id.* at 54-64. The IG stated that one company had particular capabilities to conduct community of interest searches, which it made available to the FBI under contract.

[546]   *See* 47 C.F.R. § 42.6.

[547]   Scott Shane and Colin Moynihan, Drug Agents Use Vast Phone Trove, Eclipsing N.S.A.'s, The New York Times (Sept. 1, 2013).

[548]   See Part 3 of this Report for a more detailed description of the NSA's collection and analysis of telephone calling records.

This arrangement provides the government with three main logistical advantages: greater speed, greater historical depth, and greater breadth of records available for analysis.

1. Speed

Under the NSA's bulk telephone records collection program, at the point when the agency learns that a particular telephone number may be associated with terrorism and worth investigating, the agency's database already contains the calling records of numbers that have been in contact with the number to be investigated. The only significant delay comes from the time required for agency personnel to assure themselves that the "reasonable articulable suspicion" standard for that number has been met — and, with respect to a number believed to be used by a U.S. person, that the agency's suspicions are not based solely on activity protected by the First Amendment. Once the necessary reviews have been conducted, the calling records associated with a telephone number — up to three "hops" away from that number — can be retrieved nearly instantaneously.

In contrast, obtaining the calling records of a particular number by subpoena or NSL might take days or longer. And this process would normally reveal only the direct contacts of the target number, although as noted, it could be possible to acquire contacts out to two hops. This alternative process would require separate subpoenas or NSLs to be directed to each provider; the NSA would then need to compile the results and check for connections among them.

2. Historical Depth

By collecting telephone records soon after they are created and storing them for five years, the NSA guarantees their continued availability during that period. Thus when the agency searches for the records of a telephone number of interest, it will have at its disposal calling records extending back five years.

In contrast, if the NSA waited to collect the records of a particular number until it came under suspicion, much of the older calling history of that number may not be available. As noted, telephone companies are required to maintain the records of an individual telephone call for eighteen months only. Beyond that, retention periods vary widely. A company receiving a government request for the records of a particular number might be able to furnish only a year and a half of records.

The farther back a telephone number's calling records stretch, the more telephone calls they will reveal. The NSA asserts that a greater historical depth of records therefore is more likely to show connections with numbers of interest. A larger historical repository of a suspect's calling records also may permit the NSA to better understand the typical communications pattern of that suspect, alerting the agency to unusual or aberrational activity.

3. Breadth

Once the NSA develops reasonable suspicion about a particular telephone number, the agency is able to view and analyze all the telephone contacts made by that number (a first "hop"), all the contacts made by every number identified at the first tier (a second "hop"), and all the contacts made by every number identified at the second tier (a third "hop"). In contrast, obtaining telephone records through alternative means — absent the community of interest approach described above — would normally provide the agency with only the first tier: the immediate contacts of the original number. Although investigators could then pursue the full calling records of any of those contacts, based upon the information discernable at the first tier, automatic access to additional tiers provides insight that might not be gained any other way.

For instance, if target A is in contact with another number, B, that is unknown to the NSA, and if the timing, frequency, and pattern of their calls suggest nothing out of the ordinary, the agency might have no articulable reason to obtain the full calling records of B. Those records, however, might show that B is in contact with C, a number that is of high interest to the agency. Notwithstanding the agency's lack of information about B, the calling records thus would have shown a "two hop" link between A and C. Such information could help analysts piece together a connection between suspects who were not previously known to be connected. The same information might also suggest that B is a number of potential interest to the agency — something that would not be fully apparent from the mere fact that B had been in contact with A.

In another hypothetical example, the same calling records might show that target A frequently contacts numbers D, E, and F. Viewing the full calling records of those three numbers might reveal that E and F also frequently communicate with each other, and always around the same time that one of them has been in touch with A. Number D, on the other hand, might have no evident connection to any of A's other contacts. This information might lead investigators to prioritize E and F in their inquiry, while deemphasizing D. The relationship between E and F would not have been apparent by looking only at A's first-tier contacts, and as a result investigators might not have explored those two numbers further.

Thus, immediate access to a second tier of contacts offers the promise of fleshing out networks of linked individuals in a way that working step-by-step, one tier of contacts at a time, may not. The difference is not merely that additional time is saved because the agency does not have to make a new request for each number. Rather, as a matter of practical reality, that new number might never be pursued at all. Simply put, the pressures of limited time and resources may deter investigators from further examining some important first-tier contacts whose significance becomes apparent only when a second tier of calling records is automatically available. Losing that automatic access may translate into losing some degree of analytic insight.

IV.   Demonstrated Efficacy of the NSA's Bulk Collection of Telephone Records

Clearly, the NSA's bulk acquisition of telephone records provides the government with certain capabilities that would otherwise be lacking in the endeavor to combat terrorism. But the question remains whether those capabilities have demonstrably enhanced the government's efforts to safeguard the nation. Answering this question requires examining the instances in which telephone records obtained by the NSA under Section 215 of the Patriot Act were used in counterterrorism investigations. That examination in turn must seek to ascertain whether similar results could have been achieved using telephone records obtained through other means.

Any attempt to assess the value of the NSA's telephone records program must be cognizant of a few considerations. First, the information that the NSA obtains through Section 215 is not utilized in a vacuum. Rather, it is combined with information obtained under different legal authorities, including the Signals Intelligence that the NSA captures under Executive Order 12333, traditional wiretaps and other electronic surveillance of suspects conducted under FISA court authority, the interception of telephone calls and emails authorized by the FISA Amendments Act of 2008, the collection of communications metadata through FISA's pen register and trap and trace provision, physical surveillance, and the development of informants. The intelligence community views the NSA's Section 215 program as complementing and working in tandem with these and other intelligence sources, enabling analysts to paint a more comprehensive a picture when examining potential national security threats.

Moreover, what the Section 215 program yields is the identification of telephone numbers of potential interest, or the revelation of connections between telephone numbers of interest, which must be passed on to the FBI or other agencies as leads for further investigation. Any assessment of the program's value, and any expectations about what it can be expected to accomplish, must bear this consideration in mind.

Finally, an intelligence-gathering tool like the NSA's Section 215 program can provide value that materially enhances the safety of the nation even if it never provides the single critical piece of insight enabling the government to thwart an imminent terrorist attack. Because the work of intelligence gathering and analysis is cumulative, it is rare that any particular technique or legal authority can be identified as the key component without which a terrorist plot would have succeeded. Intelligence-gathering tools can provide value

144

in more indirect ways, by helping to advance investigations and focus efforts in ways that are sometimes more difficult to measure.

That being said, in the Board's view, an intelligence-gathering tool with significant ramifications for privacy and civil liberties cannot be regarded as justified merely because it provides *some* value in protecting the nation from terrorism. Particularly when an intelligence program reaches as broadly as the NSA's bulk collection of telephone records — potentially touching the lives of nearly every American, and in the process investing considerable power in the hands of the government to monitor the communication patterns of its citizens — we believe it is necessary to measure the value provided by the program by considering whether comparable results could be achieved through less intrusive means and whether any unique value offered by the program outweighs its implications for privacy and civil liberties.

In our effort to carry out this balancing task with respect to the NSA's Section 215 program, we have examined a wealth of classified materials regarding the operation of the program. As we have reviewed such materials, the intelligence community has provided us with follow-up information responding to specific questions or concerns we have posed to them. We have taken public testimony from government officials and have received a series of classified briefings with a range of personnel from the NSA and other elements of the intelligence community. We have spoken with representatives of private companies who have received and complied with court orders under the NSA's surveillance program. We have heard from academics, technology experts, civil liberties advocates, and former government officials through written submissions provided to us and through commentary at public workshops that we have conducted.

In particular, we have closely scrutinized the specific cases cited by the government as instances in which telephone records obtained under Section 215 were useful in counterterrorism investigations. In the wake of the unauthorized disclosures during the summer of 2013, the intelligence community compiled a list of fifty-four counterterrorism events in which Section 215 or Section 702 of the FISA Amendments Act of 2008 "contributed to a success story." Twelve of those incidents involved the use of Section 215. We have examined those incidents in depth, attempting to discern precisely what was accomplished in each case through the use of Section 215 records and whether similar results could have been achieved using more tailored means of gathering telephone records.

Our deliberations have led us to conceptualize seven broad ways in which an intelligence-gathering tool such as the NSA's bulk telephone records program can provide value in safeguarding the nation from terrorism. We explain these seven categories of success below and discuss how often the NSA's Section 215 program has achieved each of them.

Our analysis suggests that where the telephone records collected by the NSA under its Section 215 program have provided value, they have done so primarily in two ways. The first is by offering additional leads regarding the contacts of terrorism suspects already known to investigators, which can help investigators confirm suspicions about the target of an inquiry or about persons in contact with that target. But our review suggests that the Section 215 program offers little unique value here, instead largely duplicating the FBI's own information-gathering efforts. The second is by demonstrating that known foreign terrorism suspects do *not* have U.S. contacts or that known terrorist plots do *not* have a U.S. nexus. This can help the intelligence community focus its limited investigatory resources by avoiding false leads and channeling efforts where they are needed most. But the value of this benefit must be kept in perspective, as discussed below.

Based on the information provided to the Board, we have not identified a single instance involving a threat to the United States in which the telephone records program made a concrete difference in the outcome of a counterterrorism investigation. Moreover, we are aware of no instance in which the program directly contributed to the discovery of a previously unknown terrorist plot or the disruption of a terrorist attack. And we believe that in only one instance over the past seven years has the program arguably contributed to the identification of an unknown terrorism suspect. In that case, moreover, the suspect was not involved in planning a terrorist attack and there is reason to believe that the FBI may have discovered him without the contribution of the NSA's program.

Even in those instances where telephone records collected under Section 215 offered additional information about the contacts of a known terrorism suspect, in nearly all cases the benefits provided have been minimal — generally limited to corroborating information that was obtained independently by the FBI. And in those few cases where some information not already known to the government was generated through the use of Section 215 records, we have seen little indication that the same result could not have been obtained through traditional, targeted collection of telephone records. The classified briefings and materials the Board has received have not demonstrated that the increased speed, breadth, and historical depth of the Section 215 program have produced any concrete results that were otherwise unattainable. In other words, we see little evidence that the unique capabilities provided by the NSA's *bulk* collection of telephone records actually have yielded material counterterrorism results that could not have been achieved without the NSA's Section 215 program.

As noted, the Board has examined closely the twelve cases compiled by the intelligence community in which telephone records collected under Section 215 "contributed to a success story" in a counterterrorism investigation. We have assigned each of these cases to one or more of seven "categories of success" that we have devised to illustrate the different forms of value that a counterterrorism program like this one could provide. We do not ascribe any talismanic significance or scientific precision to these broad, non–mutually exclusive categories. But we believe they help illustrate what the Section 215 program has and has not accomplished to date. These seven categories, and our analysis of how the government's twelve examples fit within them, are as follows:

1. *Enabling "Negative Reporting."* Analysis of telephone calling records can establish that a known terrorism suspect overseas has *not* been in telephone contact with anyone in the United States, suggesting that a known terrorist or terrorist plot in a foreign country does *not* have a U.S. nexus. Such information can help the government focus its limited investigative resources where they are needed most. We found five instances in which Section 215 records were used in this way.

2. *Adding or Confirming Details.* Analysis of telephone calling records can also help focus investigative efforts by providing additional information about terrorism suspects or plots already known to the government. The information obtained might confirm suspicions about a suspect, enable greater understanding about that suspect's connections, or establish links between known suspects. We found seven instances in which Section 215 telephone records served this function. The value provided by the records, however, was limited. In nearly every case, the information supplied by the NSA through Section 215 offered no unique value, but simply mirrored or corroborated information that the FBI obtained independently using other means. And in none of these cases did the rapid speed with which Section 215 records can be analyzed lead to any tangible benefits. In sum, we believe that the limited value provided by the Section 215 program in these cases could have been achieved without the NSA's bulk collection of telephone records.

3. *"Triaging."* In time-sensitive scenarios, where investigators have reason to believe that a terrorist attack may be imminent, or where they are otherwise conducting a fast-breaking investigation, prompt analysis of a suspect's telephone records may help the government prioritize leads based on their urgency. While this category is not fundamentally different from the previous one, as it also involves adding more information about plots or suspects already known to the government, its special value may lie in the potentially critical production of swift results. We identified four instances in which telephone numbers derived from the Section 215 program were disseminated quickly to the FBI in this type of scenario. In none of these cases, however, did the information contribute to the disruption of a terrorist attack.

4. *Identifying Terrorism Suspects.* Analysis of telephone records can contribute to the discovery of terrorism suspects previously unknown to the government. We found only one instance in which Section 215 telephone records arguably served this purpose and helped to identify a previously unknown suspect. In that case, however, the suspect was not involved in planning a terrorist attack — rather, he had sent money to support a foreign terrorist organization — and there is reason to believe that the FBI may have discovered him without the information it received from the NSA.

5. *Discovering U.S. Presence of Known Terrorism Suspects.* The use of Section 215 records theoretically could help alert the government that a known terrorism suspect has entered the United States from abroad. We are not aware of any instances in which this has occurred.

6. *Identifying Terrorist Plots.* The Board is not aware of any instances in which the use of Section 215 telephone records directly contributed to the discovery of a terrorist plot.

7. *Disrupting Terrorist Plots.* The Board is not aware of any instances in which the use of Section 215 telephone records directly contributed to the disruption of a terrorist plot.

To help illustrate the concrete benefits provided by the NSA's Section 215 program, we elaborate below on four counterterrorism investigations that members of the intelligence community have cited as demonstrating successful use of the program. These cases, which are among the twelve "success stories" referenced above, have been discussed by government officials in public statements, legal filings, and congressional testimony.[549] We believe that scrutiny of these examples demonstrates the limited value provided by the NSA's Section 215 program.

---

[549] Although the Board has benefitted from classified information obtained directly from members of the Intelligence Community, some information about these four cases has been made available to the public. *See, e.g.*, Declaration of Acting Assistant Director Robert J. Holley, Federal Bureau of Investigation, ¶¶ 24-26, *ACLU v. Clapper*, No. 13-3994 (S.D.N.Y. Oct. 1, 2013); Hearing of the Senate Appropriations Committee on Cybersecurity: Preparing for and Responding to the Enduring Threat, 113th Cong. (June 12, 2013); Hearing of the House Permanent Select Committee on Intelligence on How Disclosed NSA Programs Protect Americans, and Why Disclosure Aids Our Adversaries, 113th Cong. (June 18, 2013); Hearing of the House Judiciary Committee on Oversight of the Administration's Use of the Foreign Intelligence Surveillance Act (FISA) Authorities, 113th Cong. (July 17, 2013); Hearing of the Senate Judiciary Committee on Strengthening Privacy Rights and National Security: Oversight of FISA (Foreign Intelligence Surveillance Act) Surveillance Programs, 113th Cong. (July 31, 2013). Transcripts of much of this congressional hearing testimony are available at http://icontherecord.tumblr.com/.

A. New York City Subway Attack Plot

Since the disclosure of the NSA's Section 215 and Section 702 programs, one of the most frequently discussed cases in which these programs were utilized has been the thwarted 2009 plot to bomb the New York City subway. Section 215, however, played no role in disrupting this attack. It made a minor contribution by providing corroborating information about one of the plot's already known coconspirators, who was arrested months after the plot was disrupted. There is no reason to believe that bulk collection of telephone records was necessary for this minor contribution.

On September 6 and 7, 2009, the NSA intercepted emails sent from an unknown individual in the United States to an Al Qaeda courier in Pakistan whom it was monitoring. These emails sought advice on the correct mixture of ingredients to use for certain explosives, and the urgency of their tone suggested an imminent attack. The NSA passed this information on to the FBI, which used a national security letter to identify the unknown individual as Najibullah Zazi, located near Denver, Colorado. Beginning on September 7, the FBI set up 24-hour surveillance of Zazi's residence, began monitoring his Internet activity, and undertook other investigative efforts.

On September 8, Zazi conducted Internet searches suggesting that he was looking for home improvement stores in Queens, New York, where he could purchase acid that can be used in explosives. That same day, he rented a car. The next day, Zazi began driving from Colorado to New York City, arriving on September 10. His plan, he later said, was to meet up with associates, obtain and assemble the remaining components to build explosives, and detonate them on subway lines in Manhattan.

The FBI followed Zazi as he drove from Colorado to New York. By this time, over 100 agents from the Bureau's Denver field office were working on the investigation, and the Bureau's New York field office also became involved, along with local New York City law enforcement — by one account "every terrorism squad in New York City."[550]

After arriving in New York, Zazi learned that law enforcement was monitoring him. His suspicions may have been triggered when he was pulled over by police on September 10 as he crossed the George Washington Bridge, for what he was told was a random drug search. After consenting to an inspection of his vehicle, he was allowed to proceed. Any suspicions Zazi might have had were confirmed when an associate of his tipped him off about the government's investigation. About the time of Zazi's arrival in New York, law enforcement agents working on the investigation interviewed Ahmad Wais Afzali, an imam whom the government allegedly had used in the past as an informant. These agents showed

---

[550]   Transcript of Jury Trial, *United States v. Mohammed Wali Zazi*, Crim. No. 10-0060 (E.D.N.Y. July 18, 2011) (Testimony of Eric Jurgenson, Special Agent, Federal Bureau of Investigations, Denver Field Office, National Security Squad 3).

Afzali photos of Zazi and asked questions about him. Thereafter, Afzali spoke by phone with Zazi and related to him what the authorities had asked about him.

Having been alerted about the government's investigation, Zazi purchased an airline ticket and returned to Colorado on September 12. He later stated that he and his associates abandoned their plans after learning that the government was monitoring him.

On September 14, two days after Zazi returned to Colorado, government agents searched three apartments in a Queens neighborhood. The agents found components that could be used to make bombs, along with evidence tying these materials to Zazi. The FBI first interviewed him on September 16 at the Bureau's Denver field office, where he appeared voluntarily with counsel, and he was arrested on September 19. Initially denying any involvement in terrorism, he later admitted his guilt and cooperated with investigators. Several other individuals were arrested in connection with the plot as well.

While Section 215 was used during the Zazi investigation, it played no role in thwarting the subway bombing plot. The plot was discovered through email monitoring, and its details were fleshed out through additional electronic surveillance, physical surveillance, and other traditional investigative measures. The plot was disrupted when law enforcement inadvertently tipped off Zazi that he was being monitored, leading him and his associates to abandon their plans and prompting him to return to Colorado. Although the NSA provided the FBI with a report early in the investigation showing calls made from Zazi's telephone, and later provided additional leads based on the Section 215 data, these reports did not identify Zazi's associates in New York City or the apartments where materials intended to support the bombing were found. Rather, other investigative techniques led to those discoveries.

The only concrete result obtained in the Zazi case through the use of Section 215 was to identify an unknown telephone number of one of Zazi's New York coconspirators, Adis Medunjanin. The FBI, however, already was aware of Medunjanin and his connection to Zazi's plot, having obtained that information independently using other means. And while the NSA's information may have further heightened the FBI's interest in Medunjanin, there is no indication that use of the NSA's bulk collection program was necessary for the government to identify the unknown telephone number, or that this information was not obtainable through more traditional law enforcement techniques. Despite being under suspicion from the outset of the plot's discovery in September 2009, Medunjanin was not arrested until January 2010, several months after Zazi returned to Colorado and was taken into custody. As far as we can tell, the particular speed associated with Section 215 queries offered no apparent benefit in corroborating the FBI's interest in Medunjanin. Nor did the ability to search through five years of records or to have immediate access to several "hops" of telephone calls.

The Zazi case shows how Section 215 is used to complement other investigative tools, as intelligence community officials have emphasized. In our view, it also illustrates the minimal added benefit provided by the program in light of those other tools.

B. Operation Wi-Fi

Our analysis of another 2009 case, which involved an early stage plot to attack the New York Stock Exchange, also fails to demonstrate that the Section 215 program has offered significant added value to the government's counterterrorism efforts.

While conducting Internet surveillance of an extremist based in Yemen, the NSA discovered a connection between that extremist and an unknown person in Kansas City, Missouri. The NSA provided information about this connection to the FBI. In the course of its investigation, the FBI subsequently identified the unknown person as an individual named Khalid Ouazzani, and it discovered that he was in communication with other individuals located in the United States who were in the very initial stages of devising a plan to bomb the New York Stock Exchange. All of these individuals eventually were convicted for their roles in the nascent plot.

After the FBI discovered the plot and identified the individuals involved, the NSA queried telephone numbers associated with those individuals using Section 215, providing additional telephone numbers as leads to the FBI. Those numbers simply mirrored information about telephone connections that the FBI developed independently using other authorities.

Thus, while Section 215 was used in the Operation Wi-Fi investigation, we are aware of no indication that bulk collection of telephone records was necessary to the investigation, or that the information produced by Section 215 provided any unique value.

C. David Coleman Headley Investigation

In October 2009, Chicago resident David Coleman Headley was arrested and charged for his role in plotting to attack the Danish newspaper that published inflammatory cartoons of the Prophet Mohammed. He was later charged with helping orchestrate the 2008 Mumbai hotel attack, in collaboration with the Pakistan-based militant group Lashkar-e-Taiba. He pled guilty and began cooperating with authorities.

Headley, who had previously served as an informant for the Drug Enforcement Agency, was identified by law enforcement as involved in terrorism through means that did not involve Section 215. Further investigation, also not involving Section 215, provided insight into the activities of his overseas associates. In addition, Section 215 records were queried by the NSA, which passed on telephone numbers to the FBI as leads. Those numbers, however, only corroborated data about telephone calls that the FBI obtained independently through other authorities.

Thus, we are aware of no indication that bulk collection of telephone records through Section 215 made any significant contribution to the David Coleman Headley investigation.

D. Basaaly Moalin Investigation

The investigation of Basaaly Moalin is the only case in which Section 215 records demonstrably contributed to the identification of an unknown terrorism suspect.

In 2007, the NSA provided the FBI with information showing an indirect connection between a telephone number in Somalia, which the NSA was tracking because of its association with the Al Shabaab terrorist organization, and an unknown telephone number in San Diego. The NSA reported this information to the FBI, which realized that the telephone number was linked to pending FBI investigations. Based on the NSA's report and the link between this telephone number and pending investigations, the FBI opened a preliminary investigation into the number.

Using a national security letter and database checks, the FBI identified the user of the San Diego telephone number as Basaaly Moalin, the subject of a previous FBI investigation that was closed several years earlier for lack of sufficient information. The FBI reopened the case, and through subsequent investigation it learned that Moalin and three others were providing material support to Al Shabaab. All four men were convicted in 2013 of providing funds to the terrorist organization.

The NSA's report was the catalyst that prompted the FBI to investigate Moalin's San Diego number. Even without the NSA's tip-off, however, FBI agents may well have discovered that the number was a common link among pending FBI investigations. Moreover, given that the NSA's tip came from monitoring a specific foreign number it was tracking, it is not clear to us that bulk collection of telephone records was necessary to discovering the connection between this number and Moalin's. Conventional techniques may have been less likely to discover it, or at least more time-consuming. But we know of no indication that speed or Section 215's five-year depth of records were important to the discovery.

In addition, we believe it worthy of note that Moalin and his associates were not charged or convicted of involvement in planning or executing any specific terrorist plots. Their crime was sending money to Al Shabaab. While there is a critical value in cutting off funds to deadly foreign terrorist organizations such as this one, we find it significant that in the seven-year history of the NSA's Section 215 program, this material-support prosecution remains the only time that the program has directly contributed to the identification of an unknown terrorism suspect. And even in this instance, as noted, Moalin was not entirely unknown to law enforcement, but rather was the subject of a previous FBI investigation and was the user of a telephone number already linked to pending FBI investigations.

In our view, therefore, it is telling that the Moalin case represents perhaps the strongest success story produced by the NSA's Section 215 program. Like the other three cases discussed above, the Moalin investigation shows that the program does provide some demonstrable value in supporting the government's counterterrorism efforts. But it also starkly illustrates the limits of what the program has accomplished, and perhaps what it is capable of accomplishing.

E. Remaining Success Stories

Three of the remaining cases included among the government's twelve "success stories" are similar to the narratives described above. In these three cases, the NSA queried Section 215 telephone records and passed information on to the FBI to be used as leads in its investigations. But in all three cases, that information simply mirrored or corroborated intelligence that the FBI obtained independently through other means. In none of these cases has the Board identified any unique value supplied to the FBI by the Section 215 program. Nor can the Board point to any concrete way in which the program altered the outcome of these investigations.

The last five success stories provided by the government are all examples of "negative reporting," as described above — situations in which the Section 215 data helped investigators eliminate the possibility of a U.S. connection to a foreign terrorist plot. While the value of such "peace of mind" is not to be discounted, especially in time-sensitive scenarios where it may permit investigators to better focus their attention on the true threats, it also must be kept in perspective. Particularly in light of the policy considerations discussed below, we question whether the government's routine collection of all Americans' telephone records is justified on the basis that it can be helpful to identify situations where there is *no threat* to the United States.

F. 9/11

Some have suggested that if the NSA's calling records program were in place before 9/11, it could have alerted the government that one of the future airplane hijackers was in the United States, and perhaps have led to the prevention of the attacks. For several years, beginning in the late 1990s, the NSA intercepted telephone calls to and from a prominent Al Qaeda safe house in Yemen. A number of calls were made in early 2000 between this safe house and a person named Khalid, who after 9/11 was identified as hijacker Khalid al-Mihdhar. Although the NSA was able to listen to these conversations, it did not have the telephone number that was calling the safe house, and thus it did not know that Mihdhar made the calls from San Diego, California. Had the NSA known this information, it is argued, the government could have identified Mihdhar as the caller and been aware of his presence in the United States, perhaps leading to his apprehension and the identification and detention of other hijackers.[551]

For two reasons, we do not believe the Mihdhar example supports continuance of the NSA's Section 215 program. First, the failure to identify Mihdhar's presence in the United States stemmed primarily from a lack of information sharing among federal agencies, not of a lack of surveillance capabilities. As documented by the 9/11 Commission and others, this was a failure to connect the dots, not a failure to collect enough dots. Second, in order to have identified the San Diego telephone number from which Mihdhar made his calls, it was not necessary to collect the entire nation's calling records.

As explained by the 9/11 Commission Report, the joint inquiry into the 9/11 attacks by the House and Senate intelligence committees, and a Department of Justice Inspector General report, the government had ample opportunity before 9/11 to pinpoint Mihdhar's location, track his activities, and prevent his 2001 reentry into the United States. By early 2000, the CIA was aware of Mihdhar and knew that he had a visa enabling him to travel to the United States. Yet despite having information that Mihdhar and fellow hijacker Nawaf al-Hazmi "were traveling to the United States," the CIA "missed repeated opportunities to act based on the information in its possession." The agency did not advise the FBI of what it knew or "add their names to watchlists."[552] Furthermore, at the time that Mihdhar and Hazmi were in San Diego in early 2000, when the calls to Yemen were made, they were living with "a long-time FBI asset."[553] Mihdhar left the United States in June 2000, and he was able to return in 2001 because he still had not been placed on any watchlists. And "[o]n four occasions in 2001, the CIA, the FBI, or both had apparent opportunities to refocus on

---

[551] The executive branch has highlighted the Mihdhar case in its applications to the FISA court seeking authorization for the NSA's program, in litigation defending the program in other courts, and in briefing papers provided to the congressional intelligence committees urging the extension of Section 215's sunset date. Officials have also discussed the case in congressional testimony. *See, e.g.,* Testimony of General Keith Alexander, Commander, U.S. Cyber Command, Director of the National Security Agency and Chief of the Central Security Service, Hearing of the Senate Appropriations Committee on Cybersecurity: Preparing for and Responding to the Enduring Threat, 113th Cong. (June 12, 2013); Testimony of the Honorable Robert S. Mueller, III, Director, Federal Bureau of Investigation, Hearing before the Committee on the Judiciary, House of Representatives: Oversight of the Federal Bureau of Investigation, 113th Cong. (June 13, 2013); Testimony of Sean Joyce, Deputy Director, Federal Bureau of Investigation, Hearing of the House Permanent Select Committee on Intelligence on How Disclosed NSA Programs Protect Americans, and Why Disclosure Aids Our Adversaries, 113th Cong. (June 18, 2013).

[552] Report of the U.S. Senate Select Committee on Intelligence and U.S. House Permanent Select Committee on Intelligence: Joint Inquiry into Intelligence Community Activities Before and After the Terrorist Attacks of September 11, 2001, S. Rep. No. 107-351, H.R. Rep. No. 107-792, at 12-16 (Dec. 2002).

[553] Office of the Inspector General, Department of Justice, A Review of the FBI's Handling of Intelligence Information Prior to the September 11 Attacks, Chapter 5 (Nov. 2004), *available at* http://www.justice.gov/oig/special/0506/chapter5.htm.

the significance of Hazmi and Mihdhar and reinvigorate the search for them."[554] Yet these opportunities were missed.[555]

It is argued, however, the NSA's bulk telephone records program could have made up for these intelligence lapses and failures of information sharing. Knowledge that the telephone calls from "Khalid" to the Yemen safe house were made from San Diego theoretically could have led the government to discover Mihdhar's presence in the United States. But obtaining this knowledge did not require a bulk telephone records program. The NSA knew the telephone number of the Yemen safe house. If the telephone calls with Mihdhar were deemed suspicious at the time, the government could have used existing legal authorities to request from U.S. telephone companies the records of any calls made to or from that Yemen number. Doing so could have identified the San Diego number on the other end of the calls.[556] Thus we do not believe that a program that collects all telephone records from U.S. telephone companies was necessary to identify Mihdhar's location in early 2000, nor that such a program is necessary to make similar discoveries in the future.

Finally, in the absence of evidence that the NSA's Section 215 program has made any significant contribution to counterterrorism efforts to date, some officials have suggested to us that the program should be preserved because it might do so in the future. Like a burglar alarm or a fire insurance policy, under this reasoning, the program is valuable even if it has not yet been triggered by a break-in or a fire. Yet, it is worth noting that the program supplied no advance notice of attempted attacks on the New York City subway, the failed Christmas Day airliner bombing, or the failed Times Square car bombing. Given the limited value this program has demonstrated to date, as outlined above, we find little reason to expect that it is likely to provide significant value, much less essential value, in safeguarding the nation in the future.

V. Privacy and Civil Liberties Implications of the NSA's Bulk Collection of Telephone Records

Having described what we believe to be the value of the NSA's telephone records program in combating terrorism, we now turn to the implications of that program for privacy and civil liberties. We believe those implications are serious. The design of the NSA's program shows that the government recognizes the privacy concerns raised by the

---

[554]   THE 9/11 COMMISSION REPORT: FINAL REPORT OF THE NATIONAL COMMISSION ON TERRORIST ATTACKS UPON THE UNITED STATES, at 266 (2004).

[555]   *See* 9/11 Commission Report at 266-72.

[556]   The government could have sought this information through any of the alternative means of seeking telephone records described earlier, although the speed with which telephone companies could respond to such requests would likely vary by provider.

collection and analysis of telephone calling records. The government has responded to those concerns by imposing rules that limit the NSA's *use* of telephone records after their collection by the agency. These rules offer many valuable safeguards designed to curb the intrusiveness of the program. But in our view, they cannot fully ameliorate the implications for privacy, speech, and association that follow from the government's ongoing collection of virtually all telephone records of every American.

Because telephone calling records can reveal intimate details about a person's life, particularly when aggregated with other information and subjected to sophisticated computer analysis, the government's collection of a person's entire telephone calling history has a significant and detrimental effect on that person's privacy. Beyond such individual privacy intrusions, permitting the government to routinely collect the calling records of the entire nation fundamentally shifts the balance of power between the state and its citizens. Moreover, as outlined below, this practice can be expected to have a chilling effect on the free exercise of speech and association, because law-abiding individuals and groups engaged in sensitive or controversial work cannot trust in the confidentiality of their relationships as revealed by their calling patterns. Finally, for the reasons explained below, we do not believe that these concerns are eliminated by the detailed rules placed on the NSA's use of telephone calling records after their collection.[557]

A. The Revealing Nature of Telephone Calling Records

Telephone calling records, which indicate who called whom, at what time, and for how long, but do not include the contents of any conversations, are a form of "metadata."[558] Like the address on the outside of an envelope, which announces the envelope's destination but does not reveal the content of the letter inside, telephone calling records provide information about the existence and details of a call without revealing what was said.

---

[557]   In assessing the privacy intrusions associated with the NSA's bulk collection of telephone records, the widely recognized Fair Information Practice Principles ("FIPPs") help inform our analysis. The FIPPs offer guidance for privacy safeguards that have formed the basis for the Privacy Act of 1974 and many federal agencies' approaches to privacy protection. *See* Federal Trade Commission, Fair Information Practice Principles, *available at* http://www.ftc.gov/reports/privacy3/fairinfo.shtm. The Department of Homeland Security describes the FIPPs as a set of eight principles: Transparency, Individual Participation, Purpose Specification, Data Minimization, Use Limitation, Data Quality and Integrity, Security, and Accountability and Auditing. Department of Homeland Security, Privacy Policy Guidance Memorandum, No. 2008-01, at 1 (Dec. 29, 2008), *available at* http://www.dhs.gov/xlibrary/assets/privacy/privacy_policyguide_2008-01.pdf (memorializing DHS adoption of the FIPPs).

[558]   Telephony metadata might also include cell site location information, but the NSA does not presently obtain location information as part of its collection efforts under Section 215. The technological infrastructure through which the NSA receives calling records from the telephone companies supports the collection of cell site location information but the information is filtered out. As recently as 2010 and 2011, the government has confirmed, the NSA conducted a pilot project to test the collection of cell site information about mobile telephones. *See* Charlie Savage, *In Test Project, N.S.A. Tracked Cellphone Locations*, N.Y. TIMES (Oct. 2, 2013). The information that *is* collected by the NSA under Section 215 does include telephone area codes, prefixes, and other data that allows the agency to locate callers geographically in a very broad sense.

But while telephone calling records are distinct from the spoken content of any conversation, they can be highly revealing nonetheless. As Justice Stewart noted over thirty years ago, the telephone numbers that a person dials "easily could reveal the identities of the persons and the places called, and thus reveal the most intimate details of a person's life."[559] Because the circumstances of a particular call can be highly suggestive of its content, the mere record of a call potentially offers a window into the caller's private affairs. Some illustrative examples cited by a privacy advocacy organization include the following: calling a suicide prevention hotline; calling a telephone sex service at 2:30 a.m.; calling an HIV testing service, then one's doctor, then one's health insurance company within the same hour; receiving a call from the local NRA office during a campaign against gun legislation, then calling one's congressional representatives immediately afterward; and calling one's gynecologist, speaking for half an hour, then calling the local Planned Parenthood number later that day.[560]

At bottom, telephone metadata is information about a person's conduct. Just as it reveals something about a person to know that he or she visited the doctor's office, likewise it reveals something about that person to know that he or she called the doctor's office on the telephone. When the government collects metadata about its citizens, therefore, it is collecting information about its citizens' activity.

Moreover, when the government collects *all* of a person's telephone records, storing them for five years in a government database that is subject to high-speed digital searching and analysis, the privacy implications go far beyond what can be revealed by the metadata of a single telephone call. The frequency with which two numbers are in contact with each other, along with the timing and duration of their calls, provides insight into the nature of the relationship between the two callers. When both of those numbers are in contact with a third number, the pattern of calls among these three numbers adds to the story that can be gleaned from their communications records. Thus, aggregation of numerous calling records over an extended period of time can paint a clear picture of an individual's personal relationships and patterns of behavior. This picture can be at least as revealing of those relationships and habits as the contents of individual conversations — if not more so.[561]

---

[559]   *Smith*, 442 U.S. at 748 (Stewart, J., dissenting).

[560]   Kurt Opsahl, *Why Metadata Matters*, EFF.ORG (June 7, 2013), *available at* https://www.eff.org/deeplinks/2013/06/why-metadata-matters.

[561]   All four expert technologists who testified at the Board's July 2013 public workshop agreed on this point. *See* Privacy and Civil Liberties Oversight Board, Transcript of Workshop Regarding Surveillance Programs Operated Pursuant to Section 215 of the USA PATRIOT Act and Section 702 of the Foreign Intelligence Surveillance Act, at 140-41 (July 9, 2013) (statement of Ashkan Soltani, Independent Researcher and Consultant) ("The metadata is actually more sensitive at times than the content."); *id.* at 184-85 (statement of Daniel Weitzner, MIT Computer Science and Artificial Intelligence Lab ("Metadata at scale is at least as revealing as content."); *id.* at 189-90 (statement of Steven Bellovin, Columbia University Computer Science Department); *id.* at 137 (statement of Marc Rotenberg, Electronic Privacy Information Center),

The power of such communications metadata to illustrate a person's social connections with stark accuracy has been illustrated vividly by technology researchers.[562]

Based on our consideration of this issue, the Board is convinced that telephone calling records, when collected in bulk and subjected to powerful analytic tools, can reveal highly sensitive personal information. The government acknowledges as much, arguing that "sophisticated analytic tools" can reveal "chains of communication" and "connections between individuals."[563] As one former general counsel of the NSA recently was quoted as saying: "Metadata absolutely tells you everything about somebody's life. . . . [It's] sort of embarrassing how predictable we are as human beings. . . . If you have enough metadata you don't really need content."[564]

There is a paradox here. We have concluded, based on the evidence provided by the government, that the NSA's Section 215 program has not proven useful in identifying unknown terrorists or terrorist plots, in part because the program often merely corroborates information about connections among individuals that have already been obtained independently through other means. Yet we also conclude that telephone calling records, if used in more expansive ways than the government currently employs them, can reveal a great deal about an innocent person's habits, private affairs, and network of social, familial, and professional connections. This capability is magnified when calling records are aggregated across customers and carriers and over a long period of time. The very power that inheres in the analysis of telephone calling records — a power that the government has emphasized in defending the intelligence value of the NSA's Section 215 program — illustrates the depth of the privacy implications entailed by the program without proving its effectiveness as a counterterrorism tool.[565]

---

available at http://www.pclob.gov/. *See also* Steven Bellovin, Submission to the Privacy and Civil Liberties Oversight Board: Technical Issues Raised by the Section 215 and Section 702 Programs, at 2-4 (July 31, 2013) ("Metadata is often far more revealing than content").

[562]   For instance, researchers at the Massachusetts Institute of Technology have developed a program called "Immersion" that can generate a telling visual rendering of an individual's web of social connections simply through the use of email metadata — the record of who sent email messages to whom. *See* Immersion: A People-Centric View of Your Email Life, *available at* https://immersion.media.mit.edu/. *See also* Abraham Riesman, *What Your Metadata Says About You*, Boston Globe (June 29, 2013).

[563]   Administration White Paper, Bulk Collection of Telephony Metadata under Section 215 of the USA PATRIOT Act, at 13-14 (Aug. 9, 2013).

[564]   Alan Rusbridger, *The Snowden Leaks and the Public*, N.Y. Review of Books (Nov. 21, 2013) (quoting former NSA general counsel Stewart Baker).

[565]   While the apparent lack of a case in which the 215 program actually detected terrorist activity may be a paradox in light of the revealing nature of call detail records, it should not be a surprise. In 2008, the National Research Council of the Academies of Science published a report in which a committee comprised of some of the nation's leading experts on computer science, data mining, behavioral science, terrorism and law concluded, after two years of study, the same thing we find here: "Modern data collection and analysis techniques have had remarkable success in solving information-related problems in the commercial sector;

B. Privacy Implications of Bulk Collection of Telephone Calling Records

Given the ability of telephone calling records to reveal intimate details of a person's life, significant privacy interests are at stake when the government collects all of a person's calling records, particularly when it retains this information for years in a database that enables swift mapping of one's pattern of communications and network of contacts.

At the most basic level, routine government collection of telephone records defeats the core concept of information privacy — the ability of individuals to control information about themselves. This loss of control is heightened when it is *the government* collecting personal records. With its powers of compulsion and criminal prosecution, the government poses unique threats to privacy when it collects data on its own citizens.[566] Allowing it to gather vast quantities of information about the conduct of individuals as a routine matter where those individuals are not suspected of any crimes affects the balance of power between the state and its people.[567]

Collection and analysis of information on the scale of the NSA's Section 215 program also heightens the risk of the types of mistakes that often accompany the implementation of large information systems. Indeed, privacy violations, including the inadvertent collection of unauthorized personal data, improper use of the data collected, or dissemination of that data to persons or entities not approved to receive it, may be inevitable.[568] As discussed in detail in Part 4 above, since the NSA began collecting telephone and Internet metadata

---

for example, they have been successfully applied to detect consumer fraud. But such highly automated tools and techniques cannot be easily applied to the much more difficult problem of detecting and preempting a terrorist attack, and *success in doing so may not be possible at all.*" National Research Council, Protecting Individual Privacy in the Struggle Against Terrorists: A Framework for Program Assessment, at 2 (National Academies Press, 2008) (emphasis added). *See also* Constitution Project, *Principles for Government Data Mining: Preserving Civil Liberties in the Information Age* at 10 (2010) (examining data mining programs and finding the value of programs to identify potential terrorists "is unclear due to the particular difficulties of developing a predictive model to identify plans for terrorist acts."). These studies only focus on the power to detect terrorist activity and do not address other potential benefits from the 215 program discussed above.

[566] *See, e.g.*, Jim Harper, *Understanding Privacy — and the Real Threats to It (Cato Policy Analysis No. 520)* (Aug. 4, 2004).

[567] *See* Neil Richards, *The Dangers of Surveillance*, 126 Harvard Law Review 1934, 1952-53 (2013) ("the gathering of information affects the power dynamic between the watcher and the watched, giving the watcher greater power to influence or direct the subject of surveillance.").

[568] As Professor Steven Bellovin explained: "It is a truism in the computer security business that data that does not exist cannot be compromised. This includes both organizational misuse and misuse by individuals. Conversely, databases that do exist can be and are misused. . . . I am by no means suggesting that intelligence agencies should not collect or store information. That said, any form of collection does pose additional risks to personal privacy and security; an evaluation of the desirability of creating new databases of this type should take potential misuse into account as well. Put bluntly, it *will* happen; technical and personnel precautions will at best limit the extent." Steven Bellovin, Submission to the Privacy and Civil Liberties Oversight Board: Technical Issues Raised by the Section 215 and Section 702 Programs, at 8 (July 31, 2013) (emphasis in original).

under the supervision of the FISA court, there have been repeated instances of precisely these sorts of violations.[569]

Government collection of personal information on such a massive scale also courts the ever-present danger of "mission creep." At the moment, telephone records obtained by the NSA under Section 215 may exclusively be used in furtherance of clearly defined counterterrorism efforts, and only in the manner prescribed by the FISA court's orders. Once collected, however, information is always at risk of being appropriated for new purposes. Thus, when the government assembles a database containing the calling histories of millions of individuals, proposals to make this information available for other important governmental functions may be inevitable.[570] Already, it has been reported in the press, officials from numerous federal agencies have exerted pressure on the NSA to share its data and surveillance tools for investigations into "drug trafficking, cyberattacks, money laundering, counterfeiting and even copyright infringement."[571]

An even more compelling danger is that personal information collected by the government will be misused to harass, blackmail, or intimidate, or to single out for scrutiny individuals or groups adhering to minority religions or holding unpopular views. To be clear, the Board has seen no evidence suggesting that anything of the sort is occurring at the NSA. But while the danger of such abuse may seem remote, it is more than merely theoretical. The government's rampant misuse of its surveillance authority during the twentieth century to squelch domestic dissent in the name of national security was amply documented by the reports of the Church Committee, and was in fact the impetus for passage of the Foreign Intelligence Surveillance Act. In recent months, allegations have emerged at the national and local level involving the targeting of particular groups based on their ideology or religion — whether it be the Internal Revenue Service's reported singling out of Tea Party–affiliated organizations or the New York Police Department's alleged secret labeling of entire mosques as terrorist organizations. Prudence cautions

---

[569]   See pages 46 to 56 of this Report for a discussion of compliance issues in the NSA's bulk telephone records program.

[570]   *See* Privacy and Civil Liberties Oversight Board, Transcript of Workshop Regarding Surveillance Programs Operated Pursuant to Section 215 of the USA PATRIOT Act and Section 702 of the Foreign Intelligence Surveillance Act, at 127 (July 9, 2013) (Bellovin statement) ("One of the things that's the biggest problem in privacy is not the primary uses of data collected for a legitimate reason but the secondary uses that are often found later on for some particular database."); *id.* at 137-38 (Rotenberg statement) ("Once you have information collected and stored in a database, you will not surprisingly find new uses for it. In fact, it would be surprising if you didn't find new uses"). *See also* Ashkan Soltani, Watching the Watchers: Increased Transparency and Accountability for NSA Surveillance Programs, Submission to the PCLOB, at 9-10 (July 9, 2013).

[571]   Eric Lichtblau & Michael S. Schmidt, *Other Agencies Clamor for Data N.S.A. Compiles*, N.Y. Times (Aug. 3, 2013). According to this report, the NSA generally has fended off these requests, but not without reportedly generating complaints from other agencies that its stance has "undermined their own investigations into security matters." *Id.*

against assuming that abuse of surveillance powers is a problem that will never reoccur, and any decision to invest the government with a broad surveillance power must duly take into account the abuse that this power could enable, whether or not such abuse is evident today. Regardless of the good faith with which it may be wielded today, the immense power afforded the government by routine collection of all telephone records enables significant abuse and intrusion into Americans' privacy.

C. Chilling of Free Speech and Association

The NSA's bulk collection of telephone records also directly implicates freedom of speech and association. The readiness with which individuals engage in certain political and social activities understandably may be chilled by knowledge that the government collects a record of virtually every telephone call made by every American. Inability to expect privacy vis-à-vis the government in one's telephone communications means that people engaged in wholly lawful activities — but who for various reasons justifiably do not wish the government to know about their communications — must either forgo such activities, reduce their frequency, or take costly measures to hide them from government surveillance. Among the important freedoms that may be threatened by this chilling effect are the rights to participate in political activism, communicate with and benefit from the press, and promote novel or unpopular ideas.

"Awareness that the Government may be watching chills associational and expressive freedoms," as Justice Sonia Sotomayor noted in a 2012 concurring opinion.[572] Her predecessors on the Supreme Court observed decades ago that national security cases "often reflect a convergence of First and Fourth Amendment values not present in cases of 'ordinary' crime" and that "[h]istory abundantly documents the tendency of Government — however benevolent and benign its motives — to view with suspicion those who most fervently dispute its policies."[573] Years earlier, the Court recognized the "vital relationship between freedom to associate and privacy in one's associations," explaining: "Inviolability of privacy in group association may in many circumstances be indispensable to preservation of freedom of association, particularly where a group espouses dissident beliefs."[574] More recently, in discussing NSA surveillance, President Obama has acknowledged that privacy in communications is part of "our First Amendment rights and expectations in this country."[575]

---

[572] *United States v. Jones*, 132 S. Ct. 945, 956 (2012) (Sotomayor, J., concurring).

[573] *United States v. U.S. Dist. Court for E. Dist. of Mich., S. Div.*, 407 U.S. 297, 313 (1972).

[574] *Nat'l Ass'n for Advancement of Colored People v. State of Ala. ex rel. Patterson*, 357 U.S. 449, 462 (1958).

[575] Josh Gernstein, *Obama plans new limits on NSA surveillance*, POLITICO.COM (Dec. 5, 2013).

Following public disclosure of the NSA's bulk telephone records program, numerous advocacy organizations from across the political spectrum have joined legal challenges to the program, asserting that it hinders their ability to communicate confidentially with members, donors, legislators, whistleblowers, members of the public, and others.[576]

For instance, the NRA has asserted in a legal filing that, as an organization advancing often-controversial political stances, it "has jealously guarded information about its members and supporters" who have expressed concern about "repercussions either at work or in their community" if their NRA membership were disclosed.[577] The organization likens the government's bulk telephone records program to a compelled disclosure of its membership list, because the program supplies the government with the calling records of "everyone who might communicate with the NRA or its affiliates by phone."[578] In a different lawsuit, organizations ranging from environmentalists to gun-rights activists to religious and political advocacy groups have filed affidavits declaring that they have been chilled in their ability to associate with their supporters.[579] For example, Greenpeace has declared that it "cannot reassure those who contact Greenpeace" or "those we actively seek out for collaboration that their communications with Greenpeace will be confidential" — frustrating the organization's advocacy mission, which depends on "free and open communication with colleagues, members, experts, and leaders of government and industry," as well as the ability to receive confidential tips about threats to the organization's protest activities.[580]

Knowledge that the government continuously gathers a comprehensive record of the nation's telephone calls may also deter whistleblowers from calling attention to corporate or government wrongdoing, for fear of reprisals if their identities become known.[581] More broadly, these considerations may constrain the work of anyone who seeks

---

[576]   *See* Complaint ¶¶ 3, 24-27, *ACLU v. Clapper*, No. 13-3994 (S.D.N.Y. June 11, 2013); Complaint ¶¶ 2, 17-39, *First Unitarian Church of Los Angeles v. NSA*, No. 13-3287 (N.D. Cal. Oct. 30, 2013).

[577]   Brief of Amicus Curiae, National Rifle Association of America, Inc., in Support of Plaintiff, at 7, *ACLU v. Clapper*, No. 13-3994 (S.D.N.Y. Sept. 4, 2013).

[578]   *Id.*

[579]   In the lawsuit, *First Unitarian Church of Los Angeles v. NSA*, No. 13-3287 (N.D. Cal.), twenty-two organizations have filed affidavits making such assertions.

[580]   Declaration of Deepa Padmanabha for Greenpeace, Inc., in Support of Plaintiffs' Motion for Partial Summary Judgment, ¶¶ 11, 14-15, *First Unitarian Church of Los Angeles v. NSA*, No. 13-3287 (N.D. Cal. Oct. 30, 2013).

[581]   In support of a legal challenges to the NSA's calling records program, the Patient Privacy Rights Foundation, which seeks to "protect citizens' rights to health information privacy," claims that "phone calls are essential for discussion of sensitive matters concerning hidden use, disclosure, and sale of the nation's personal health information." Declaration of Deborah C. Peel, MD, for Patient Privacy Rights Foundation, ¶¶ 3-6, 9, *First Unitarian Church of Los Angeles v. NSA*, No. 13-3287 (N.D. Cal. Oct. 29, 2013). The organization reports in its declaration that following public disclosure of the NSA's program it experienced a significant

to communicate with activists, dissidents, and others involved in sensitive work as part of his or her research and writing. Stunting the unimpeded exchange of ideas on which such writers thrive carries implications for freedom of information as well as freedom of expression. As argued in a legal filing by the PEN American Center, a nonprofit association of writers, "[t]he prospect that telephone metadata can reveal the entire web of a writer's associations and interactions — and the contacts of all the writer's contacts, and their contacts — will inevitably limit and deter valuable interactions."

> Writers in the United States who support human rights or who communicate with human rights activists, for instance, are acutely aware of the dangers that comprehensive telephone metadata may create. The government's records of calling activity may permit reprisals or sanctions to be visited on writers, or on people with whom they speak, or on those people's families and friends, here and in other countries where they may be more vulnerable.[582]

Awareness that complete connection data on all telephone communications is stored in a government database may have debilitating consequences for journalism as well. Sources in a position to offer crucial information about newsworthy topics may remain silent out of fear that their telephone records could be used to trace their contacts with journalists — or they may be deterred by the onerous measures required to avoid leaving such a record.

Reporters and news organizations recently have warned about the danger of "self-censorship from sources and harm to the public discourse."[583] Pointing out that many significant pieces of American journalism have relied heavily on confidential sources, the Reporters Committee for Freedom of the Press, joined by thirteen other news organizations, has asserted: "When the risk of prosecution reaches such sources, quality reporting is diminished. Since the public has become aware of the call tracking, many reporters at major news outlets have said that this program and other NSA surveillance efforts have made sources less willing to talk with them, even about matters not related to national security."[584]

---

decrease in telephone calls from whistleblowers and others who would have reason to communicate anonymously. *Id.*

[582]   Brief of Amicus Curiae PEN American Center in Support of Plaintiffs' Motion for a Preliminary Injunction and in Opposition to Defendants' Motion to Dismiss, at 20, *ACLU v. Clapper*, No. 13-3994 (S.D.N.Y. Sept. 4, 2013).

[583]   Brief Amici Curiae of Reporters Committee for Freedom of the Press and 13 Other News Organizations in Support Plaintiffs' Motion for Partial Summary Judgment, at 3, *First Unitarian Church of Los Angeles v. NSA*, No. 13-3287 (N.D. Cal. Nov. 18, 2013).

[584]   Brief Amici Curiae of Reporters Committee for Freedom of the Press and 13 Other News Organizations in Support Plaintiffs' Motion for Partial Summary Judgment, at 1-2, *First Unitarian Church of*

These accounts describe changes in behavior on the part of journalists, sources, whistleblowers, activists, dissidents, and others upon learning that the government maintains a comprehensive and daily updated repository of call detail records on their telephone calls. The Board believes that such a shift in behavior is entirely predictable and rational. Although we cannot quantify the full extent of the chilling effect, we believe that these results — among them greater hindrances to political activism and a less robust press — are real and will be detrimental to the nation.

All of these accounts cited above refer to a chilling effect created by the *collection* of telephone calling records. The journalists, members of political organizations, and ordinary Americans discussed above assert that they are inhibited in their associations by the knowledge that the government is compiling a comprehensive record of phone calls that are then available for government review and analysis. While the government urges that the odds of any particular telephone record being reviewed by analysts is very small — noting that the NSA only queried the database for fewer than 300 "selectors" in 2012 — the government acknowledges that the number of individuals whose phone records are returned through this query process is substantially larger than 300 per year.[585] Under the automated system approved by the FISC, the results of all queries may be compiled in the "corporate store" database. As explained elsewhere in this Report, the compiled records that may be aggregated in the corporate store could contain the complete calling records of 1.5 million telephone numbers — which could encompass records of telephone calls made between these numbers and over 100 million other numbers.[586] Once contained in the corporate store, analysts may further examine these records without the need for any new reasonable articulable suspicion determination. With such vast numbers of telephone records readily subject to review, it would not be speculative for these individuals to fear that their own records may be culled from the NSA's collection repository and subject to review by government analysts.

Los Angeles v. NSA, No. 13-3287 (N.D. Cal. Nov. 18, 2013). In addition, a report by the Committee to Protect Journalists spearheaded by the former Executive Editor of the *Washington Post* examined the combined impact of the Section 215 and 702 programs on journalism. It quoted one journalist as noting that "I worry now about calling somebody because the contact can be found out through a check of phone records or e-mails. . . . It leaves a digital trail that makes it easier for the government to monitor those contacts." Leonard Downie Jr. & Sara Rafsky, Committee to Protect Journalists, *The Obama Administration and the Press: Leak Investigations and Surveillance in Post-9/11 America* (Oct. 10, 2013), http://cpj.org/reports/2013/10/obama-and-the-press-us-leaks-surveillance-post-911.php.

[585]   Declaration of Teresa H. Shea, Signals Intelligence Director, National Security Agency, ¶ 24, *ACLU v. Clapper*, No. 13-3994 (S.D.N.Y. Oct. 1, 2013). While fewer than 300 identifiers were used to query the NSA's call detail records in 2012, that number "has varied over the years." *Id.* ¶ 24.

[586]   See pages 29 to 31 of this Report.

D. Significance of Rules Limiting the NSA's Use of Telephone Records

In the government's view, concerns about the privacy and civil liberties implications of the NSA's bulk acquisition of calling records should be allayed by the detailed rules that limit the agency's use of those records after collection. We disagree.

To begin with, the current rules governing the NSA's Section 215 program permit analysts to view the complete calling records of individuals who have no suspected connections to terrorist activity. In defense of the program, the government emphasizes that NSA analysts may access telephone records collected under Section 215 only through a "query" that begins with a telephone number reasonably suspected of being associated with terrorism. As described earlier in this Report, when designated agency personnel develop "reasonable articulable suspicion" or "RAS" that a number is "associated" with terrorism, they are permitted to enter that number (the "seed") into the NSA's database of Section 215 records and identify all numbers (say, seventy-five) that have been in contact with the seed over the course of five years (the "first hop"). Most if not all of the individuals behind those seventy-five numbers will have no connection with terrorism. Yet the program rules allow the system to search those seventy-five numbers against the full database with no RAS determination (the "second hop") and acquire all of the numbers (say, seventy-five) that have been in touch with each of the first seventy-five numbers over the course of five years (amounting now to 5,625 numbers). Again, the vast majority of the individuals behind those 5,625 numbers would have no connection with terrorism and quite likely none would, yet the rules allow all 5,625 to be searched against the database (the "third hop") with no RAS determination, yielding possibly over 400,000 phone numbers of individuals called or receiving calls from the 5,625.

Moreover, under the new technical system that has received FISA court approval,[587] the results of those queries (the full calling records of over 5,000 numbers generated by a three hop analysis of one seed) are placed into a central repository termed the "corporate store."[588] The NSA has estimated that in the year 2012 approximately 300 numbers were approved as reasonably suspicious and used as seeds to query its database. If that figure holds true, then during the course of one year the corporate store could acquire the complete calling records of 1.5 million telephone persons (5,625 times 300, since the third hop produces full calling records on the 5,625 numbers yielded by the second hop) — which could encompass records of telephone calls made between these numbers and over 100 million other numbers (1.5 million persons, each calling or receiving a call from seventy-five other numbers). The rules of the FISA court for the 215 program impose no

---

[587] *See* Primary Order at 11 & n.11, *In re Application of the Federal Bureau of Investigation for an Order Requiring the Production of Tangible Things*, No. BR 13-158 (FISA Ct. Oct. 11, 2013).

[588] *See id.*

limits on how long data can be held in the corporate store, in contrast to the five-year retention limit on collection store data.

Furthermore, under the rules approved by the FISA court, NSA personnel may then search any phone number, including the phone number of a U.S. person, against the corporate store — as long as the agency has a valid foreign intelligence purpose in doing so — without regard to whether there is "reasonable articulable suspicion" about that number.[589] Unlike with respect to the initial RAS query, the FISA court's orders specifically exempt the NSA from maintaining an audit trail when analysts access records in the corporate store.[590] The Board does not believe that this system adequately protects individual privacy, particularly as to those who are not reasonably suspected of any involvement in terrorism.

Not only do we find the existing rules inadequate in light of the depth and breadth of the data collected by the government, but we also must note again the difficulties that the NSA has had in following those rules, as described earlier in this Report. The complexity of a system like the NSA's Section 215 program may unavoidably entail inadvertent violations of the rules that govern the handling of individuals' calling records. From the beginning of the Section 215 program, the government assured the FISA court that software measures would prevent analysts from viewing calling records of telephone numbers that had not been approved for searching. Yet those assurances turned out to be wrong, leading the FISA court to conclude in 2009 that, from the inception of the program, "the NSA's data accessing technologies and practices were never adequately designed to comply with the governing minimization procedures."[591] Since then, a range of inadvertent violations resulting from the complexity of the program and the NSA's technological systems has continued up to the present day. And beyond the government's self-reported compliance failures (the reporting of which is laudable), the FISA court has acknowledged that it has little independent means of verifying whether the NSA's program is being implemented according to the court's orders and in a manner that protects privacy interests.[592]

Finally, we note the risk that rules could be changed. The government could, in the future, be permitted to use the NSA's Section 215 records for purposes other than the narrow counterterrorism efforts for which they are authorized now. It might be permitted to store the records for longer than five years, or to disseminate them more broadly among federal agencies and personnel than current standards permit. The "reasonable articulable suspicion" standard could be loosened or eliminated.

---

[589] *See* Primary Order at 11 & n.11, *In re Application of the Federal Bureau of Investigation for an Order Requiring the Production of Tangible Things*, No. BR 13-158 (FISA Ct. Oct. 11, 2013).

[590] *See id.* at 7 n.6. All records in the corporate store will be the results of RAS-approved queries.

[591] Order at 14-15, *In re Production of Tangible Things*, No. BR 08-13 (FISA Ct. Mar. 2, 2009).

[592] *See, e.g., id.* at 12.

The rules could also be impacted by changes in technology. That is in evidence right now, as the NSA moves to an updated system of handling its Section 215 records that involves a new system of automated queries (described above) that places substantial information outside the database controlled by the court-imposed rules. Technology upgrades also present opportunities for mistakes and miscommunication regarding the manner in which individuals' calling records are being treated, a problem that has occurred in the past with the Section 215 data.

In sum, even under the rules that are in place today, the permissibility of three-hop querying makes a huge number of telephone records pertaining to innocent Americans subject to viewing by intelligence analysts. Moreover, under the new automated query process approved by the FISA court, all of those records may be retained indefinitely and analyzed through a variety of means without auditing. Even if the data were subject to stricter rules, the record casts doubt on whether those outside the government could reasonably be assured that those rules were being complied with. Thus, even if such stricter rules, consistently followed, were adequate to prevent invasions of privacy, they could not fully ameliorate the legitimate concerns raised by the government's possession of such a comprehensive dataset. Under the Section 215 program, individuals and groups who desire privacy in their activities and associations must contend with a novel and troubling dynamic: all of their calling records must be presumed to be in the hands of the government, under circumstances that give them no ability to know whether the government is scrutinizing their records or disseminating them to other agencies. That scenario threatens to impose a unique chilling effect on speech and association.

VI.   Conclusion

The 9/11 Commission, noting that the Patriot Act "vested substantial new powers in the investigative agencies of the government" and acknowledging "concerns regarding the shifting balance of power to the government," made the following recommendation: "The burden of proof for retaining a particular governmental power should be on the executive, to explain," among other things, "that the power actually materially enhances security."[593] Based on our study of the NSA's bulk telephone records program, which has included access to classified material and numerous briefings with intelligence officials, we do not believe the government has demonstrated that the program materially enhances security to a degree that justifies its effects on privacy, free speech, and free association.

If the program's implications for privacy and civil liberties were minor, then the showing made by the government might perhaps warrant retention of the program on the

---

[593]   9/11 Commission Report at 394-95.

chance that it may offer critical counterterrorism insights in the future, even if it has not yet done so. As we have explained above, however, in our view the daily governmental collection of the telephone calling records of nearly every American has deep privacy ramifications, fundamentally alters the relationship between citizens and the state, and threatens to substantially chill the speech and associational freedoms that are essential to our democracy. Any governmental program that entails such costs requires a strong showing of efficacy. We do not believe the NSA's telephone records program conducted under Section 215 meets that standard.

VII. Recommendations for Section 215 Program

Recommendation 1. The government should end its Section 215 bulk telephone records program.

The Section 215 bulk telephone records program is not sustainable from a legal or policy perspective. As outlined in this Report, the program lacks a viable legal foundation under Section 215, implicates constitutional concerns under the First and Fourth Amendments, raises serious threats to privacy and civil liberties as a policy matter, and has shown only limited value. For these reasons, the government should end the program.

As intelligence community officials have emphasized, the Section 215 program is but one tool used in the government's counterterrorism efforts. Without the program, the government would still be able to seek telephone calling records directly from communications providers for records held in their own databases, through national security letters or, in investigations of potential criminal conduct, with grand jury subpoenas, court orders or warrants.[594] And the government would still be able to use pen registers and trap and trace devices under FISA and, in criminal investigations, under Title 18 for the prospective collection of new calling records as they are generated. The Board believes that the Section 215 program has contributed only minimal value in combating terrorism beyond what the government already achieves through these and other alternative means. Cessation of the program would eliminate the privacy and civil liberties concerns associated with bulk collection without unduly hampering the government's efforts, while ensuring that any governmental requests for telephone calling records are tailored to the needs of specific investigations.

---

[594]   We recognize that the use of national security letters, which are issued without judicial approval, present its own privacy and civil liberties concerns and has been the subject of extensive debate. In this study, we did not examine the government's use of NSLs. We merely recognize here that they remain a tool available to the government for the acquisition of telephone calling records on a particularized basis.

The Board does not recommend that the government impose data retention requirements on communications providers in order to facilitate any system of seeking records directly from private databases. The Board also does not recommend creating a third party to hold the data; such an approach would pose difficult questions of liability, accountability, oversight, mission creep, and data security, among others.

Once the Section 215 bulk collection program has ended, the government should purge the database of telephone records that have been collected and stored during the program's operation, subject to limits on purging data that may arise under the federal records laws or as a result of any pending litigation. This should include purging both the "collection store," which contains all records obtained under the program over the past five years, and the "corporate store," which contains the results of all automated contact chaining queries. NSA and other agencies could retain copies of data already disseminated in reports.

The Board also recommends against the enactment of legislation that would merely codify the existing program or any other program that collected bulk data on such a massive scale regarding individuals with no suspected ties to terrorism or criminal activity. While new legislation could provide clear statutory authorization for a program that currently lacks a sound statutory footing, any new bulk collection program would still pose grave threats to privacy and civil liberties. If the government and Congress seek to develop a new program to replace the Section 215 program, any such new program should be crafted far more narrowly, and the government should demonstrate that its effectiveness will clearly outweigh any intrusions on privacy and civil liberties interests.[595]

Moreover, the Board's constitutional analysis above should provide a message of caution to policymakers. As Fourth Amendment doctrine continues to evolve in order to address powerful new electronic surveillance technologies, the Supreme Court may be on the cusp of modifying the third-party doctrine on which the Section 215 program rests. Freedoms under the First Amendment, such as free speech, religion, and association, are clearly implicated by bulk collection of information on telephone communications. It is not necessary to find constitutional violations in order to urge — as a policy matter — that Congress should exercise restraint to respect the important individual interests involved. Given the significant privacy and civil liberties interests at stake, Congress should seek the least intrusive alternative and should not legislate to the outer bounds of its authority.

---

[595] In theory the government could seek authorization from Congress for a new and significantly more targeted program, limited, for example, to telephone numbers that are more likely to be associated with potential terrorists, if such a program could be developed. The government might seek the private sector's assistance in developing a methodology for targeting this narrower, more relevant pool of information.

The Board recognizes that immediate shutdown of the 215 program could be disruptive, and the government may need a short period of time to explore and institutionalize alternative approaches, and believes it would be appropriate for the government to wind down the 215 program over a short interim period. If the government does find the need for a short wind-down period, the Board urges that it should follow the procedures under Recommendation 2 below.

Recommendation 2. The government should immediately implement additional privacy safeguards in operating the Section 215 bulk collection program.

The Board recommends that the government immediately implement several additional privacy safeguards to mitigate the privacy impact of the present Section 215 program. The recommended changes can be implemented without any need for congressional or FISC authorization. Specifically, the government should:

(a) reduce the retention period for the bulk telephone records program from five years to three years;

(b) reduce the number of "hops" used in contact chaining from three to two;

(c) submit the NSA's "reasonable articulable suspicion" determinations to the FISC for review after they have been approved by NSA and used to query the database; and

(d) require a "reasonable articulable suspicion" determination before analysts may submit queries to, or otherwise analyze, the "corporate store," which contains the results of contact chaining queries to the full "collection store."

At present, the NSA retains all collected call detail records for five years, but this retention period can and should be limited to three years. Over time, people change their telephone numbers as well as their patterns of contacts and communications. Government officials have already said that reducing the retention period from five years to three would preserve the greatest value that the program offers.[596]

Similarly, changing program rules to limit contact chaining to two hops — that is, permitting each query to return only records of calls from the selector number out to the telephone numbers it calls, and from those "first hop" telephone numbers out to the numbers they have called — would not unduly diminish the value of the telephony

---

[596]   Privacy and Civil Liberties Oversight Board, Transcript of Public Hearing, Consideration of Recommendations for Change: The Surveillance Programs Operated Pursuant to Section 215 of the USA PATRIOT Act and Section 702 of the Foreign Intelligence Surveillance Act, at 118 (Nov. 4, 2013) (testimony of Rajesh De, General Counsel, NSA) ("[T]hree years probably would be where the knee of the curve is in terms of the greatest value"), *available at* http://www.pclob.gov/.

metadata program. No third hops (the telephone numbers called by the second hop numbers) should be permitted based on a single RAS determination. If the government wishes to search for connections from identifiers it obtained at the second hop, it should be required to obtain a new RAS approval for each such telephone number. Each additional hop from the original "selector" makes the connection more remote and adds exponentially greater numbers of "false positives" to the query results. The value of connections becomes more limited as the contact chain is extended and it becomes more difficult to sift through the results.

The third immediate change that the Board recommends is that the NSA should submit its RAS determinations to the FISC for review after queries have been run. NSA officials would still make the RAS determinations under existing minimization rules and this would provide sufficient authorization to run a query. The NSA would submit these RAS determinations to the FISC periodically over the coming months or as part of the next renewal application for the program. Submission of RAS determinations would allow the FISC to assess whether the RAS standard has properly been met as part of the evaluation of whether to renew the program and potentially modify its terms and protections.

The Board notes that review of RAS determinations will increase the workload of the FISC, and urges Congress to take into account the growing responsibilities of the FISC overall as it considers the judiciary's budget, but the Board does not believe that the burden will be excessive. The government has stated that in 2012 there were fewer than 300 RAS-approved selectors over the course of the entire year, so the number of RAS determinations submitted to the FISC for any quarterly renewal application should be manageable. Further, this after the fact procedure would not present the time pressure of individualized FISC review prior to querying the database.

The fourth immediate change is to extend privacy safeguards to the database that contains all of the metadata generated by queries run on RAS-approved selectors. As described above, NSA uses RAS-approved selectors to run queries on the full database of calling records termed the "collection store." Under the automated query process approved by the FISC, the results of all queries, containing millions of call detail records retrieved through contact chaining, are compiled in a database called the "corporate store." The vast majority of the call detail records transferred will concern U.S. persons as to whom there is no suspicion of any connection to terrorism. In essence, the corporate store will contain an ever-growing subset of telephone calling records. Under the current minimization procedures approved by the FISC, analysts may query the corporate store database with any selector, without prior RAS approval — so long as they have a valid foreign intelligence purpose — and seemingly may engage in data mining or other forms of analysis besides querying. The Board recommends that this rule be changed. Telephony metadata on presumptively innocent Americans, whether in the large database or a subset, should be subject to query only based on the same reasonable articulable suspicion standard.

Part 8:
DISCUSSION AND RECOMMENDATIONS REGARDING THE
FOREIGN INTELLIGENCE SURVEILLANCE COURT

I. Overview of the Foreign Intelligence Surveillance Court

The Foreign Intelligence Surveillance Court ("FISC" or "FISA court") is a critical component of the system of checks and balances that our nation has created around the exercise of national security powers. When Congress created the court in 1978 in response to concerns about the abuse of electronic surveillance,[597] it represented a major restructuring of the domestic conduct of foreign intelligence surveillance, with constitutional implications. Until then, successive Presidents of both parties had authorized national security wiretaps and other searches solely on the basis of their powers under Article II of the Constitution. The Foreign Intelligence Surveillance Act ("FISA") of 1978 provided a procedure under which the Attorney General could obtain a judicial warrant authorizing the use of electronic surveillance in the United States for foreign intelligence purposes.[598] As the House Permanent Select Committee on Intelligence explained in its 1978 report recommending adoption of FISA:

> The history and law relating to electronic surveillance for "national security" purposes have revolved around the competing demands of the President's constitutional powers to gather intelligence deemed necessary to the security of the nation and the requirements of the fourth amendment. The U.S. Supreme Court has never expressly decided the issue of whether the President has the constitutional authority to authorize warrantless electronic surveillance for foreign intelligence purposes. Whether or not the President has an "inherent power" to engage in or authorize warrantless electronic surveillance and, if such power exits, what limitations, if any, restrict the scope of that power, are issues that have troubled constitutional scholars for decades.[599]

---

[597] *See* S. Rep. No. 95-604(I), at 7 (1978) ("Senate Judiciary Committee Report") ("The legislation is in large measure a response to the revelations that warrantless electronic surveillance in the name of national security has been seriously abused."); H.R. Rep. No. 95-1283(I), at 111 (1978) ("HPSCI Report") (dissenting views of Reps. Wilson, McClory, Robinson and Ashbrook) ("No one can deny that abuses of electronic surveillance have taken place in the past under the claim of 'national security.'").

[598] Senate Judiciary Committee Report at 5. When enacted, FISA did not cover activities occurring outside the United States. By and large, that remains true today, the only exception being acquisitions of foreign intelligence that intentionally target a U.S. person reasonably believed to be outside the United States, which were brought within the jurisdiction of the FISC under the FISA Amendments Act of 2008. *See* 50 U.S.C. § 1881c.

[599] HPSCI Report at 15.

In essence, FISA represented an agreement between the executive and legislative branches to leave that debate aside[600] and establish a special court to oversee foreign intelligence collection. While the statute has required periodic updates, national security officials have agreed that it created an appropriate balance among the interests at stake, and that judicial review provides an important mechanism regulating the use of very powerful and effective techniques vital to the protection of the country.[601]

Currently, the FISA court is comprised of eleven judges. The Chief Justice of the United States appoints these judges from among sitting U.S. district court judges, who previously have been appointed by the President and confirmed by the Senate. The Chief Justice also appoints one of the FISC judges to serve as presiding judge. These judges serve on the FISC for staggered seven-year terms while continuing to maintain a full docket of cases in their home districts. FISA requires that the judges be drawn from at least seven different U.S. judicial circuits. At least three of the eleven must reside within twenty miles of Washington, D.C.,[602] to ensure that there will be a judge available to hear emergency matters.

Over time, the scope of FISA and the jurisdiction of the FISA court have evolved. When FISA was first enacted, the jurisdiction of the court was limited to reviewing applications for "electronic surveillance." That term has its own unique and complex definition under the statute but largely it concerns the acquisition of the contents of electronic communications.[603] In 1994, Congress amended FISA to permit applications for and orders authorizing physical searches.[604] In 1998, Congress further amended the statute

---

[600]   "[T]he bill does not recognize, ratify, or deny the existence of any Presidential power to authorize warrantless surveillance in the United States in the absence of the legislation. It would, rather, moot the debate over the existence or non-existence of this power[.]" HPSCI Report at 24. This agreement between Congress and the executive branch to involve the judiciary in the regulation of intelligence collection activities did not and could not resolve constitutional questions regarding the relationship between legislative and presidential powers in the area of national security. *See In re: Sealed Case*, 310 F.3d 717, 742 (FISA Ct. Rev. 2002) ("We take for granted that the President does have that authority [inherent authority to conduct warrantless searches to obtain foreign intelligence information] and, assuming that is so, FISA could not encroach on the President's constitutional power.").

[601]   *See, e.g., FISA Hearing: Hearing before the Permanent Select Committee on Intelligence*, 110th Cong. (2007) (statement of Michael McConnell, Director of National Intelligence) ("It is my steadfast belief that the balance struck by the Congress in 1978 was not only elegant, it was the right balance to allow my Community to conduct foreign intelligence while protecting Americans."); Joint Statement for the Record of James R. Clapper, Director of National Intelligence, and General Keith B. Alexander, Director, National Security Agency, before the Senate Committee on the Judiciary, at 9 (Oct. 2, 2013) ("On the issue of FISC reform, we believe that the *ex parte* nature of proceedings before the FISC is fundamentally sound and has worked well for decades in adjudicating the Government's applications for authority to conduct electronic surveillance or physical searches in the national security context under FISA.").

[602]   50 U.S.C. § 1803(a). The Patriot Act expanded the number of judges on the FISC from seven to eleven and added the requirement that three of the judges must reside within twenty miles of Washington, D.C.

[603]   50 U.S.C. § 1801(f).

[604]   Pub. L. No. 103-359, § 807, 108 Stat. 3423, 3443 (1994) (codified at 50 U.S.C. §§ 1821 to 1829).

to add authority for the FISC to review and approve applications for the installation and use of pen registers and trap and trace devices to collect foreign intelligence.[605] Also in 1998, Congress amended the statute to create a "business records" provision, which authorized the FISA court, at the government's request, to order a common carrier, public accommodation facility, physical storage facility, or vehicle rental facility to release records in its possession pertaining to a foreign power or agent of a foreign power.[606] That authority was substantially amended by Section 215 of the Patriot Act.[607]

However, despite these changes, the main business of the Court prior to 2004 remained the consideration of government applications relating to a specific person, a specific place, or a specific communications account or device. Numerically, consideration of such particularized applications still constitutes the vast majority of the court's workload. In considering these applications, judges sitting on the FISC perform a role very similar to that performed by judges and magistrates in ordinary criminal cases. Proceedings are conducted *ex parte*; that is, with only government attorneys appearing before the court, which is the same way that applications for a search warrant or a wiretap are considered in criminal proceedings. Such individualized applications tend to be very fact-specific; often the only question is whether the application meets the express standard set forth in FISA. As a former judge of the FISA court recently explained, "approving search warrants and wiretap orders and trap and trace orders and foreign intelligence surveillance warrants one at a time is familiar ground for judges."[608]

There is one major difference between these individualized FISC and criminal proceedings. FISA applications and the proceedings associated with them are not only *ex parte,* they are also secret, to a degree that makes it very difficult for a target of surveillance to ever challenge the legality of the government's actions.[609] As Judge James G. Carr, a senior district court judge and former member of the FISA court, has pointed out "[T]he subject of a conventional Fourth Amendment search warrant knows of its execution, can challenge its lawfulness if indicted, and can, even if not indicted, seek to recover seized property or possibly sue for damages. In contrast, except in very, very rare instances,

---

[605]   Pub. L. No. 105-272, § 601, 112 Stat. 2396, 2404 (1998) (codified at 50 U.S.C. §§ 1841 to 1846).

[606]   Pub. L. No. 105-272, § 602, 112 Stat. 2396, 2410 (1998) (codified at 50 U.S.C. §§ 1861 to 1863).

[607]   Pub. L. No. 107-56, § 215, 115 Stat. 272, 287 (2001) (codified at 50 U.S.C. § 1861). See pages 40 to 41 of this Report for a discussion of this expanded authority.

[608]   Privacy and Civil Liberties Oversight Board, Transcript of Workshop Regarding Surveillance Programs Operated Pursuant to Section 215 of the USA PATRIOT Act and Section 702 of the Foreign Intelligence Surveillance Act, at 35 (July 9, 2013) (statement of Judge James Robertson), *available at* http://www.pclob.gov/.

[609]   FISA directs that the "record of proceedings under this Act, including applications made and orders granted, shall be maintained under security measures established by the Chief Justice in consultation with the Attorney General and the Director of National Intelligence." 50 U.S.C. § 1803(c).

suppression or other means of challenging the lawfulness of a FISA order is simply not available to the subject of a FISA order."[610] Although criminal defendants must be notified if the government intends to enter into evidence or otherwise use against them evidence derived from FISA surveillance, special procedures under the statute limit what can be disclosed to defendants, and proceedings on a motion to suppress must be held *ex parte* if the Attorney General files an affidavit that disclosure or an adversary hearing would harm the national security of the United States.[611] In practice, the government always files such an affidavit, and it appears that no defendant has ever obtained a copy of the government's statement of probable cause or other documents that served as the basis for FISA surveillance.[612]

II.   The FISC's Role after 9/11

Beginning in 2004, the role of the FISA court changed as a result of two significant developments. First, in 2004, the government approached the court with a request to approve a program involving what is now referred to as "bulk collection." Specifically, the government requested that the court approve, under the FISA provisions for pen registers and trap and trace devices, the bulk collection of "to and from" data concerning the Internet communications of many unspecified persons. Both the government and the court recognized that the application raised novel legal issues not presented in the individualized applications that had characterized the court's work until then. The government submitted a lengthy memorandum of law supporting its request, and the court, when it approved the request, issued a lengthy opinion addressing the legal issues presented. That request for collection of Internet metadata was followed by one in 2006 concerning telephony metadata, filed under a different provision of FISA and thus presenting further unique questions.

---

[610]   Prepared Remarks of James G. Carr, Senior U.S. District Judge, N.D. Ohio, *Senate Judiciary Committee Hearing: Strengthening Privacy Rights and National Security: Oversight of FISA Surveillance Programs* (July 31, 2013), *available at* http://www.judiciary.senate.gov/pdf/7-31-13CarrTestimony.pdf.

[611]   50 U.S.C. § 1806(f).

[612]   Jimmy Gurulé, *FISA and the Battle Between National Security and Privacy*, JURIST (Feb. 17, 2012) (noting that no court has ever disclosed FISA documents to a defendant and concluding that defendants face "insurmountable legal hurdles" to suppress evidence derived from electronic surveillance or physical searches authorized under FISA). It is our understanding that these practices will not be affected by the DOJ's recent decision to notify defendants when surveillance under FISA leads to other evidence that the government intends to introduce against them. *See* Charlie Savage, *Door May Open for Challenge to Secret Wiretaps*, N.Y. TIMES (Oct. 16, 2013) (reporting that the DOJ had been taking a narrow view of "derived from" and had not been notifying defendants if they had been targeted under FISA but the information obtained was not itself introduced but had led to other evidence that was introduced).

A second major development occurred when Congress enacted the FISA Amendments Act of 2008 ("FAA"), which authorized the Attorney General and the Director of National Intelligence ("DNI") to target the electronic communications of persons reasonably believed to be located outside the United States, for the purpose of acquiring foreign intelligence information. The FAA authorized the Attorney General and the DNI to issue directives requiring electronic communications service providers to assist the government in collecting these communications. In contrast to other acquisitions of content authorized under FISA, the FAA did not require the government to seek the FISA court's approval of its decisions about which individuals to target; instead, the Act authorized the court to review annual "certifications" by the government and to review the targeting and minimization procedures adopted by the government for this program. The required certifications must include an affidavit by an appropriate official attesting that there are targeting and minimization procedures in place that meet statutory requirements and stating that a significant purpose of the acquisition is to obtain foreign intelligence information.[613] The FAA required the government to assess its compliance with the targeting and minimization procedures and to report its assessment to the court on a semi-annual basis and to report other implementation details to the court on an annual basis. From time to time, in response to compliance lapses brought to the FISA court's attention by the government[614] the FISC has conducted detailed inquiries into specific technical and constitutional issues arising in the implementation of the government's authority.

III.   Process for FISC Review of Government Applications

Whether the FISA court is considering a particularized request or a programmatic one such as the bulk metadata collection program under Section 215, even before an application reaches the court, it undergoes extensive review in the executive branch. It is first reviewed by lawyers at the FBI, the NSA, or other agencies, and then by lawyers at the National Security Division of the Department of Justice ("NSD"), who present the government's applications to the court. Review by the NSD frequently involves substantial back and forth between the agency seeking authorization and the DOJ lawyers, as the lawyers seek additional factual details about the target of the surveillance, technical information about the surveillance methodology, or assurances about how the information acquired will be used and disseminated. Agency personnel would say that at times these interactions are quasi-adversarial. At the conclusion of the process, the application will generally be quite lengthy and may have extensive supporting documentation, and it must

---

[613]   50 U.S.C. § 1881a(g).

[614]   See pages 46 to 56 of this Report for a discussion of these compliance incidents.

be approved by the Attorney General, the Deputy Attorney General, or upon designation, the Assistant Attorney General for National Security.[615]

At the FISC, each week one of the eleven judges who comprise the court is on duty in Washington.[616] Normally, a proposed application must be submitted to the duty judge by the DOJ at least seven days before the government seeks to have the matter entertained. Upon the court's receipt of a proposed application, a member of the FISA court's legal staff will review the application and evaluate whether it meets the legal requirements under FISA. The FISC's legal staff are career employees who have developed substantial expertise in FISA. They are much more senior and experienced than typical judicial law clerks in federal courts, who are often recent law school graduates. However, the legal staff's job responsibilities and role are analogous to those of most judicial law clerks in that they serve as staff to the judges rather than as advocates.[617] They conduct research to probe whether the government's application should be granted. While their role includes identifying any flaws in the government's statutory or constitutional analysis, it does not reach to contesting the government's arguments in the manner of an opposing party. As part of their evaluation of a proposed application, the court attorneys will often have one or more telephone conversations with the DOJ lawyers to seek additional information and/or raise concerns about the application.[618] The legal staff will prepare a written analysis of the application for the duty judge, which includes an identification of any weaknesses, flaws or other concerns. For example, the court attorney may recommend that the judge consider requiring the addition of information to the application; imposing special reporting requirements; or shortening the requested duration of an application.

The duty judge will then review the proposed application along with the legal staff's analysis and will make a preliminary determination about how to proceed. The judge's

---

[615]   50 U.S.C. § 1801(g) (defining Attorney General to include delegation to other specified officials); *id* § 1804(g) (Attorney General approval required).

[616]   The description of the FISC's procedures in this section is based on its published Rules of Procedure and on two detailed letters from FISC presiding judge Reggie B. Walton to the chairman of the Senate Judiciary Committee. *See* United States Foreign Intelligence Surveillance Court, Rules of Procedure (Nov. 1, 2010); Letter from the Honorable Reggie B. Walton, Presiding Judge, U.S. Foreign Intelligence Surveillance Court, to the Honorable Patrick J. Leahy, Chairman, Committee on the Judiciary, U.S. Senate (July 29, 2013) ("Walton Letter of July 29, 2013"); Letter from the Honorable Reggie B. Walton, Presiding Judge, U.S. Foreign Intelligence Surveillance Court, to the Honorable Patrick J. Leahy, Chairman, Committee on the Judiciary, U.S. Senate (Oct. 11, 2013) ("Walton Letter of Oct. 11, 2013").

[617]   *See*, David Kris, *On the Bulk Collection of Tangible Things*, LAWFARE RESEARCH PAPER SERIES, at 38-39 (Sept. 29, 2013), *available at* http://www.lawfareblog.com/. Kris notes that Congress could expand the number of FISC legal advisers and "allow and encourage" FISC judges to designate one or more to draft briefs opposing the DOJ attorneys' legal arguments.

[618]   The legal staff interact with the government by telephone on a daily basis; they meet in person with the government as often as two to three times a week, or as few as one to two times a month, in connection with the various matters pending before the court. *See* Walton Letter of July 29, 2013, at 6.

responses might include indicating to the court staff that he or she is prepared to approve the application without a hearing; indicating an inclination to impose conditions on the approval of the application; determining that additional information is needed about the application; determining that a hearing would be appropriate before deciding whether to grant the application; or indicating an inclination to deny the application. The staff attorney will then relay the judge's inclination to the government, and the government will then submit a final application, which may include additional information in response to the court's feedback. The government may seek a hearing, for example, to challenge the judge's proposed conditions. In some cases, the government may decide not to submit a final application or to withdraw one that has been submitted, after learning that the judge does not intend to approve it. Unless the government withdraws the application, the FISC judge, either with or without a hearing, will decide whether to approve or deny it or to approve it with conditions.

When a FISA court judge holds a hearing, it will be attended, at a minimum, by the Department of Justice attorney who prepared the application and a fact witness from the agency seeking the Court's authorization. FISC judges have the authority to take testimony, for example, from government employees familiar with the technical issues associated with a particular technique or program or from personnel responsible for the operation of a program. Although it is an open question, in theory, at least, the court could also hear from outside experts on technical questions.[619]

It is frequently reported that the FISA court approves a very large percentage of government applications. In fact, however, the approval rate for wiretap applications in ordinary criminal cases is higher than the approval rate for FISA applications.[620] Moreover, the FISA statistics do not take into account the changes to the final applications that are ultimately submitted, made as a result of the back and forth between the FISC legal staff and government attorneys. Nor does the percentage of approvals take into account the applications that are withdrawn or never submitted in final form due to concerns raised by the court or its legal staff. The FISA court has recently kept track of such actions and has found that, during the three month period from July through September 2013, 24.4% of matters submitted to the FISA court ultimately involved substantive changes to the

---

[619]   Judge James Carr, former FISC judge, and James Baker, who previously practiced before the FISC, both testified at the PCLOB's hearing on November 4, 2013, about the role of in-house legal counsel and the court's ability to consult outside technologists. *See* Privacy and Civil Liberties Oversight Board, Transcript of Public Hearing, Consideration of Recommendations for Change: The Surveillance Programs Operated Pursuant to Section 215 of the USA PATRIOT Act and Section 702 of the Foreign Intelligence Surveillance Act, at 175-77, 204-08 (Nov. 4, 2013), *available at* http://www.pclob.gov/.

[620]   Walton Letter of July 29, 2013, at 3 n.6.

information provided by the government or to the authorities granted as a result of court inquiry or action.[621]

Applications that are novel or more complex, such as applications under Section 702 and applications for renewal of bulk phone call metadata collection under Section 215, are handled using a process that is similar to the one described above, but more exacting. The government typically submits a proposed application of this type more than one week in advance; in the case of Section 702, proposed applications are typically filed approximately one month before filing a final application. Programmatic applications are accompanied by even more detailed information than an individualized application, and the court attorney who reviews that application spends more time reviewing it, as does the judge. In addition, under the court's rules, if an application involves an issue not previously presented to the court, including novel issues of technology or law, the government must advise the FISC in writing of the nature and significance of the issue and submit a memorandum explaining the novel technique, novel implementation of an existing technique, or legal issue not previously considered by the court.[622]

FISA does not provide a mechanism for the FISC to invite non-governmental parties to provide views on pending government applications or otherwise participate in FISA court proceedings prior to approval of an application. After an order has been issued, the statute and the FISC rules provide opportunities for recipients of such orders (or of government directives issued under Section 702) to challenge those orders or directives.[623] Such challenges are very rare. There has been one instance in which the court heard arguments from a non-governmental party that sought to substantively contest a directive from the government.[624] In another case that did not address the legality of a particular order but concerned service providers' ability to disclose information about the number of orders they had received, the court heard from outside lawyers, but even though those outside attorneys had security clearances, they were not granted full access to the

---

[621]   *See* Walton Letter of Oct. 11, 2013, at 1-2.

[622]   FISC Rule of Procedure 11.

[623]   In the case of particularized orders issued under Title I of FISA, a recipient of an order can refuse to comply, in which case the government may seek to compel, setting up the opportunity for the recipient to challenge the order. The FAA provides that an electronic communication service provider receiving a directive issued under Section 702 may file a petition to modify or set aside such directive with the FISC, which shall have jurisdiction to review such petition. *See* 50 U.S.C. § 1881a(h)(4). Likewise, a person receiving a production order under Section 215 may challenge the legality of that order or of the nondisclosure provision that accompanies Section 215 orders by filing a petition with FISC. *See* 50 U.S.C. § 1861(f).

[624]   Specifically, in 2007, the government issued directives to Yahoo!, Inc., pursuant to the Protect America Act of 2007. Yahoo! refused to comply, and the government filed a motion with the FISC to compel compliance. The court ordered and received briefing from both parties. *See In Re Directives,* 551 F.3d 1004 (FISA Ct. Rev. 2008).

information that DOJ attorneys submitted to the FISC.[625] Outside parties have participated as an amicus or friend of the court in several matters before the FISA court, but to date, those have involved proceedings seeking the release of various records and not an assessment of the government's legal authorization to conduct surveillance.[626]

FISA also established a Foreign Intelligence Court of Review ("FISCR"), comprised of three judges drawn from U.S. district courts or courts of appeals. These judges are also appointed by the Chief Justice of the United States and also serve staggered seven-year terms. The appellate jurisdiction of the FISCR was originally limited to reviewing the denial of applications.[627] Since 2006, when recipients of FISC orders under Section 215 were permitted to challenge those orders, the statute was amended to allow appeal to the FISCR whenever the FISA court denies a challenge to a Section 215 order.[628] Likewise, the FISA Amendments Act of 2008 granted electronic communication service providers the right to appeal FISC decisions denying challenges to directives issued under the FAA.[629] Appeals to the FISCR have been rare.[630] FISA does not provide a way for the FISCR to receive the views of other non-governmental parties on appeals pending before it. However, the court has in one case accepted amicus curiae or friend of the court briefs on a significant legal question pending before it.[631] FISA also provides that the Supreme Court of the United

---

[625]   At the PCLOB's November 4, 2013, hearing, Marc Zwillinger, of ZwillGen PLLC, testified regarding his experience representing Internet service providers before the FISC, including a challenge by five Internet service providers seeking the right to disclose information about the number of FISA orders they receive. He noted that the outside counsel in the case with security clearances were denied access to certain government filings. *See* Privacy and Civil Liberties Oversight Board, Transcript of Public Hearing, Consideration of Recommendations for Change: The Surveillance Programs Operated Pursuant to Section 215 of the USA PATRIOT Act and Section 702 of the Foreign Intelligence Surveillance Act, at 156-59 (Nov. 4, 2013), *available at* http://www.pclob.gov/. The litigation in this matter is ongoing.

[626]   *See* Walton Letter of July 29, 2013. Recently, the Center for National Security Studies sought permission to file an amicus brief urging that Section 215 does not permit bulk collection of telephone records in connection with the renewal of the Section 215 program. The FISC granted permission for CNSS to file such an amicus brief, but only in a miscellaneous docket where it can be accessed by any FISC judge. *See* Memorandum Opinion, *In re Application of the Federal Bureau of Investigation for an Order Requiring the Production of Tangible Things* No. BR 13-158 (FISA Ct. Dec. 18, 2013).

[627]   50 U.S.C. § 1803(b).

[628]   *See* 50 U.S.C. § 1861(f)(2). This provision was added as part of the modifications to Section 215 by the USA PATRIOT Improvement and Reauthorization Act of 2005, Pub. L. No. 109-177, 120 Stat. 191 (2006).

[629]   Electronic communications service providers may also appeal an adverse decision when the DOJ has moved to compel their compliance with such a directive. *See* 50 U.S.C. § 1881a(h)(6).

[630]   Only two opinions from the FISCR have been released. These are *In Re Sealed Case,* 310 F.3d 717 (FISA Ct. Rev. 2002) (an appeal by the government), and *In Re Directives,* 551 F.3d 1004 (FISA Ct. Rev. 2008) (an appeal by Yahoo! in the case described above). Based upon the best information available to the Board, these are the only two cases decided by the FISCR to date.

[631]   *See In Re Sealed Case,* 310 F.3d 717 (FISA Ct. Rev. 2002).

States has jurisdiction to review FISCR decisions,[632] but to date, no FISC decision has come before the Supreme Court for review.[633]

IV.   Proposals for Reform of the FISC Process

In recent months, numerous proposals have been offered to modify the process by which the FISA court considers government applications, especially in cases involving novel legal or technical issues. These proposals have arisen in part from a concern that the FISC's *ex parte*, classified proceedings do not take adequate account of positions other than those of the government. In considering these proposals, the Board gives great weight to two points: that the FISC, its judges, their staff, and the government lawyers who appear before the court operate with integrity and give fastidious attention and review to surveillance applications; but also that it is critical to the integrity of the process that the public have confidence in its impartiality and rigor.[634]

Proposals to change the FISA court process must take into account the imperative of secrecy in the application of some of the nation's most sensitive intelligence collection techniques; the importance of speed in responding to often fast-breaking events posing severe risk to the national security; the resource limits faced by the court and its judges (who carry an ordinary civil and criminal caseload in their "home" districts); and constitutional issues.

With those considerations in mind, we believe that some reforms are appropriate and would help bolster public confidence in the operation of the court. The most important reforms concern three sets of issues: (1) providing a greater range of views and legal arguments to the FISC as it considers novel and significant issues; (2) facilitating appellate review of such decisions; and (3) providing increased opportunity for the FISC to receive technical assistance and legal input from outside parties. In addition, in the next section of this Report, we discuss and make recommendations regarding the need for greater public transparency for the legal opinions adopted by the court.

---

[632]   50 U.S.C. § 1803(b), § 1861a(f), § 1881a(h)(6), § 1881a(i)(4).

[633]   The Supreme Court has not heard any appeals of FISC orders, nor has it ever considered the merits of a FISA order or ruled on the constitutionality of the statue. In *Clapper v. Amnesty International USA*, 133 S. Ct. 1138 (2013), the Court held that the petitioners lacked standing to bring a constitutional challenge to the FAA, and on November 18, 2013, the Court denied a mandamus petition filed by the Electronic Privacy Information Center that had sought to challenge the FISC's order approving the Section 215 telephony metadata program. *See In Re Electronic Privacy Information Center*, No. 13-58 (U.S. Nov. 18, 2013).

[634]   The PCLOB heard from three judges who formerly served on the FISC. Judge James Robertson, who served on the FISC from 2002 through 2005, participated in the Board's July 9, 2013, public workshop; Judge James Carr, who served on the FISC from 2002 through 2008, participated in our November 4, 2013, public hearing; Judge John Bates, who served on the Court from 2006 to February, 2013 and as its presiding judge from 2009 to 2013, met with the Board on October 16, 2013.

V.   Recommendations Regarding FISC Operations

Recommendation 3. Congress should enact legislation enabling the FISC to hear independent views, in addition to the government's views, on novel and significant applications and in other matters in which a FISC judge determines that consideration of the issues would merit such additional views.

Although the FISC continues to review applications for individualized FISA warrants, in the past decade it has also been called upon to evaluate requests for broader collection programs, such as the 215 telephony metadata program, and to review extensive compliance reports regarding the implementation of the surveillance authorized under Section 702. This expansion of the FISC's jurisdiction has presented it with complex and novel issues of law and technology. Currently, these issues are adjudicated by the court based only on filings by the government, supplemented by the research and analysis of the judges and their experienced legal staff.

Our judicial system thrives on the adversarial presentation of views. As Judge Robertson noted:

> [A]nybody who has been a judge will tell you that a judge needs to hear both sides of a case before deciding. It's quite common, in fact it's the norm to read one side's brief or hear one side's argument and think, hmm, that sounds right, until we read the other side.[635]

Nonetheless, the *ex parte* process works well when the FISC is considering individualized applications presenting no novel legal or technical questions. The inquiry there is fact-based, and the legal standard is familiar and explicit in the statute. Consideration of individualized surveillance applications is a function that judges in other courts all over the country routinely perform on an *ex parte* basis, and it is no less appropriate in the national security context.

However, there is a growing consensus that the *ex parte* approach is not the right model for review of novel legal questions or applications involving broad surveillance programs that collect information about the communications of many people who have no

---

[635]   Privacy and Civil Liberties Oversight Board, Transcript of Workshop Regarding Surveillance Programs Operated Pursuant to Section 215 of the USA PATRIOT Act and Section 702 of the Foreign Intelligence Surveillance Act, at 34 (July 9, 2013) (statement of Judge James Robertson); *see also* Privacy and Civil Liberties Oversight Board, Transcript of Public Hearing, Consideration of Recommendations for Change: The Surveillance Programs Operated Pursuant to Section 215 of the USA PATRIOT Act and Section 702 of the Foreign Intelligence Surveillance Act, at 151 (Nov. 4, 2013) (testimony of Judge James Carr) ("[I]t's how we [judges] work, through the adversary process."), *available at* http://www.pclob.gov/.

apparent connection to terrorism. [636] The Board believes that, when FISC judges are considering requests for programmatic surveillance affecting numerous individuals or applications presenting novel issues, they should have the opportunity to call for third-party briefing on the legal issues involved. In addition to assisting the court, a mechanism allowing FISC judges to call upon independent expert advocates for a broader range of legal views could bolster the public's trust in its operations and in the integrity of the FISA system overall.

Accordingly, the Board recommends that Congress amend FISA to authorize the FISC to create a pool of "Special Advocates" who would be called upon to present independent views to the court in important cases. Even in the absence of such legislative authority, the Board believes the court has discretion to call upon outside lawyers, if they have the necessary national security clearances, to offer analysis of legal or technical issues, and the Board would urge the court to amend its rules to allow for such advocacy. However, it would be preferable to have a statutory basis for such a system.

The Board has examined the myriad bills introduced in Congress and proposals offered by advocates, scholars and others. The Board does not attempt to draft legislative language or to express views on which program details should be expressed in statute and which may be left to court rules of procedure. However, the Board has identified key elements of an advocacy process that should offer the court the benefit of outside expert participation without unduly disturbing the structure or functioning of the vast majority of the court's proceedings.

To serve this purpose, Congress should authorize the establishment of a panel of outside lawyers to serve as Special Advocates before the FISC in appropriate cases. These lawyers would not become permanent government employees, but would be available to be called upon to participate in particular FISC proceedings. The presiding judge of the FISC should select the attorneys to serve on the panel. The attorneys should be drawn from the private sector, and the Board expects that they would possess expertise in national security, privacy and civil liberties issues and be capable of obtaining appropriate security clearances. The attorneys would need office space with appropriate secure facilities, ideally within the FISA court. Congress should ensure that the FISC has adequate appropriations to

---

[636]   *See* Transcript of July 9, 2013 Public Workshop, *supra*, at 34-37 (statement of Judge James Robertson); Transcript of November 4, 2013 Hearing, *supra*, at 148-52 (testimony of Judge James Carr). Judge Carr also presented his views in a *New York Times* op-ed, *see* James G. Carr, *A Better Secret Court*, N.Y. TIMES (July 22, 2013), and in testimony before the Senate Judiciary Committee. *See* Prepared Remarks of James G. Carr, Senior U.S. District Judge, N.D. Ohio, *Senate Judiciary Committee Hearing: Strengthening Privacy Rights and National Security: Oversight of FISA Surveillance Programs* (July 31, 2013), *available at* http://www.judiciary.senate.gov/pdf/7-31-13CarrTestimony.pdf.

implement and operate the Special Advocate program. The Board is confident that such a system would not raise any serious constitutional issues.[637]

In the Board's view, the FISC should have discretion to choose the applications or other matters on which it would seek the Special Advocate's views. In such cases, the FISC judge assigned to the matter would call upon one of the lawyers on the Special Advocate panel to participate in it. The FISC can establish specific rules for inviting a Special Advocate's participation, including whether the lawyers on the panel would be invited on a rotating basis. The Board expects that the court would invite the Special Advocate to participate in matters involving interpretation of the scope of surveillance authorities, other matters presenting novel legal or technical questions, or matters involving broad programs of collection, but would not mandate the participation of the Special Advocate in any particular case. In addition, the Board would leave flexibility for a FISC judge to identify other matters that merit Special Advocate participation. The Board does not believe it is necessary or appropriate for Special Advocates to participate in all applications for individualized FISA orders, but the court should have the option of seeking input when such applications present novel legal or technical questions.

The role of the Special Advocate, when invited by the court to participate, would be to make legal arguments addressing privacy, civil rights, and civil liberties interests. The Board does not propose requiring the Special Advocate to serve as the government's adversary, as opposing lawyers would do in traditional litigation. The Special Advocate should not be expected to oppose every argument made by the government. Rather, the Special Advocate would review the government's application and exercise his or her judgment about whether the proposed surveillance or collection is consistent with law or unduly affects privacy and civil liberties interests. The Special Advocate would rely on both statutory and constitutional arguments as appropriate. The Special Advocate would have discretion to make legal arguments opposing the application in its entirety, advocating modifications to the application that would address privacy and civil liberties-related legal concerns, or to conclude that the application was lawful and did not unduly burden privacy or civil liberties.

As noted above, current FISC Rule of Procedure 11 requires that if an application involves any novel issues, including novel issues of technology or law, the government must advise the FISC in writing of the nature and significance of the issue and submit a memorandum explaining the novel technique or legal interpretation. This existing

---

[637] For example, the Appointments Clause would not be implicated because the role we suggest would not provide the Special Advocate with the requisite legal authority to qualify as an officer under this clause. *See* Andrew Nolan, Richard M. Thompson II, & Vivian S. Chu, *Introducing a Public Advocate into the Foreign Intelligence Surveillance Act's Courts: Select Legal Issues*, CONGRESSIONAL RESEARCH SERVICE, at 8-13 (Oct. 25, 2013) (outlining circumstances under which a public advocate role might cause an Appointments Clause problem).

requirement provides a useful mechanism to trigger consideration of whether Special Advocate participation would be beneficial. If the presiding judge determined that Special Advocate participation would be helpful based on the government's Rule 11 submission, the judge could immediately invite Special Advocate participation. Otherwise, FISC rules could require that, upon receiving such a notification, the presiding judge should seek a Special Advocate's preliminary views on whether the matter poses privacy or civil rights issues and whether the judge's resolution of these issues would benefit from Special Advocate participation. Upon reviewing the Special Advocate's submission, the judge would determine whether to invite his or her full participation.

However, the circumstances prescribed in FISC Rule 11 are not the only circumstances where participation by the Special Advocate might be appropriate. FISC judges should also consider inviting Special Advocate participation for applications to *renew* already approved programs or implementations of techniques. This may be appropriate in matters that raised issues that were novel or significant at the time the *original* application was filed but were not fully considered at that time; matters in which intervening circumstances have raised issues that did not exist at the time of the original application; or in other matters where the judge concludes that it would be helpful to have a more thorough briefing with a diversity of views presented.

Once a Special Advocate has been invited to participate with respect to an application or other matter, the Special Advocate should be permitted to participate in all proceedings related to that application or matter and should have access to all government filings.

The procedures for participation by a Special Advocate should recognize that Special Advocate participation might not be possible in emergency circumstances before electronic surveillance begins. Tracking the existing rules for emergency employment of electronic surveillance under FISA, the procedures should permit the Special Advocate to participate when the court subsequently reviews the application after commencement of the emergency surveillance.

The Board does not intend this proposal to confer on the Special Advocate any absolute right to participate in any matter. Instead, the Board intends that Special Advocate participation would be at the discretion of the court. Based on statements by former FISC judges, the Board believes that the FISC judges themselves will find value in hearing the views of independent advocates in difficult cases. Their experience with and dedication to the more expansive proceedings in their regular district court roles will insure that the Special Advocate will be invited to participate in the type of novel and difficult cases that have inspired the current debate.

One of the policy underpinnings of the Board's recommendation is that providing an independent voice in FISC proceedings will increase public confidence in the integrity of those proceedings. Toward this end, the Board recommends that the rules for the Special Advocate program be made public and that the Attorney General provide regular and public reports on the program's operation. Those recommendations are discussed in detail in the next section of this Report concerning transparency.

Recommendation 4. Congress should enact legislation to expand the opportunities for appellate review of FISC decisions by the FISCR and for review of FISCR decisions by the Supreme Court of the United States.

Over the past decade, the FISC has generated a significant body of law interpreting FISA authorities and other potentially applicable statutes, and analyzing related constitutional questions. However, FISC opinions have been much less likely to be subject to appellate review than the opinions of ordinary federal courts. Virtually all proponents of FISC reform, including judges who have served on the court, agree that there should be a greater opportunity for appellate review of FISC decisions by the FISCR and for review of the FISCR's decisions by the Supreme Court of the United States.[638] Providing for greater appellate review of FISC and FISCR rulings will strengthen the integrity of judicial review under FISA. Providing a role for the Special Advocate in seeking that appellate review will further increase public confidence in the integrity of the process.

Identifying the precise mechanism by which the Special Advocate could seek appellate review of a FISC decision that has rejected arguments based on alleged infringements of privacy or civil liberties is a hard task, but such a mechanism should not be impossible to design.

There are two basic ways in which the Special Advocate could seek judicial review of a FISC order: by directly filing a petition for review with the FISCR of orders that the Special Advocate believes are inconsistent with FISA or the Constitution; or by requesting that the FISC certify an appeal of its order. Under either approach, the Board would expect the Special Advocate, in deciding whether to seek an appeal, to exercise his or her judgment about the importance of the legal questions at stake and the severity of the implications for

---

[638]   *See, e.g.,* Transcript of November 4, 2013 Hearing, *supra,* at 148-52 (testimony of Judge James Carr) ("[C]ertainly, in my day-to-day functions as an ordinary Article III judge, it [appellate review] is very important."). *See also* Angela Canterbury (Project On Government Oversight), Kel McClanahan (National Security Counselors), & Patrice McDermott (OpenTheGovernment.org), Submission to the Privacy and Civil Liberties Oversight Board, at 4 (Aug. 1, 2013) (recommending that attorney representing the public "have the opportunity to appeal adverse decisions"), *available at* http://www.regulations.gov/#!documentDetail;D=PCLOB-2013-0005-0029; Gregory T. Nojeim (Center for Democracy and Technology), Submission to the Privacy and Civil Liberties Oversight Board, at 6-7 (Aug. 1, 2013) (recommending that ombudsman representing civil liberties interests be able to address "whether an order that is granted should be appealed to the FISA Court of Review"), *available at* http://www.regulations.gov/#!documentDetail;D=PCLOB-2013-0005-0034.

privacy or civil liberties. The Special Advocate would not be considered an adversary in the traditional sense, and would not be required to seek an appeal of every order that did not adopt the position he or she took before the FISC.

If Congress were to adopt the first approach, the Board would recommend a structure allowing the Special Advocate to file a petition with the FISCR seeking review of a FISC order and giving the FISCR discretionary review of the petition. This would be similar to the process of seeking certiorari in the Supreme Court of the United States. Congress or the FISCR could enact or adopt standards by which the FISCR would decide which petitions to grant, similar to the standards by which the Supreme Court decides when to grant a petition for certiorari.[639] If the FISCR granted review, the Special Advocate would be permitted to participate in the matter, just as in the FISC. Similarly, Congress could authorize the Special Advocate to file a petition for certiorari seeking the Supreme Court's review of a FISCR decision in which the Special Advocate had participated. This approach would be consistent with the Board's recommendation above, which grants the court some discretion to manage the Special Advocate's role in proceedings. It also would have the benefit of allowing the Special Advocate to appeal without the permission of the court that issued the order in question.

Under the second approach, Congress would enact legislation authorizing FISC judges to certify their decisions to the FISCR for review. The Special Advocate would be eligible to file a motion with the FISC requesting the court to certify its decision to the FISCR and, if it were denied by the FISC, to appeal that denial. The Special Advocate could participate in any appellate proceedings that followed. In addition, Congress could amend 28 U.S.C. § 1254(2) to add the FISCR as a court authorized to certify a question of law to the Supreme Court for review,[640] and the Special Advocate could be authorized to petition the FISCR to certify its decision to the Supreme Court for review. Under this approach, the decision whether to certify a case for review to the FISCR would be left to the discretion of the FISC or the FISCR, and the decision whether to certify a case for review to the Supreme Court would be left to the discretion of the FISCR.

Both approaches avoid concerns by some commentators that a Special Advocate lacks Article III standing to directly appeal a FISC decision.[641]

---

[639]   *See* Rules of the Supreme Court of the United States, Rule 10 (July 1, 2013), *available at* http://www.supremecourt.gov/ctrules/2013RulesoftheCourt.pdf.

[640]   This statute currently provides that one of the methods by which cases in the courts of appeals may be reviewed by the U.S. Supreme Court is as follows: "By certification at any time by a court of appeals of any question of law in any civil or criminal case as to which instructions are desired, and upon such certification the Supreme Court may give binding instructions or require the entire record to be sent up for decision of the entire matter in controversy." 28 U.S.C. § 1254(2).

[641]   *See e.g.,* Andrew Nolan, Richard M. Thompson II, & Vivian S. Chu, *Introducing a Public Advocate into the Foreign Intelligence Surveillance Act's Courts: Select Legal Issues*, CONGRESSIONAL RESEARCH SERVICE, at 20-24

Our recommendations for enhancing appellate review are based on the assumption that, as with traditional litigation in federal court, a FISC order would take effect immediately unless the court granted a stay of its order. Thus, when a Special Advocate appeals or seeks certification of an appeal of a FISC order, the surveillance approved by the FISC should generally be permitted to proceed pending any further review. The Special Advocate should be permitted to file a motion for a stay pending appeal that, if granted, would prohibit the government from immediately undertaking the approved surveillance. The government should be allowed to oppose this order and, as with similar stay motions in U.S. District Court, the FISC judge should determine whether to grant the stay. If the motion is denied, the Special Advocate should also be permitted to file similar motions in the FISCR and Supreme Court. FISA Section 103(f) already makes clear that judges of the FISC and FISCR and justices of the Supreme Court have the authority to order such stays pending review.

Recommendation 5. The FISC should take full advantage of existing authorities to obtain technical assistance and expand opportunities for legal input from outside parties.

FISC judges should take advantage of their ability to appoint Special Masters or other technical experts to assist them in reviewing voluminous or technical materials, either in connection with initial applications or in compliance reviews.

In addition, the FISC and the FISCR should develop procedures to facilitate amicus participation by third parties in cases involving questions that are of broad public interest, where it is feasible to do so consistent with national security. The Board recognizes that it will be difficult to take advantage of amicus participation by parties who lack national security clearances and cannot be privy to the facts of the case. Nevertheless, the fact that there has already been a case in which the FISCR has accepted input from amici and the FISC's recent order granting permission for the filing of an amicus brief[642] demonstrate that it is sometimes possible. The Special Advocate could advise the FISC or FISCR that amicus participation would be helpful in a particular case and ask the court to provide appropriate public notice of the opportunity for amicus participation.

(Oct. 25, 2013); Marty Lederman & Steve Vladeck, *The Constitutionality of a FISA "Special Advocate,"* JUST SECURITY (Nov. 4, 2013), http://justsecurity.org/2013/11/04/fisa-special-advocate-constitution/. The Board does not take a position on whether these concerns about lack of standing would ultimately prevail in litigation.

[642] *See* Memorandum Opinion, *In re Application of the Federal Bureau of Investigation for an Order Requiring the Production of Tangible Things* No. BR 13-158 (FISA Ct. Dec. 18, 2013).

Part 9:
DISCUSSION AND RECOMMENDATIONS REGARDING TRANSPARENCY

I.   Introduction

In a representative democracy, the tension between openness and secrecy is inevitable and complex. The challenges are especially acute in the area of intelligence collection, where the powers exercised by the government implicate fundamental rights and our enemies are constantly trying to understand our capabilities in order to avoid detection. In this context, both openness and secrecy are vital to our survival, and we must strive to develop and implement intelligence programs in ways that serve both values.[643]

Transparency is one of the foundations of democratic governance.[644] Our constitutional system of government relies upon the participation of an informed electorate. This in turn requires public access to information about the activities of the government. Transparency supports accountability. It is especially important with regard to activities of the government that affect the rights of individuals, where it is closely interlinked with redress for violations of rights.

There are also instrumental benefits to openness, as summarized by the Moynihan Commission:

> Broad access to information promotes better decisions. It permits public understanding of the activities of government and promotes more informed debate and accountability. It increases the Government's ability to respond to criticism and justify its actions to the public. It makes possible the free exchange of scientific information and encourages new discoveries that foster economic growth. By allowing a better understanding of our history, it provides opportunities to learn lessons from the past, and it makes it easier to quash unfounded speculation about the Government's past actions. Reducing the amount of information in the classification system allows for better management and cost controls of that system and increases respect for the information that needs to stay protected. Greater access thus provides ground in which the public's faith in its government can flourish.[645]

---

[643]   "Protecting information critical to our Nation's security and demonstrating our commitment to open Government . . . are equally important priorities." Exec. Order No. 13,526 (Dec. 29, 2009).

[644]   *See* Exec. Order No. 13,292 (Mar. 25, 2003) ("Our democratic principles require that the American people be informed of the activities of their Government").

[645]   Report of the Commission on Protecting and Reducing Government Secrecy ("Moynihan Commission Report"), S. Doc. No. 105-2 at 49-50 (1997), *available at* http://www.fas.org/sgp/library/moynihan/index.html. The Moynihan Commission report remains one of

In the intelligence context, transparency regarding collection authorities and their exercise can increase public confidence in the intelligence process and in the monumental decisions that our leaders make based on intelligence products.[646] With respect to electronic surveillance in particular, where the government depends on the cooperation of service providers and those service providers in turn depend for their commercial success on the trust of their customers, transparency, if coupled with a system of appropriate controls, can help boost public confidence in the security and confidentiality of communications services. Public disclosure showing that certain techniques are applied with more precision and under stricter controls than many fear can help allay concerns, benefiting U.S.-based companies in the global marketplace. Transparency also works in tandem with other forms of oversight and control, alerting Congress, courts, inspectors general and others, including this Board, to issues that merit deeper scrutiny in public and classified settings. As the 9/11 Commission noted, "[s]ecrecy, while necessary, can also harm oversight."[647]

However, we must also recognize the critical functions served by government secrecy. To quote again from the Moynihan Commission:

> Effective secrecy has proven indispensable to the functioning of government, serving the interests not only of the officials in power but of the governed as well. . . . The primary objective of government secrecy in the national security realm . . . is to protect U.S. interests by controlling information that provides an advantage (including the element of surprise) over an adversary or prevents that adversary from gaining an advantage that could damage the United States. . . . The maintenance of secrecy has proven essential to the successful development, implementation, and completion (or, conversely, the abandonment) of plans and missions. . . . The successful conduct of plans and missions in turn may depend on protecting key technologies. . . . Secrecy also is essential to the effective conduct of diplomatic negotiations. . . . Closely linked to [these] is the protection of internal policy deliberations: the negotiations among government officials that precede and accompany the development of the plans, missions, and external negotiations cited above. . . . Thus, drafts and memoranda used in negotiations often remain classified

---

the best sources on both the importance of protecting secrets and the costs of secrecy. *See id.* at 6-10 (discussing both principles).

[646]   *See* Nick Hopkins, *Former NSA Chief: Western Intelligence Agencies must be more Transparent*, THE GUARDIAN (Sept. 30, 2013) (quoting former NSA Director Michael Hayden: "It's clear to me now that in liberal democracies the security services don't get to do what they do without broad public understanding and support. And although the public cannot be briefed on everything, there has to be enough out there so that the majority of the population believe what they are doing is acceptable.").

[647]   9/11 Commission Report, *supra*, at 103.

even when the final positions and statements do not. . . . Finally, secrecy is essential in protecting confidential relationships with individuals.[648]

Despite widespread support for balancing openness and secrecy, there has been equally widespread consensus within and without the government that the system tilts too far in the direction of secrecy.[649] Even officials who themselves have implemented the classification system have long been saying that the government has far too many secrets.[650]

Undoubtedly, "we can, and must, be more transparent."[651] The question is how. Generalities about the value of transparency do not go far in answering the hard questions of what can be disclosed and what must remain secret. Instead, progress may best be achieved by considering specific problems.[652] In that spirit, our focus here will be on transparency with regard to the Section 215 program, the opinions of the FISC, and statistical reporting on the government's use of FISA authorities. Insights garnered with respect to those three concrete matters may have broader value regarding transparency about other legal authorities of the government that affect the rights of individuals and about the scope of the exercise of those powers.

---

[648]   Moynihan Commission Report, *supra*, at 6-7.

[649]   There is a long history of official studies finding that too much information is classified. In 1956, the Defense Department Committee on Classified Information found that "overclassification has reached serious proportions." DEF. DEP'T COMM. ON CLASSIFIED INFO., REPORT TO THE SECRETARY OF DEFENSE BY THE COMMITTEE ON CLASSIFIED INFORMATION 6 (1956). Forty years later, the Moynihan Commission found that the information classification system sought to protect far too much information while not effectively protecting the most important secrets. *See* Moynihan Commission Report, *supra*. Fifteen years after that, the Public Interest Declassification Board ("PIDB"), an advisory committee established by Congress, concluded that the current classification system "keeps too many secrets, and keeps them too long." Public Interest Declassification Board, *Transforming the Security Classification System*, at 2 (Nov. 2012), *available at* http://www.archives.gov/declassification/pidb/recommendations/transforming-classification.html. For summaries of other official condemnations of overclassification, *see* Steven Aftergood, *Reducing Government Secrecy: Finding What Works*, 27 YALE L. & POL'Y. REV. 399, 404-07 (2009).

[650]   *See, e.g.*, IC21: The Intelligence Community in the 21st Century: Hearing before H. Permanent Select Comm. on Intelligence, 104th Cong., at 204 (July 27, 1995) (testimony of former National Security Advisor Brent Scowcroft) ("I think there is no question that we classify too much."). Former Deputy Under Secretary of Defense for Intelligence and Security Carol Haave told a House subcommittee in 2004 that the amount of defense information that is overclassified or unnecessarily classified could be as much as fifty percent. Too Many Secrets: Overclassification as a Barrier to Critical Information Sharing: Hearing before the Subcomm. On National Security, Emerging Threats and International Relations before H. Comm. on Gov't Reform, 108th Cong., at 82 (Aug. 24, 2004) (testimony of Carol Haave).

[651]   President Barack Obama, Remarks by the President in a Press Conference at the White House (Aug. 9, 2013), *available at* http://www.whitehouse.gov/the-press-office/2013/08/09/remarks-president-press-conference.

[652]   *See* Steven Aftergood, *Reducing Government Secrecy: Finding What Works*, *supra*, at 407-14.

We expect to return to transparency in our future work.[653] In our first semi-annual report, issued before the Snowden leaks, the Board identified transparency as a cross-cutting issue that it intended to pursue. In part, this Report contributes to that goal, as we seek to describe the Section 215 telephone metadata program in a more comprehensive and accurate way than has been done anywhere else so far.[654] We plan to provide a similarly detailed picture of the Section 702 program in a subsequent report.

II.   Recent Developments

In the aftermath of the Snowden disclosures, the government has released a substantial amount of information on the leaked government surveillance programs. These official disclosures have helped foster greater public understanding of government surveillance programs, although there remains a deep well of distrust.

In August 2013, following the President's directive, the Office of the Director of National Intelligence ("ODNI") created a new public website, "IC on the Record." Through this website, the ODNI has released thousands of pages of documents related to the Section 215 and 702 programs as well as other material regarding FISA and the operation of the FISC more generally. The site also compiles a variety of public statements by government officials on these topics, including press statements and congressional testimony.

The FISA court has also newly created a website where it posts pleadings, orders and other materials.[655] Recently, public interest groups have initiated proceedings in the

---

[653]   Promoting appropriate transparency in counterterrorism programs is an express part of the PCLOB's statutory mandate. Our authorizing statute charges the Board with making our reports public, holding public hearings, and otherwise informing the public of our activities, as appropriate and in a manner consistent with the protection of classified information and applicable law. *See* 42 U.S.C. § 2000ee(f).

[654]   A group of 53 non-governmental organizations joined in a letter to the PCLOB on July 9, 2013, asking that the PCLOB seek disclosure "of sufficient information to enable the public to understand the existing legal authorities for national security surveillance of Americans and the administration's interpretation of their scope, and to permit an informed public debate on government surveillance."

[655]   U.S. Foreign Intelligence Surveillance Court Public Filings (Beginning June 2013), *available at* http://www.uscourts.gov/uscourts/courts/fisc/index.html.

FISC seeking release of FISC decisions[656] and seeking the ability to participate in proceedings on future government applications for renewal of FISA programs.[657]

There have also been increased disclosures under the Freedom of Information Act, a cornerstone of our system of transparency whose limitations in the national security arena are well known. Some of the documents newly released to the public by the government have been released in lawsuits filed under FOIA years before the Snowden leaks.[658] After the Snowden leaks, the government has confirmed the existence of these programs, defined the scope of documents discoverable in the litigation relatively broadly, and moved expeditiously to create redacted versions of classified documents for release.

However, to date the official disclosures relate almost exclusively to specific programs that had already been the subject of leaks, and we must be careful in citing these disclosures as object lessons for what additional transparency might be appropriate in the future. Any harm to national security was already done with Snowden's illegal disclosures. Additional material has been officially disclosed to correct misperceptions caused by fragmentary leaks, but in part such disclosures were considered appropriate because it was judged that the marginal additional harm to national security would be minimal.

The reactive nature of the government's disclosures gives little insight into what principles should guide transparency in any programs not yet disclosed or still on the drawing board. Nor do we yet have insights into what in retrospect the intelligence

---

[656]   In one case pending before the FISC where public interest groups sought disclosure of a FISC opinion issued on February 19, 2013 interpreting Section 215, Judge Saylor ordered the government to submit a detailed explanation of its conclusion that it was unable to create a redacted version of that opinion. *In re: Orders of this Court Interpreting Section 215 of the Patriot Act*, No. Misc. 13-02 (FISA Ct. Nov. 20, 2013), *available at* http://www.uscourts.gov/uscourts/courts/fisc/misc-13-02-order-131120.pdf. The government responded on December 20, 2013, indicating that it had created a proposed redacted opinion for the court's review. *See* Submission of the United States in Response to the Court's November 20, 2013 Order. *Id.* (FISA Ct. December 20, 2013), *available at* http://www.uscourts.gov/uscourts/courts/fisc/br13-02-order-131230.pdf.

[657]   In addition to seeking permission to file an amicus brief, as described earlier, the Center for National Security Studies' petition sought to require the government to file a public application and have the FISC sit en banc when the FISC considered renewal of Section 215 orders in January 2014. Although the FISC granted permission for CNSS to file an amicus brief, it denied the other requests. *See In re: Application of the FBI for an Order Requiring the Production of Tangible Things*, No. BR 13-158 (FISA Ct. December 18, 2013), *available at* http://www.uscourts.gov/uscourts/courts/fisc/br13-158-Memorandum-131218.pdf.

[658]   Years before the Snowden leaks, the American Civil Liberties Union and the Electronic Frontier Foundation had filed FOIA lawsuits seeking information on the government's interpretation and application of Sections 215 and 702. *See American Civil Liberties Union v. Federal Bureau of Investigation*, No. 11-7562 (S.D.N.Y. 2011) (FOIA suit seeking records concerning the FBI's use and interpretation of Section 215); *Electronic Frontier Foundation v. U.S. Department of Justice*, No. 11-5221 (N.D. Cal. 2011) (Section 215 FOIA); *see also Electronic Frontier Foundation v. U.S. Department of Justice*, No. 12-1441 (D.D.C. 2012) (Section 702 FOIA).

community believes might have been disclosed earlier in the case of the leaked programs without unreasonable risk to national security.

The Board believes that the government must take the initiative and formulate long-term solutions that promote greater transparency for government surveillance policies more generally, in order to inform public debate on technology, national security, and civil liberties going beyond the current controversy over the Section 215 and 702 programs. In this effort, all three branches have a role.

There are some guideposts for how to draw the lines that need to be drawn to actually implement transparency in a responsible way. Some recent examples suggest possible criteria for transparency.

III.   Transparency by the Executive Branch

On March 22, 2012, the Office of the Director of National Intelligence and the Department of Justice announced that they had adopted revised guidelines on the access, retention, use, and dissemination by the National Counterterrorism Center ("NCTC") of information in databases of other agencies containing non-terrorism information. The ODNI and DOJ issued a press release about the guidelines[659] and posted the guidelines themselves on the Internet.[660] The announcement attracted immediate media attention.[661] Public interest organizations published analyses of the guidelines.[662] The ACLU produced a redline comparing the revised guidelines to the prior version.[663] *The Wall Street Journal* further investigated the background of the guidelines' development and published a major

---

[659]   Office of the Director of National Intelligence and U.S. Department of Justice Joint Statement, "Revised Guidelines Issued to Allow the NCTC to Access and Analyze Certain Federal Data More Effectively to Combat Terrorist Threats" (Mar. 22, 2012), *available at* http://www.dni.gov/index.php/newsroom/press-releases/96-press-releases-2012/528-odni-and-doj-update-guidelines-for-nctc-access,-retention,-use,-and-dissemination-of-information-in-datasets-containing-non-terrorism-information.

[660]   Guidelines for Access, Retention, Use, and Dissemination by the National Counterterrorism Center and Other Agencies of Information in Datasets Containing Non-Terrorism Information (March 2012), *available at* http://www.nctc.gov/docs/NCTC%20Guidelines.pdf.

[661]   *See* Charlie Savage, *U.S. Relaxes Limits on Use of Data in Terror Analysis*, N.Y. TIMES (Mar. 22, 2012).

[662]   John Malcom, Jessica Zuckerman and Andrew Kloster, *New National Counterterrorism Center Guidelines Require Strong Oversight*, HERITAGE FOUNDATION (Feb. 21, 2013), *available at* http://www.heritage.org/research/reports/2013/02/new-national-counterterrorism-center-guidelines-require-strong-oversight; Chris Calabrese, *The Biggest New Spying Program You've Probably Never Heard Of*, ACLU (July 30, 2012), *available at* https://www.aclu.org/blog/national-security-technology-and-liberty/biggest-new-spying-program-youve-probably-never-heard; Rachel Levinson-Waldman, *What the Government Does with Americans' Data*, BRENNAN CENTER FOR JUSTICE, at 19-22 (Oct. 2013), *available at* http://www.brennancenter.org/publication/what-government-does-americans-data.

[663]   2008 National Counterterrorism Center Guidelines Redlined with 2012 Changes, ACLU (July 27, 2012), *available at* https://www.aclu.org/national-security/2008-national-counterterrorism-center-guidelines-redlined-2012-changes.

story in December 2012.[664] Later, the ODNI's privacy office issued an information paper describing the civil liberties and privacy protections in the updated guidelines.[665]

The government's decision to write the guidelines in unclassified form not only supported press and advocacy inquiry, but also served to bring the guidelines to the attention of oversight entities, which could then pursue further classified oversight. In fact, soon after PCLOB members began substantive work, in December 2012, we sought and received one of several in-depth briefings on the guidelines from the NCTC, followed by a briefing from the Department of Homeland Security.

The release of the NCTC guidelines is only one example of the preparation and release of key policy documents in unclassified form. The Attorney General Guidelines on FBI investigations, which govern not only criminal investigations but also investigations for foreign intelligence purposes, are unclassified. The FBI's massive manual of investigative procedures is largely public, covering not only criminal investigations, but also national security matters, and describing in great detail the situations in which various investigative techniques are used.[666] Key criteria for operation of the nation's airline passenger screening system were publicly developed through a notice and comment proceeding,[667] and substantial information about the program, including a Privacy Impact Assessment, is published online.[668]

These and other disclosures about key national security programs that involve the collection, storage and dissemination of personal information show that it is possible to describe practices and policies publicly, even those that have not been otherwise leaked, without damage to national security or operational effectiveness. Of course, the targets of investigation are secret, and may remain so indefinitely in the case of national security investigations. But a very wide range of legal authorities is laid out, along with the criteria for exercising them.

---

[664]   Julia Angwin, *U.S. Terrorism Agency to Tap a Vast Database of Citizens*, WALL STREET JOURNAL (Dec. 13, 2012).

[665]   Office of the Director of National Intelligence, Civil Liberties and Privacy Office, "Description of Civil Liberties and Privacy Protections Incorporated in the Updated NCTC Guidelines" (January 2013), *available at* http://www.nctc.gov/docs/CLPO_Information_Paper_on_NCTC_AG_Guidelines_-_1-22-13.pdf.

[666]   FBI Domestic Investigations and Operations Guide (DIOG) (2011 Version), *available at* http://vault.fbi.gov/FBI%20Domestic%20Investigations%20and%20Operations%20Guide%20%28DIOG%29/fbi-domestic-investigations-and-operations-guide-diog-2011-version/.

[667]   Department of Homeland Security, Transportation Security Administration, Secure Flight Program Final Rule, 73 Fed. Reg. 64018 (Oct. 28, 2008), *available at* http://www.gpo.gov/fdsys/pkg/FR-2008-10-28/html/E8-25432.htm.

[668]   Transportation Security Administration, Secure Flight Program, http://www.tsa.gov/stakeholders/secure-flight-program.

IV. Transparency in the Legislative Process

When Section 215 was adopted in 2001 to authorize applications for FISA court orders requiring production of "any tangible things," there was no mention in the public record that it was intended to provide legal justification for the bulk collection of business records. (There is also no indication that there was any non-public discussion of using the statute in that way, as the bulk collection programs were just beginning when Section 215 was adopted and those nascent bulk programs were proceeding under different legal theories not involving approval of the FISA court). When the statute was revised and reauthorized in 2005–2006, there was no also indication on the public record that it would provide the legal justification for bulk collection, although by then the existence of bulk collection programs was known to some members of Congress. During the 2005-2006 reauthorization debate, critics of Section 215 speculated that it could be used to acquire entire data sets, although none speculated that it could be used to justify ongoing collection, and the government's public statements did not address bulk collection. By the time Section 215 was up for renewal in 2011, it was known to some members of Congress that the statute was being used to support bulk collection, and the DOJ provided Congress with a classified description of the NSA's telephone and Internet bulk collection programs.[669] But public references by Senators familiar with the program to "sensitive sources and collection methods" and "secret legal interpretations"[670] were so guarded that there was no public discussion of bulk collection.[671]

With full respect for the pressure confronting Congress and the executive branch in the years after 9/11 and up until this very day, we do not believe that the process surrounding the application of Section 215 to bulk collection comported with the kind of public debate that best serves the development of policy affecting the rights of Americans.[672] Even where classified intelligence operations are involved, the "purposes

---

[669]   See pages 97 to 99 of this Report.

[670]   Statement of Senator Ron Wyden re: Patriot Act Reauthorization (May 26, 2011) ("[W]hen the American people find out how their government has secretly interpreted the Patriot Act, they will be stunned and they will be angry.... Members of the public have no access to the executive branch's secret legal interpretations, so they have no idea what their government thinks this law means.") *available at* http://www.wyden.senate.gov/news/press-releases/in-speech-wyden-says-official-interpretations-of-patriot-act-must-be-made-public.

[671]   In an indication of how little information was made available to the public, one close observer of the surveillance debates mistakenly concluded in 2011 that there was "fairly persuasive" evidence that Senator Wyden was referring to the collection of geolocation data — the one piece of metadata that the government was in fact *not* collecting under the 215 program. *See* Julian Sanchez, *Atlas Bugged: Why the "Secret Law" of the Patriot Act is Probably About Location Tracking*, CATO AT LIBERTY (May 27, 2011), http://www.cato.org/blog/atlas-bugged-why-secret-law-patriot-act-probably-about-location-tracking.

[672]   Referring generally to the "many legal novelties and legal hurdles that the administration faced after 9/11," former Assistant Attorney General Jack Goldsmith concluded, "The administration's failure to engage Congress deprived the country of national debates about the nature of the threat and its proper response that

and framework" of a program for domestic intelligence collection should be debated in public.[673] Here we are talking specifically about the legislative process and programs that are intended to be ongoing; different considerations may apply, for example, when a statute is being applied case-by-case to unique fact situations. Also, during the process of developing legislation, some hearings and briefings may need to be conducted in secret to ensure that policymakers fully understand the intended use of a particular authority. But the government should not base an ongoing program affecting the rights of Americans on an interpretation of a statute that is not apparent from a natural reading of the text. Either the statute should be amended or, if the statute is subject to periodic reauthorization, the legal interpretation extending the statute to a new program should be made public before the statute is reauthorized.

In the case of Section 215, the government should have made it publicly clear in the reauthorization process that it intended for Section 215 to serve as legal authority to collect data in bulk on an ongoing basis. It should have been possible for the government to describe criteria for selecting categories of data for acquisition as well as procedures around storage and use of such data. It may have been appropriate to withhold the specific categories of data (telephony metadata) that the government intended to collect. Certainly, once the program was statutorily authorized, it would be appropriate to keep secret the names of the telephone carriers subject to the FISC orders. A description of the power sought would have avoided the many legal questions now being raised about the government's interpretation of Section 215, such as the scope of the "relevance" standard, the use of the statute for ongoing disclosures, and the extent to which bulk collection under Section 215 may conflict with other statutes.

---

would have served an educative and legitimating function regardless of what emerged from the process. The go-it-alone strategy minimized the short-term discomforts to the Executive branch of public debate, but at the expense of medium-term Executive Branch mistakes. When the Executive Branch forces Congress to deliberate, argue, and take a stand, it spreads accountability and minimizes the recriminations and other bad effects of the risk taking that the President's job demands." *See* Preserving the Rule of Law in the Fight Against Terrorism, Hearing before the Senate Judiciary Committee (Oct. 2, 2007) (statement of Jack Landman Goldsmith), *available at* http://www.judiciary.senate.gov/hearings/testimony.cfm?id=e655f9e2809e5476862f735da12ecadc&wit_id =e655f9e2809e5476862f735da12ecadc-1-1.

[673]   Privacy and Civil Liberties Oversight Board, Transcript of Public Hearing, Consideration of Recommendations for Change: The Surveillance Programs Operated Pursuant to Section 215 of the USA PATRIOT Act and Section 702 of the Foreign Intelligence Surveillance Act, 290-93 (Nov. 4, 2013) (testimony of Jane Harmon, former Member of Congress and Member of House Armed Services, Homeland Security, and Intelligence Committees), *available at* http://www.pclob.gov/.

V.   Release of FISC and FISCR Opinions

Since 9/11, and especially since 2004, the FISA court has confronted novel and significant legal questions, as the government has brought various programs under the FISA system, as the statute itself has been amended, including to add new authorities, and as technology and the government's capabilities have evolved. Consequently, in the past ten years the court has issued a substantial body of opinions on statutory and constitutional questions.[674] These opinions discuss and approve the underlying legal rationale for government activities and address the implications of compliance issues and other matters raised by the sometimes unique conditions judges are imposing on the operation of approved programs. In short, these opinions describe (often in very accessible language) the scope of the government's authority and the ways in which that authority is implemented in contexts affecting the rights of Americans. There is thus public interest in the disclosure of these opinions.

FISA requires that "The record of proceedings under this chapter, including applications made and orders granted, shall be maintained under security measures established by the Chief Justice in consultation with the Attorney General and the Director of National Intelligence."[675] Until recently, with two exceptions from 1981 and 2002, FISC opinions were written in a totally classified fashion, without an eye to publication in any form, with facts and law tightly interwoven. The recent release of opinions regarding already leaked programs offers, in itself, little insight into how to maximize disclosure of legal opinions.

Nevertheless, there is precedent for public disclosure of opinions on sensitive intelligence matters. Early in the history of FISA, a FISC opinion was written in unclassified form on a question of law (whether the court had the authority to issue orders approving physical searches).[676] Since 9/11, two opinions of the FISCR were released at the time they were issued, with relatively few redactions.[677] Regular Article III courts have been

---

[674]   If our recommendations on creation of a Special Advocate are implemented, the number of opinions may increase at an even greater rate. And while the FISCR has heard relatively few cases, that too would change if our recommendations are implemented for creating a path for appellate review of FISC decisions.

[675]   50 U.S.C. § 1803(c).

[676]   *In re Application of the United States for an Order Authorizing the Physical Search of Nonresidential Premises and Personal Property*, slip op. (FISA Ct. June 11, 1981) (in case preceding enactment of amendment to FISA providing explicit authority for physical searches, court found that it lacked such authority). *See also In Re All Matters Submitted to the Foreign Intelligence Surveillance Court*, 218 F. Supp.2d 611 (FISA Ct. 2002) (addresses government request to permit greater sharing of information between law enforcement and intelligence personnel in the aftermath of September 11th), *rev'd sub nom. In Re Sealed Case* 310 F.3d 717 (FISA Ct. Rev. 2002).

[677]   *In Re Sealed Case* 310 F.3d 717 (FISA Ct. Rev. 2002), and *In Re Directives*, 551 F.3d 1004 (FISA Ct. Rev. 2008). Based upon the best information available to the Board, these are the only two cases decided by the FISCR to date.

grappling with secrecy issues in opinions on habeas petitions by Guantanamo detainees and in other matters. Combining the best of the methods applied by judges so far, redactions can be grouped together so that the rest of the text remains uninterrupted and comprehensible, the significance of the redacted information to the holding could be explained, and unclassified summaries of the redacted paragraphs could be added.[678]

In recent months, we are told that the FISC judges have begun drafting their opinions with the expectation that they may be declassified and released in redacted form.[679] We believe that, as a general rule, FISA court judges can write their opinions in such a way as to separate specific facts peculiar to the case at hand from broader legal analyses. This trend is one that we view as a significant step toward greater transparency not only with regard to already disclosed programs, but also with respect to other matters that may arise. Prospectively, we encourage the FISA court to write opinions with an eye to declassification. We also believe that there is significant value in producing declassified versions of earlier opinions. We realize that the process of redacting opinions written during a period of presumed secrecy will be more difficult and will burden individuals with other pressing duties, but we believe that it is appropriate to make the effort where those opinions and orders complete the historical picture of the development of legal doctrine regarding matters within the jurisdiction of the FISC.

We therefore recommend that the government undertake a classification review of all significant FISC opinions and orders involving novel interpretations of law, beginning with opinions describing the legal theories relied upon for widespread collection of metadata from Americans not suspected of terrorist affiliations, to be followed by opinions involving serious compliance issues.

We note one other transparency matter concerning the FISC. Should the government adopt our recommendation for a Special Advocate in the FISC, the nature of that advocate's role must be transparent to be effective. The FISC should publicly disclose any rules the court adopts governing the advocate's participation in proceedings. In addition, the Attorney General should regularly and publicly report statistics on the frequency of Special Advocate participation including the number of times Special Advocates have sought review of FISC decisions in the FISCR and the U.S. Supreme Court.

---

[678] Michael A. Sall, *Classified Opinions: Habeas at Guantanamo and the Creation of Secret Law*, 101 GEO. L.J. 1147, 1167 (citing, *inter alia*, *Parhat v. Gates*, 532 F.3d 834, 844 (D.C. Cir. 2008)).

[679] For example, Judge Eagan's August 29, 2013 opinion and order reauthorizing the Section 215 bulk telephony metadata program were released in redacted form less than one month after issuance. The declassified version of the opinion as well as the accompanying order containing Judge Eagan's legal analysis includes very few redactions. *See* Amended Memorandum Opinion, *In re Application of the Federal Bureau of Investigation for an Order Requiring the Production of Tangible Things*, No. BR 13-109 (FISA Ct. Aug. 29, 2013).

VI.   Increased Public Reporting

One important way to understand and assess any government program is numerically — to categorize its critical elements and count them. Periodic public reporting on surveillance programs is a valuable tool promoting accountability and public understanding. When the government was seeking reauthorization of the Patriot Act, it publicly released detailed numerical information about the use of sunsetting authorities as a way of reassuring Congress and the public that the authorities were being used in a targeted and limited fashion.[680] When FISA was first adopted in 1978, it included a provision requiring the Attorney General every year to transmit to Congress a report setting forth the total number of applications made for FISA surveillance and the total number of such orders either granted, modified, or denied.[681] The reports, while skeletal, have never been classified.[682] Since 1978, Congress amended FISA to require the government to provide to Congress additional information, including a breakdown of the number of persons targeted under the statute's various authorities.[683] These more detailed reports, however, are classified and the granularity of public reporting remains very limited.

We recommend that the government should also increase the level of detail in its unclassified reporting to Congress and the public regarding surveillance programs. It is important to ensure that any public reporting does not aid our adversaries. However, we believe that publication of additional numerical information on the frequency with which various surveillance authorities are being used would be possible without allowing terrorists to improve their tradecraft. To ensure that such information is meaningful, the government would have to distinguish between particularized programs and those involving bulk collection. In the case of targeted programs, the government should disclose how many orders have been issued and how many individuals have been targeted.

---

[680]   *See, e.g.*, Hearing before the Subcommittee on Crime, Terrorism, and Homeland Security of the House Judiciary Committee, 109th Cong. at 8-9 (April 28, 2005) (statement of Kenneth Wainstein) ("As of March 30, 2005, federal judges have reviewed and granted the Department's request for a section 215 order 35 times. To date, the provision has only been used to obtain driver's license records, public accommodations records, apartment leasing records, credit card records, and subscriber information, such as names and addresses, for telephone numbers captured through court-authorized pen registers and trap-and-trace orders (a pen register records the numbers a telephone dials and a trap-and-trace device records the numbers from which it receives calls). The Department has not requested a section 215 order to obtain library or bookstore records, medical records, or gun sale records."), *available at* http://www.justice.gov/archive/ll/subs/testimony/042805-usa-wainstein.pdf.

[681]   Pub. L. 95-511, 92 Stat. 1783, 1795 (1978) (codified at 50 U.S.C. § 1807).

[682]   For a collection of these reports, see the Federation of American Scientists' website: https://www.fas.org/irp/agency/doj/fisa/#rept.

[683]   *See* 50 U.S.C. §§ 1862, 1871.

In recent years, U.S. companies have begun publishing reports showing, country by country, how many government demands they receive for disclosure of user data (and how often they receive demands for takedown of content.) The companies find these reports useful in building and maintaining customer trust. However, the secrecy of FISA orders and National Security Letters limits the ability of private sector entities to disclose to their customers the scope of government surveillance or data disclosure demands. The United States is one of few countries that permit any publication of figures on government surveillance, but the unique position of the United States in the global communications infrastructure puts unique pressure on companies headquartered here. Some Internet service providers have sought permission to voluntarily disclose statistics regarding the number of government FISA requests they have received and the number of their customers affected.[684] Government officials have opposed these requests in part on the grounds that such statistics would reveal government capabilities and could indicate to would-be terrorists which providers to favor and which to avoid. The government has indicated, however, that it may be possible to provide aggregate statistics in a way that does not jeopardize national security in this fashion. We urge the government to work with the companies to reach agreement on standards allowing reasonable disclosures of aggregate statistics that would be meaningful without revealing sensitive government capabilities or tactics.

Beyond public reporting, FISA requires the Attorney General to "fully inform" the Senate and House Intelligence and Judiciary Committees regarding the government's activities under certain sections of FISA including Section 215.[685] FISA also requires the government to provide the congressional committees with copies of "all decisions, orders, or opinions of the FISC or FISC that include significant construction or interpretation" of the provisions of FISA. These two reporting requirements facilitate congressional oversight. The Board urges the government to extend this complete reporting to the PCLOB as well, to facilitate the Board's oversight role.

---

[684] Google, Inc., Microsoft Corporation, Yahoo! Inc., Facebook, Inc., and LinkedIn Corporation have filed declaratory judgment actions in the FISC seeking permission to disclose such statistics, and additional providers have filed motions seeking permission to participate in the cases as friends of the court. The FISC has created a public docket of these filings. *See* FISA Ct., Nos. Misc. 13-03, Misc. 13-04, Misc. 13-05, Misc. 13-06, & Misc. 13-07, *available at* http://www.uscourts.gov/uscourts/courts/fisc/index.html.

[685] *See* 50 U.S.C. §§ 1808, 1846, 1862, 1871, 1881f. Reporting requirements under Sections 1808 and 1862 do not include the House Judiciary Committee, but the other sections include all four committees.

VII.   Recommendations to Promote Transparency

Recommendation 6. To the maximum extent consistent with national security, the government should create and release with minimal redactions declassified versions of new decisions, orders and opinions by the FISC and FISCR in cases involving novel interpretations of FISA or other significant questions of law, technology or compliance.

FISC judges should continue their recent practice of drafting opinions in cases involving novel issues and other significant decisions in the expectation that declassified versions will be released to the public. This practice has facilitated declassification review. The government should promptly create and release declassified versions of these FISC opinions.

Recommendation 7. Regarding previously written opinions, the government should perform a declassification review of decisions, orders and opinions by the FISC and FISCR that have not yet been released to the public and that involve novel interpretations of FISA or other significant questions of law, technology or compliance.

Although it may be more difficult to declassify older FISC opinions drafted without expectation of public release, the release of such older opinions is still important to facilitate public understanding of the development of the law under FISA. The government should create and release declassified versions of older opinions in novel or significant cases to the greatest extent possible consistent with protection of national security. This should cover programs that have been discontinued, where the legal interpretations justifying such programs have ongoing relevance. The Board acknowledges the cumulative burden of these transparency recommendations, especially as the burden of review for declassification may fall on the same individuals who are responsible for preparing new FISA applications, overseeing compliance with existing orders, and carrying out other duties. The Board urges the government to develop and announce some prioritization plan or approach. We recommend beginning with opinions describing the legal theories relied upon for widespread collection of metadata from Americans not suspected of terrorist affiliations, to be followed by opinions involving serious compliance issues.

Recommendation 8. The Attorney General should regularly and publicly report information regarding the operation of the Special Advocate program recommended by the Board. This should include statistics on the frequency and nature of Special Advocate participation in FISC and FISCR proceedings.

These reports should include statistics showing the number of cases in which a Special Advocate participated, as well as the number of cases identified by the government as raising a novel or significant issue, but in which the judge declined to invite Special

Advocate participation. The reports should also indicate the extent to which FISC decisions have been subject to review in the FISCR and the frequency with which Special Advocate requests for FISCR review have been granted. The Attorney General can make such reports without the need for a congressional directive. However, Congress might amend FISA's reporting requirement to require the Attorney General to report in unclassified form on the number of matters in which the government notified the court of a novel issue under Rule 11 and, in such cases, the number of times the FISC invited Special Advocate participation.[686] In addition to providing such regular public reports, the Attorney General should include statistics and information on operation of the Special Advocate as part of the Attorney General's obligation under 50 U.S.C. § 1871(a)(5) to submit to congressional committees copies of all decisions or opinions of the FISC that include significant construction or interpretation of the provisions of FISA.

The FISC should also make public any rules adopted by the FISC governing the Special Advocate's participation in court proceedings.

> ***Recommendation 9. The government should work with Internet service providers and other companies that regularly receive FISA production orders to develop rules permitting the companies to voluntarily disclose certain statistical information. In addition, the government should publicly disclose more detailed statistics to provide a more complete picture of government surveillance operations.***

The Board understands that the government has engaged in discussions with certain communications service providers that are seeking permission to publish statistics about the number of government surveillance and data disclosure requests they receive per year. The Board urges the government to pursue these discussions to determine the maximum amount of information that could be published in a way that is consistent with protection of national security. In addition, the government should itself release annual reports showing in more detail the nature and scope of FISA surveillance for each year. The government disclosures showing the number of orders or demands directed to private entities could be provided in numerical ranges and aggregated for all providers, but they should be separated by the type of FISA authority involved. Thus, for example, all Section

---

[686]   Since FISA first came into effect, the government has filed in unclassified form the report required under Section 107 of the Act covering certain annual statistics regarding the number of FISA applications and orders. 50 U.S.C. § 1807. Over the years, those reports have become somewhat longer with the addition of further reporting requirements. Compare the report for 1979, https://www.fas.org/irp/agency/doj/fisa/1979rept.html, with the report for 2012, https://www.fas.org/irp/agency/doj/fisa/2012rept.pdf.   Section 502 of the Act, 18 U.S.C. § 1862, regarding business records, specifically requires unclassified reporting of these statistics, and Section 118 of the USA PATRIOT Improvement and Reauthorization Act, Pub. L. 109-177, 120 Stat. 192, 217 (2006), requires unclassified reports on use of National Security Letter authorities.

215 requests for all companies could be aggregated, but Section 215 statistics would be reported separately from requests under other FISA authorities.

The Board recognizes that company-by-company reporting presents certain difficulties, as does reporting of the number of customers affected. On the one hand, so long as one FISA order can encompass multiple accounts, a simple statement of the number of demands received will not indicate how many accounts or customers are affected. On the other hand, if a company is allowed to report the number of customers affected (even in ranges), if its numbers suddenly jump from the range of hundreds or thousands of customers affected to millions or hundreds of millions, that would immediately signal that that particular company has received a bulk collection demand, a fact that may be operationally sensitive. At the very least, both government and companies need to agree on the rules for reporting numbers of customers affected. Perhaps, the content versus non-content distinction is relevant: Companies could be permitted to disclose the number of customers or accounts affected by FISA acquisitions of content, but not by bulk collections of metadata.[687]

The problem could be further mitigated if the Board's recommendation regarding transparency of bulk collection authorities is adopted. The government could indicate how many orders for bulk collection it has obtained, and under which legal authority, without disclosing which companies have received bulk collection orders. Otherwise, if a statute such as Section 215 continues to be used as the basis both for individualized collection and bulk collection, the mere number of Section 215 orders could be misleading. Despite the attention that has been given to numerical reporting, mere numbers can be misleading. A key thrust of the Board's recommendations is that the government should first and foremost explain, to the extent possible, what it is doing and should contextualize the numbers that it issues.

> ***Recommendation 10. The Attorney General should fully inform the PCLOB of the government's activities under FISA and provide the PCLOB with copies of the detailed reports submitted under FISA to the specified committees of Congress. This should include providing the PCLOB with copies of the FISC decisions required to be produced under Section 601(a)(5).***

> ***Recommendation 11. The Board urges the government to begin developing principles and criteria for transparency.***

---

[687]   Our suggestions here focus on FISA authorities and are also relevant to National Security Letters. Our recommendations do not address reporting of activities under Executive Order 12333. It has become clear in recent months that E.O. 12333 collection poses important new questions in the age of globalized communications networks, but the Board has not yet attempted to address those issues.

The Board has offered some initial suggestions about how lines can be drawn in the future around the disclosure of legal authorities. The Board urges the Administration to commence the process of articulating principles and criteria for deciding what must be kept secret and what can be released as to existing and future programs that affect the American public.

Recommendation 12. The scope of surveillance authorities affecting Americans should be public.

In particular, the Administration should develop principles and criteria for the public articulation of the legal authorities under which it conducts surveillance affecting Americans. If the text of the statute itself is not sufficient to inform the public of the scope of asserted government authority, then the key elements of the legal opinion or other document describing the government's legal analysis should be made public so there can be a free and open debate regarding the law's scope. This includes both original enactments such as 215's revisions and subsequent reauthorizations.

The Board's recommendation distinguishes between "the purposes and framework" of surveillance authorities and factual information specific to individual persons or operations. While sensitive operational details regarding the conduct of government surveillance programs should remain classified, and while legal interpretations of the application of a statute in a particular case may also be secret so long as the use of that technique in a particular case is secret, the government's interpretations of statutes that provide the basis for ongoing surveillance programs affecting Americans can and should be made public. This includes intended uses of broadly worded authorities at the time of enactment as well as post-enactment novel interpretations of laws already on the books.

Part 10:
CONCLUSION

Our nation is protected by men and women devoted to the rule of law. In talking to dozens of career employees throughout the intelligence agencies, we found widespread dedication to the Constitution and eagerness to comply with whatever rules are laid down by Congress and the judiciary. We are grateful to the employees of the intelligence community for their cooperation with this study, and for working tirelessly to keep us safe. None of the comments in this Report should be read in any way as a criticism of their integrity. We hope that this Report is viewed as a contribution to our shared mission of protecting America from terrorism while also preserving "the precious liberties that are vital to our way of life."[688]

---

[688] National Security Intelligence Reform Act, § 1061(b)(1), as amended by Pub. L. 110-53, section 801 (2007) (codified at 42 U.S.C. § 2000ee(b)).

<u>**ANNEX A**</u>

Separate Statement by Board Member Rachel Brand

I commend the Board and our tiny staff for putting together this comprehensive Report while simultaneously struggling to establish our still-infant agency. Although I disagree with much of the Report's discussion and some of its recommendations, this may be the most thorough description and analysis of the Section 215 bulk telephony metadata collection program ("Section 215 program") that has been published to date.

I concur in most of the Board's recommendations, and I am pleased that we were able to achieve unanimity on so many of them. However, I write separately to briefly note several points on which I disagree with the Report. Most importantly, I dissent from the Board's recommendation to shut down the Section 215 program without establishing an adequate alternative.

Where I agree with the Board's Report

I join the Board's proposal to create a process for appointing an independent advocate to provide views to the Foreign Intelligence Surveillance Court ("FISC") in important or novel matters. (Recommendations 3-5.) Although I believe the FISC already operates with the same integrity and independence as other federal courts, I agree with the Board that some involvement by an independent third party will bolster public confidence in the FISC's integrity and strengthen its important role.

Of course, the devil is in the details. Meddling in a system that already works well is risky. Any proposal to change the FISC's operations must, among other things, ensure that the FISC can continue to operate very quickly; not jeopardize the security of the sensitive materials reviewed by the court; provide adequate resources to account for an increased burden on the court; and allow the FISC's judges to retain discretion and control over the participation of an independent advocate in any given case. I believe this Board's recommendations account for all of these considerations better than any of the other proposals that have been offered.

I also sign on to most of the Board's recommendations to provide greater transparency about the government's counterterrorism programs. (Recommendations 6-11.) I agree with the Board that additional transparency, where possible, promotes public confidence in our national security agencies. However, it is important to note that the Board recommends that transparency measures be adopted *to the extent consistent with national security.* It is this qualification that enables me to sign on to the core of those recommendations. I suspect I have a different view than some of my colleagues about how to implement each of the recommendations, but those details will be worked out in the future.

I do not sign on to the Board's discussion concerning Recommendation 12, because I do not believe that an intelligence program or legal justification for it must necessarily be known to the public to be legitimate or lawful.

Finally, I join the Board's recommendations for immediately modifying the Section 215 program (Recommendation 2) because I believe these changes will ameliorate privacy concerns while preserving the operational value of the program.

Where I disagree with the Board's Report

I cannot sign on to the substance of much of the Board's analysis. I am concerned that the Report gives insufficient weight to the need for a proactive approach to combating terrorism, and I hope that the Report will not contribute to what has aptly been described as cycles of "timidity and aggression" in the government's approach to national security.[689] After September 11, 2001, the public demanded to know why the government had not stopped those attacks. Fingers were pointed in every direction, and civil liberties and privacy considerations took a backseat in the public debate immediately following the attacks. Of course, the legal structure under which the agencies operated prior to 9/11 had been put into place in the 1970s as a reaction to the Church Committee's revelations of prior excesses and abuses by the Intelligence Community. Since the recent leaks of classified programs, the pendulum seems to be swinging sharply back in that direction. But I have no doubt that if there is another large-scale terrorist attack against the United States, the public will engage in recriminations against the Intelligence Community for failure to prevent it. These swings of the pendulum, though they may be an inevitable result of human nature, are an unfortunate way to craft national security policy, and they do a disservice to the men and women dedicated to keeping us safe from terrorism.

The primary value that this bipartisan, independent Board can provide is a reasoned, balanced approach, taking into account (as our statute requires) *both* civil liberties and national security interests. We should not overreact to the crisis or unauthorized disclosure du jour, but take a longer view.

With these background considerations in mind, I turn to my reasons for dissenting from the Board's recommendation to shut down the Section 215 program.

The Board concludes that the Section 215 program is not legally authorized. I cannot join the Board's analysis or conclusion on this point.

---

[689] *See, e.g.,* Jack Goldsmith, The Terror Presidency, Law and Judgment Inside the Bush Administration 163-64 (2007).

The statutory question—whether the language of Section 215 authorizes the telephony bulk metadata program—is a difficult one. But the government's interpretation of the statute is at least a reasonable reading, made in good faith by numerous officials in two Administrations of different parties who take seriously their responsibility to protect the American people from terrorism consistent with the rule of law. Moreover, it has been upheld by many Article III judges, including over a dozen FISC judges and Judge Pauley in a thorough opinion in a regular, public proceeding in U.S. District Court.[690]

In light of this history, I do not believe this is a legal question on which the Board can meaningfully contribute. If we were addressing this as a matter of first impression, advising the government on whether to launch the program in the first place, we would need to grapple with this question of statutory construction. But we do not approach this question as a matter of first impression. It has been extensively briefed and considered by multiple courts over the course of several years. Some of those cases are ongoing. This *legal* question will be resolved by the courts, not by this Board, which does not have the benefit of traditional adversarial legal briefing and is not particularly well-suited to conducting *de novo* review of long-standing statutory interpretations. We are much better equipped to assess whether this program is sound as a *policy* matter and whether changes could be made to better protect Americans' privacy and civil liberties while also protecting national security.

Because the Board also concludes that the program should be shut down as a policy matter, it seems to me unnecessary and gratuitous for the Board to effectively declare that government officials and others have been operating this program unlawfully for years. I am concerned about the detrimental effect this superfluous second-guessing can have on our national security agencies and their staff. It not only undermines national security by contributing to the unfortunate "cycles of timidity and aggression" that I mentioned earlier, but is also unfair, demoralizing, and potentially legally harmful to the individuals who carry out these programs.

Turning to the constitutionality of the Section 215 program, I agree with the Board's ultimate conclusion that the program is constitutional under existing Supreme Court caselaw.[691] The Board appropriately states that government officials are entitled to rely on current law when taking action. But in speculating at great length about what might be the future trajectory of Fourth Amendment caselaw, it implicitly criticizes the government for not predicting those possible changes when deciding whether to operate the program.

---

690   *See* Memorandum & Order, *ACLU v. Clapper*, No. 13-3994 (S.D.N.Y. Dec. 27, 2013).

691   One federal judge recently reached the opposite conclusion, holding that the Section 215 program is likely unconstitutional. *See* Memorandum Opinion, *Klayman v. Obama*, No. 13-0851 (D.D.C. Dec. 16, 2013). This demonstrates that these are difficult legal questions that ultimately will be resolved by the courts.

Perhaps the Supreme Court will amend its views on the third-party doctrine or other aspects of Fourth Amendment jurisprudence in future cases. But that is beside the point in a Report addressing whether the government's actions were legal at the time they were taken and now. Surely government officials should be able to rely on valid Supreme Court precedent without being second-guessed years later by a Board musing on what legal developments might happen in the future.

Of course, the government must seriously consider whether it *should* take actions that intrude on privacy even if it *can* take them as a legal matter. Whether the Section 215 program should continue as a matter of good policy is a question squarely within the Board's core mandate and one that courts have not addressed and cannot resolve. However, I do not agree with the Board's conclusion that the program should be shut down.

Whether the program should continue boils down to whether its potential intrusion on privacy interests is outweighed by its importance to protecting national security.

Starting with the privacy question, on the one hand, any collection program on this scale gives me pause. As the Board discusses, metadata can be revealing, especially in the aggregate (though I do not agree with the Board's statement that metadata may be even "more" revealing than contents). Whenever the government possesses large amounts of information, it could theoretically be used for dangerous purposes in the wrong hands without adequate oversight. Even if there is no actual privacy violation when information is collected but never viewed, accessed, analyzed, or disseminated in any way, as is true of the overwhelming majority of data collected under the Section 215 program, collection and retention of this much data about American citizens' communications creates at least a *risk* of a serious privacy intrusion.

This is why I join the Board's recommendations for immediate modifications to the program (Recommendation 2), including eliminating the third "hop" and reducing the length of time the data is held. Based in part on the Board's lengthy discussions with government officials, I believe these changes would increase privacy protections without sacrificing the operational value of the program.

On the other hand, the government does not collect the content of any communication under this program. It does not collect any personally identifying information associated with the calls. And it does not collect cell site information that could closely pinpoint the location from which a cell phone call was made. The program is literally a system of numbers with no names attached to any of them. As such, it does not sweep in the most sensitive and revealing information about telephone communications. This seems to have gotten lost in the public debate.

In addition, the program operates within strict safeguards and limitations. The Board's Report describes these procedures, but it bears repeating just how hard it is for the government to make any use of the data collected under this program. For example, before even looking at what the database holds on a particular phone number, an NSA analyst must first be able to produce some evidence—enough to establish "reasonable, articulable suspicion" or "RAS"—that that particular phone number is connected to a specific terrorist group listed in the FISC's order. Only a handful of trained analysts are authorized do this. Before typing the phone number into a search field, the analyst must document the "RAS" determination in writing. And if the results of the query reveal a pattern of calls that seems worth investigating further, the analyst must jump through a series of additional hoops before gathering more information about the communications or distributing that information to other agencies. As a result, only an infinitesimal percentage of the records collected are ever viewed by any human being, much less used for any further purpose. [692]

With the safeguards already in place and the additional limitations this Board recommends, I believe the *actual* intrusion on privacy interests will be small.

On the other side of the equation is the national security value of the program. The Board concludes that the program has little, if any, benefit. I cannot join this conclusion.

There is no easy way to calculate the value of this program. But the test for whether the program's potential benefits justify its continuation cannot be simply whether it has already been the key factor in thwarting a previously unknown terrorist attack. Assessing the benefit of a preventive program such as this one requires a longer-term view.

The overwhelming majority of the data collected under this program remains untouched, unviewed, and unanalyzed until its destruction. But its immediate availability *if it is needed* is the program's primary benefit. Its usefulness may not be fully realized until we face another large-scale terrorist plot against the United States or our citizens abroad. But if that happens, analysts' ability to very quickly scan historical records from multiple service providers to establish connections (or avoid wasting precious time on futile leads) could be critical in thwarting the plot.

Evidence suggests that if the data from the Section 215 program had been available prior to the attacks of September 11, 2001, it could have been instrumental in preventing

---

[692]   As the Board discusses, there have been lapses in compliance with the program's limitations. Most of these violations have been minor and technical. A few have been significant, though apparently unintentional. Compliance problems are always a matter of concern and demonstrate the need for robust oversight. But it is important to remember that the lapses the Board mentions came to light only because the government *self-reported* violations to the FISC. Those problems were then corrected, under the supervision of the FISC. And these corrective measures and self-reporting occurred *before* these programs were publicly disclosed. That is, they were identified and fixed not because of the scrutiny brought about by an unlawful leak of classified information, but because existing oversight mechanisms worked.

those attacks.[693] The clear implication is that this data could help the government thwart a future attack. Considering this, I cannot recommend shutting down the program without an adequate alternative in place, especially in light of what I view to be the relatively small actual intrusion on privacy interests.

That said, if an adequate alternative that imposes less risk of privacy intrusions can be identified, the government should adopt it. The President appears to believe that the government can craft an alternative that retains the important intelligence capabilities of the program but reduces privacy concerns by storing the data outside the government. Although I expect this Board to have a role in crafting any such alternative and I look forward to those discussions, I doubt I could support a solution that transfers responsibility for the data to telephone service providers. This approach would make sense only if it both served as an effective alternative and assuaged privacy concerns, but I am skeptical it would do either. Because service providers are not required to retain all telephony metadata for any particular length of time, asking the service providers to hold the data could not be an effective alternative without legislatively mandating data retention. But data retention could increase privacy concerns by making the data available for a wide range of purposes other than national security, and would raise a host of questions about the legal status and handling of the data and the role and liabilities of the providers holding it. In my view, it would be wiser to leave the program as it is with the NSA than to transfer it to a third party.

Whatever happens to the Section 215 program in the short term, the government should frequently assess whether it continues to provide the potential benefits it is currently believed to have, including whether the incremental benefit provided by the program is eroded by the development of additional investigative tools. This process of re-evaluation should not consist merely of ad hoc conversations among individuals involved in the programs, but should be formalized, conducted at regular intervals with involvement by this Board, approved by officials at the highest levels of the Executive Branch, and briefed to the Intelligence and Judiciary Committees. I look forward to working with the intelligence agencies in conducting this analysis.

---

[693] *See, e.g., Oversight of the Federal Bureau of Investigation: Hearing before the H. Comm. on the Judiciary,* 113th Cong. 25-26 (2013) (statement of Robert S. Mueller III, Director, Federal Bureau of Investigation) (testifying that if the data from the Section 215 program had been available to investigators before 9/11, it would have provided an "opportunity" to prevent those attacks); Decl. of Teresa H. Shea, Signals Intelligence Director, Nat'l Sec. Agency, ¶ 35, Dkt. 63, in *Am. Civil Liberties Union v. Clapper, supra* note 2; Michael Morell, *Correcting the Record on the NSA Review,* WASH. POST, Dec. 27, 2013 (had data from the Section 215 program been available at the time, "it would likely have prevented 9/11").

ANNEX B

Separate Statement by Board Member Elisebeth Collins Cook

I appreciate the thorough work of my colleagues, as well as the staff, and agree with almost all of the recommendations of the Report. I think it bodes well for the future effectiveness of the Board that we are virtually unanimous as to the policy-based recommendations reflected in the Report, and I urge that serious consideration be given to each of recommendations two through eleven. I agree that to date the Executive Branch has failed to demonstrate that the program, as currently designed, justifies its potential risks to privacy, and for that reason I join the recommendations to immediately modify its operation. I also agree with the Board that modifications to the operations of the Foreign Intelligence Surveillance Court ("FISC") and an increased emphasis on transparency are warranted—to the extent such changes are implemented in a way that would not harm our national security efforts.

I must part ways with the Report, however, as to several points. First, although I believe the Section 215 program should be modified, I do not believe it lacks statutory authorization or must be shut down. Second, I do not agree with the Board's constitutional analysis of the program, as it is concerned primarily with potential evolution in the law, and the potential risks from programs that do not exist. Third, I write separately to emphasize that our transparency and FISC recommendations must be implemented in a way that is fully cognizant of their potential impact on national security. Finally, I disagree with the Board's analysis of the efficacy of the program.

Fundamentally, I believe that the Board has erred in its approach to this program, which has been (a) authorized by no fewer than fifteen Article III judges, (b) subject to extensive Executive branch oversight, and (c) appropriately briefed to Congress. The Board has been unanimous that as a policy matter the Program can and should be modified prospectively, including by limiting the analysis the National Security Agency ("NSA") could do with the records and the amount of time NSA could keep the records. The Board has nonetheless engaged in a lengthy and time-consuming retrospective legal analysis of the Program prior to issuing those recommendations. I am concerned that this type of backward-looking analysis, undertaken years after the fact, will impact the willingness and ability of our Intelligence Community to take the proactive, preventative measures that today's threats require. And there is no doubt that should the Intelligence Community fail to take those proactive, preventative measures, it will be blamed in the event of an attack.[694]

---

[694] By the same token, having undertaken this legal analysis, I do not understand the Board's apparent recommendation that the program it considers unauthorized continue for some interim period of time.

First, based on my own review of the statutory authorization, I conclude that the Section 215 program fits within a permissible reading of the Foreign Intelligence Surveillance Act business records provision.[695] I am not persuaded that the reading of the statute advanced by the government and accepted by the Foreign Intelligence Surveillance Court[696] and Judge Pauley of the United States District Court for the Southern District of New York[697] is the only reading of Section 215, but I am persuaded that it is a reasonable and permissible one. Perhaps as important, I think the program itself represented a good faith effort to subject a potentially controversial program to both judicial and legislative oversight and should be commended. Moreover, the program has been conducted pursuant to extensive safeguards and oversight. When mistakes were discovered (and mistakes will occur at any organization the size of the National Security Agency), they were self-reported to the court and briefed to appropriate congressional committees; corrective measures were implemented, and the program reauthorized by the FISC.[698]

Second, the Board has engaged in an extensive discussion of emerging concepts of Fourth Amendment jurisprudence, none of which I join. Our conclusion that the program does not violate the Fourth Amendment is unanimous, as it should be: *Smith v. Maryland* is the law of the land.[699] The government is entitled to rely on that decision, and the judges of the FISC (and our federal district and circuit courts) are required to do so, unless and until it is reversed. Analysis of whether, when, or how the Supreme Court may revisit that decision and its application is inherently speculative and unnecessary to the Board's report.

Nor do I join the Board's First Amendment analysis (which also informs the balancing/policy section). The First Amendment implications the Board finds compelling arise not from the Section 215 program but from perceived risks from a potential program that does not exist. Although the Board focuses on the "complete" pictures the NSA could paint of each and every American in concluding that it has a significant chilling effect, that is not an accurate description of the Section 215 program. The information the NSA receives *does not include the identity of the subscribers*. As the Board's Report acknowledges, a number is paired with its subscriber information (in other words,

---

[695]   *See* Pub. L. No. 107-56, § 215, 115 Stat. 272, 287 (2001) (codified as amended at 50 U.S.C. § 1861).

[696]   *See, e.g.,* Order, *In re Application of the Federal Bureau of Investigation for an Order Requiring the Production of Tangible Things*, No. BR 06-05 (FISA Ct. May 24, 2006); Amended Memorandum Opinion, *In re Application of the Federal Bureau of Investigation for an Order Requiring the Production of Tangible Things*, No. BR 13-109 (FISA Ct. Aug. 29, 2013).

[697]   *See* Memorandum & Order, *ACLU v. Clapper*, No. 13-3994 (S.D.N.Y. Dec. 27, 2013).

[698]   *See, e.g.,* Primary Order, *In re Application of the Federal Bureau of Investigation for an Order Requiring the Production of Tangible Things*, No. BR 09-13 (FISA Ct. Sept. 3, 2009).

[699]   *Smith v. Maryland*, 442 U.S. 735 (1979).

information that would allow the NSA or other agency to identify the person associated with the number) only after a determination is made that there is a reasonable, articulable suspicion that a number queried through the database is associated with one of the terrorist organizations identified in the FISC's orders. For a telephone number reasonably believed to be used by a U.S. person, the reasonable articulable suspicion standard cannot be met solely on the basis of activities protected by the First Amendment. Any investigative steps related to that number can be taken only after a determination that the number associated with its subscriber information has potential counterterrorism value. There is no disagreement that this process is applied to only an extraordinarily small percentage of the numbers in the database, yet the Board Report's balancing/policy and First Amendment analyses proceed as if each and every number of every American is systematically paired with its subscriber information and analyzed in great detail.

In addition, the Board nowhere meaningfully grapples with two key questions. One, what is the *marginal* constitutional and policy impact of the Section 215 program, particularly in view of the Board's assertion that essentially everything the Section 215 program is designed to accomplish can be accomplished through other existing national security and law enforcement tools? Two, is there a difference as a policy and constitutional matter between an order or program that is designed by its very terms to force disclosure of each and every individual's protected activities (such as the disclosure requirement addressed in *NAACP v. Alabama*[700]), and a program such as the one under consideration today, in which information is *collected* about innumerable individuals, but human eyes are laid on less than .0001% of individuals' information? To the Board, there is no apparent constitutional or policy difference between mere collection of information and actually accessing and using that information. I do not agree.

Third, I agree with the Report's recommendations as to transparency (except recommendation twelve) and the operations of the FISC, both sets of which are designed to foster increased confidence in the government's national security efforts. I also understand that each of our recommendations is to be implemented with full consideration of the potential impact on our national security, and without hindering the operations of the FISC. As to transparency, we have always understood that not everything can be publicly discussed, *see, e.g.,* U.S. Const. Art. I § 5, cl. 3. ("Each House shall keep a Journal of its Proceedings, and from time to time publish the same, excepting such Parts as may in their Judgment require Secrecy"), as we would like to avoid providing our adversaries with a roadmap to evade detection. The rational alternative, which occurred here, is to brief the relevant committees and members of Congress, seek judicial authorization, and subject a program to extensive executive branch oversight. In a representative democracy such as

---

[700]   *NAACP v. Alabama*, 357 U.S. 449 (1958).

ours, it is simply not the case that a particular use or related understanding of a statutory authorization is illegitimate unless it has been explicitly debated in an open forum.

Finally, I have a different view from the Board as to the efficacy and utility of the Section 215 program. Although the Report purports to consider whether the program might be valuable for reasons other than preventing a specific terrorist attack, the tone and focus of the Report make clear that the Board does believe that to be the most important (and possibly the only) metric. I consider this conclusion to be unduly narrow. Among other things, in today's world of multiple threats, a tool that allows investigators to triage and focus on those who are more likely to be doing harm to or in the United States is both good policy and potentially privacy-protective. Similarly, a tool that allows investigators to more fully understand our adversaries in a relatively nimble way, allows investigators to verify and reinforce intelligence gathered from other programs or tools, and provides "peace of mind," has value.

I would, however, recommend that the NSA and other members of the Intelligence Community develop metrics for assessing the efficacy and value of intelligence programs, particularly in relation to other tools and programs. The natural tendency is to focus on the operation of a given program, without periodic reevaluations of its value or whether it could be implemented in more privacy-protective ways. Moreover, the natural tendency of the government, the media, and the public is to ask whether a particular program has allowed officials to thwart terrorist attacks or save identifiable lives. Periodic assessments would not only encourage the Intelligence Community to continue to explore more privacy-protective alternatives, but also allow the government to explain the relative value of programs in more comprehensive terms. I hope that our Board will have the opportunity to work with the Intelligence Community on such an effort.

*   *   *   *   *   *   *

In many ways, the evaluation of this long-running program was the most difficult first test this Board could have faced. Unfortunately, rather than focusing on whether the program strikes the appropriate balance between the necessity for the program and its potential impacts on privacy and civil liberties, and moving immediately to recommend corrections to any imbalance, the Board has taken an extended period of time to analyze (a) statutory questions that are currently being litigated, and (b) somewhat academic questions of how the Fourth Amendment might be applied in the future and the First Amendment implications of programs that do not presently exist. I believe that with respect to this longstanding program, the highest and best use of our very limited resources[701] is instead found in our unanimous recommendations.

The development of a modified approach to the very difficult questions raised by the government's non-particularized collection of data presents an ideal opportunity for the Board to fulfill its statutory advisory and oversight role. In this regard, I would note that some frequently mentioned alternatives pose numerous potential difficulties in their own right. For example, some have suggested that the NSA could essentially request that the telephone companies run the queries, rather than collecting and retaining records for querying. However, even assuming the companies currently keep the relevant records, there is no guarantee that those records will continue to be retained in the future. By the same token, if another terrorist attack happens, the pressure will be immense to impose data retention requirements on those companies, which would pose separate and perhaps greater privacy concerns. Finally, it is not at all clear how a third party entity to hold the data could be structured in a way that would (a) be an adequate substitute for the Section 215 program and (b) preserve the security of those records, while (c) ameliorating the perceived privacy concerns raised by that program.

There is much to consider in the near future, and I look forward to working with my colleagues on these important issues.

---

[701] Although many agencies claim to lack adequate resources, the situation of the PCLOB is particularly remarkable. The agency currently has a full-time Chairman, four part-time Members limited to 60 days of work per year, and two permanent staff members. The decision to engage in such an extended discussion of largely hypothetical legal issues was therefore not without practical consequences: the Board has delayed consideration of the 702 program, and has not addressed any of the other issues previously identified by the Board as meriting oversight. Moreover, the decision of three Members of the Board to allocate the entirety of the permanent staff's time to the drafting of the Board Report, while simultaneously drafting and refining that Report until it went to the printer, has made a comparably voluminous response impossible.

ANNEX C

AGENDA OF PUBLIC WORKSHOP

HELD ON JULY 9, 2013

Link to Workshop transcript:

http://www.pclob.gov/All%20Documents/July%209,%202013%20Workshop%20Transcript.pdf

PRIVACY AND CIVIL LIBERTIES OVERSIGHT BOARD

Workshop Regarding Surveillance Programs Operated Pursuant to Section 215 of the USA PATRIOT Act and Section 702 of the Foreign Intelligence Surveillance Act

July 9, 2013

Renaissance Mayflower Hotel – Grand Ballroom
1127 Connecticut Ave NW, Washington D.C.

AGENDA

09:00   Doors Open

09:30 – 09:45   Introductory Remarks (David Medine, PCLOB Chairman)

09:45 – 11:30   Panel I: Legal/Constitutional Perspective
               Facilitators: Rachel Brand and Patricia Wald, Board Members

               Panel Members:
               - Steven Bradbury (Formerly DOJ Office of Legal Counsel)
               - Jameel Jaffer (ACLU)
               - Kate Martin (Center for National Security Studies)
               - Hon. James Robertson, Ret. (formerly District Court and Foreign Intelligence Surveillance Court)
               - Kenneth Wainstein (formerly DOJ National Security Division/ White House Homeland Security Advisor)

12:30 – 2:00 Panel II: Role of Technology
               Facilitators: James Dempsey and David Medine, Board Members
               Panel Members:

               - Steven Bellovin (Columbia University Computer Science Department)
               - Marc Rotenberg (Electronic Privacy Information Center)

- Ashkan Soltani (Independent Researcher and Consultant)
- Daniel Weitzner (MIT Computer Science and Artificial Intelligence Lab)

2:00 – 2:15   **Break**

2:15 – 4:00   **Panel III: Policy Perspective**
Facilitators: Elisebeth Collins Cook and David Medine, Board Members

Panel Members:
- James Baker (formerly DOJ Office of Intelligence and Policy Review)
- Michael Davidson (formerly Senate Legal Counsel)
- Sharon Bradford Franklin (The Constitution Project)
- Elizabeth Goitein (Brennan Center for Justice)
- Greg Nojeim (Center for Democracy and Technology)
- Nathan Sales (George Mason School of Law)

4:00 – 4:10   **Break**

4:10 – 4:30   **Open for Public Comment**

4:30   **Closing Comments (David Medine, PCLOB Chairman)**

Affiliations are listed for identification purposes only.

ANNEX D

AGENDA OF PUBLIC HEARING

HELD ON NOVEMBER 4, 2013

Link to Hearing transcript:

http://www.pclob.gov/SiteAssets/PCLOB%20Hearing%20-%20Full%20Day%20transcript%20Nov%204%202013.pdf

PRIVACY AND CIVIL LIBERTIES OVERSIGHT BOARD
PUBLIC HEARING

Consideration of Recommendations for Change:
The Surveillance Programs Operated Pursuant to Section 215 of the USA PATRIOT Act
and Section 702 of the Foreign Intelligence Surveillance Act
November 4, 2013

Renaissance Mayflower Hotel – Grand Ballroom
1127 Connecticut Ave NW, Washington D.C.

AGENDA

08:45   **Doors Open**

09:15 – 09:30   **Introductory Remarks (David Medine, PCLOB Chairman, with Board Members**
          Rachel Brand, Elisebeth Collins Cook, James Dempsey, and Patricia Wald)

09:30 – 11:45   **Panel I: Section 215 USA PATRIOT Act and Section 702 Foreign Intelligence**
          Surveillance Act

- **Rajesh De (General Counsel, National Security Agency)**
- **Patrick Kelley (Acting General Counsel, Federal Bureau of Investigation)**
- **Robert Litt (General Counsel, Office of the Director of National Intelligence)**
- **Brad Wiegmann (Deputy Assistant Attorney General, National Security Division, Department of Justice)**

11:45 – 1:15   **Lunch Break (on your own)**

1:15 – 2:30   Panel II: Foreign Intelligence Surveillance Court

- James A. Baker (formerly DOJ Office of Intelligence and Policy Review)
- Judge James Carr (Senior Federal Judge, U.S. District Court, Northern District of Ohio and former FISA Court Judge 2002-2008)
- Marc Zwillinger (Founder, ZwillGen PLLC and former Department of Justice Attorney, Computer Crime & Intellectual Property Section)

2:30 – 2:45   Break

2:45 – 4:15   Panel III: Academics and Outside Experts

- Jane Harman (Director, President and CEO, The Woodrow Wilson Center and former Member of Congress)
- Orin Kerr (Fred C. Stevenson Research Professor, George Washington University Law School)
- Stephanie K. Pell (Principal, SKP Strategies, LLC; former House Judiciary Committee Counsel and Federal Prosecutor)
- Eugene Spafford (Professor of Computer Science and Executive Director, Center for Education and Research in Information Assurance and Security, Perdue University)
- Stephen Vladeck (Professor of Law and the Associate Dean for Scholarship at American University Washington College of Law)

4:15   Closing Comments (David Medine, PLCOB Chairman)

All Affiliations are listed for identification purposes only.

ANNEX E

Request for Public Comments on Board Study

The Federal Register

The Daily Journal of the United States Government

56952 Federal Register/Vol. 78, No. 179/Monday, September 16, 2013/Notices
PRIVACY AND CIVIL LIBERTIES OVERSIGHT BOARD

[Notice–PCLOB–2013–06; Docket No. 2013– 0005; Sequence No. 6]

Notice of Hearing

A Notice by the <u>Privacy and Civil Liberties Oversight Board</u> on <u>10/25/2013</u>

Action

Notice Of A Hearing.

Summary

The Privacy and Civil Liberties Oversight Board (PCLOB) will conduct a public hearing with current and former government officials and others to address the activities and responsibilities of the executive and judicial branches of the federal government regarding the government's counterterrorism surveillance programs. This hearing will continue the PCLOB's study of the federal government's surveillance programs operated pursuant to Section 215 of the USA PATRIOT Act and Section 702 of Foreign Intelligence Surveillance Act. Recommendations for changes to these programs and the operations of the Foreign Intelligence Surveillance Court will be considered at the hearing to ensure that counterterrorism efforts properly balance the need to protect privacy and civil liberties. Visit *www.pclob.gov* for the full agenda closer to the hearing date. This hearing was re-scheduled from October 4, 2013, due to the unavailability of witnesses as a result of the federal lapse in appropriations.

DATES:

Monday, November 4, 2013; 9:00 a.m.-4:30 p.m. (Eastern Standard Time).

Comments:

You may submit comments with the docket number PCLOB-2013-0005; Sequence 7 by the following method:

- *Federal eRulemaking Portal:* Go to *http://www.regulations.gov*. Follow the on-line instructions for submitting comments.
- Written comments may be submitted at any time prior to the closing of the docket at 11:59 p.m. Eastern Time on November 14, 2013. This comment period has been extended from October 25, 2013, as a result of the new hearing date.

All comments will be made publicly available and posted without change. Do not include personal or confidential information.

ADDRESSES:

Mayflower Renaissance Hotel Washington, 1127 Connecticut Ave. NW., Washington D.C. 20036. Facility's location is near Farragut North Metro station.

FOR FURTHER INFORMATION CONTACT:

Susan Reingold, Chief Administrative Officer, 202-331-1986. For email inquiries, please email *info@pclob.gov*.

SUPPLEMENTARY INFORMATION:

Procedures for Public Participation

The hearing will be open to the public. Individuals who plan to attend and require special assistance, such as sign language interpretation or other reasonable accommodations, should contact Susan Reingold, Chief Administrative Officer, 202-331-1986, at least 72 hours prior to the meeting date.

Dated: October 21, 2013.

Diane Janosek,
Chief Legal Officer, Privacy and Civil Liberties Oversight Board.

https://www.federalregister.gov/articles/2013/10/25/2013-25103/notice-of-hearing

ANNEX F

Index to Public Comments received to PCLOB Docket No. 2013-005 on www.regulations.gov.

Comments Received on PCLOB Docket No. 2013-005

Can also view all entries at: http://www.regulations.gov/#!docketDetail;D=PCLOB-2013-0005

Entity submitting comment - listed in order as they appear on docket	Go to URL to see comment on Docket	Additional details:
Global Network Initiative (GNI)	http://www.regulations.gov/#!documentDetail;D=PCLOB-2013-0005-0027	GNI is a multi-stakeholder group of companies, civil society organizations (including human rights and press freedom groups), investors and academics
Private individual	http://www.regulations.gov/#!documentDetail;D=PCLOB-2013-0005-0044	
Nathan Sales	http://www.regulations.gov/#!documentDetail;D=PCLOB-2013-0005-0022	Panel member at PCLOB Workshop
European Digital Rights (EDRi) and the Fundamental Rights European Experts Group (FREE)	http://www.regulations.gov/#!documentDetail;D=PCLOB-2013-0005-0024	EDRi is an association of 35 digital civil rights organizations from 21 European countries. FREE is an association whose focus is on monitoring, teaching and advocating in the EU.
Michael Davidson	http://www.regulations.gov/#!documentDetail;D=PCLOB-2013-0005-0020	Panel member at PCLOB Workshop

Project On Government Oversight (POGO), National Security Counselors, and OpenTheGovernment.org.	http://www.regulations.gov/#!documentDetail;D=PCLOB-2013-0005-0029	
Center for National Security Studies	http://www.regulations.gov/#!documentDetail;D=PCLOB-2013-0005-0033	Kate Martin was a panel member at PCLOB Workshop
Michael Davidson-second submission	http://www.regulations.gov/#!documentDetail;D=PCLOB-2013-0005-0028	Providing the July 30th opinion of the U.S. Court of Appeals for the Fifth Circuit in In re: Application of the United States of America for Historical Cell Site Data, No. 11-20884
Mr. Juan Fernando López Aguilar, Chair of the European Parliament's Civil Liberties, Justice and Home Affairs Committee	http://www.regulations.gov/#!documentDetail;D=PCLOB-2013-0005-0059	
Ashkan Soltani	http://www.regulations.gov/#!documentDetail;D=PCLOB-2013-0005-0023	Panel member at PCLOB Workshop
Alliance for Justice	http://www.regulations.gov/#!documentDetail;D=PCLOB-2013-0005-0035	
Alan Charles Raul	http://www.regulations.gov/#!documentDetail;D=PCLOB-2013-0005-0065	Has four attachments
"Three former intelligence professionals - all former employees of the National Security Agency"	http://www.regulations.gov/#!documentDetail;D=PCLOB-2013-0005-0053	Statement submitted

Private citizen anonymous	http://www.regulations.gov/#!documentDetail;D=PCLOB-2013-0005-0014	
Coalition of 53 groups- letter	http://www.regulations.gov/#!documentDetail;D=PCLOB-2013-0005-0038	This is an updated coalition letter to PCLOB
The Constitution Project	http://www.regulations.gov/#!documentDetail;D=PCLOB-2013-0005-0009	Sharon Bradford Franklin was a panel member at PCLOB Workshop
Computer and Communications Industry Association	http://www.regulations.gov/#!documentDetail;D=PCLOB-2013-0005-0025	
Private citizen anonymous	http://www.regulations.gov/#!documentDetail;D=PCLOB-2013-0005-0017	
Electronic Frontier Foundation	http://www.regulations.gov/#!documentDetail;D=PCLOB-2013-0005-0030	
-BSA -The Software Alliance Computer & Communications Industry Association (CCIA) -Information Technology Industry Council (ITI) - SIIA (Software & Information Industry Association) - TechNet	http://www.regulations.gov/#!documentDetail;D=PCLOB-2013-0005-0061	

Ashkan Soltani	http://www.regulations.gov/#!documentDetail;D=PCLOB-2013-0005-0039	Revised submission, was a panel member at PCLOB Workshop
Private citizen anonymous	http://www.regulations.gov/#!documentDetail;D=PCLOB-2013-0005-0005	
Daniel J. Weitzner, Massachusetts Institute of Technology	http://www.regulations.gov/#!documentDetail;D=PCLOB-2013-0005-0040	Panel member at PCLOB Workshop
Private citizen anonymous	http://www.regulations.gov/#!documentDetail;D=PCLOB-2013-0005-0052	
Access - AccessNow.org	http://www.regulations.gov/#!documentDetail;D=PCLOB-2013-0005-0048	
Information and Privacy Commissioner of Ontario, Canada, Dr. Ann Cavoukian	http://www.regulations.gov/#!documentDetail;D=PCLOB-2013-0005-0057	
Privacy Times	http://www.regulations.gov/#!documentDetail;D=PCLOB-2013-0005-0011	
Electronic Privacy Information Center	http://www.regulations.gov/#!documentDetail;D=PCLOB-2013-0005-0064	Marc Rotenberg was a panel member at PCLOB Workshop
ACLU Statement	http://www.regulations.gov/#!documentDetail;D=PCLOB-2013-0005-0032	Jameel Jaffer was a panel member at PCLOB Workshop
Private citizen anonymous	http://www.regulations.gov/#!documentDetail;D=PCLOB-2013-0005-0046	
Mark Sokolow	http://www.regulations.gov/#!docume	

	ntDetail;D=PCLOB-2013-0005-0018	
GodlyGlobal.org	http://www.regulations.gov/#!documentDetail;D=PCLOB-2013-0005-0019	A faith-based initiative based in Switzerland with global scope
Private citizen anonymous	http://www.regulations.gov/#!documentDetail;D=PCLOB-2013-0005-0041	
ACCESS NOW	http://www.regulations.gov/#!documentDetail;D=PCLOB-2013-0005-0047	Second posting
Coalition letter	http://www.regulations.gov/#!documentDetail;D=PCLOB-2013-0005-0010	
Center for Democracy & Technology, Gregory T. Nojeim	http://www.regulations.gov/#!documentDetail;D=PCLOB-2013-0005-0034	Gregory Nojeim was a panel member at PCLOB Workshop
Reporters Committee for Freedom of the Press	http://www.regulations.gov/#!documentDetail;D=PCLOB-2013-0005-0063	
Center for National Security Studies	http://www.regulations.gov/#!documentDetail;D=PCLOB-2013-0005-0060	Kate Martin was a panel member at PCLOB Workshop
Private citizen anonymous	http://www.regulations.gov/#!documentDetail;D=PCLOB-2013-0005-0037	
Brennan Center for Justice's Liberty and National Security Program	http://www.regulations.gov/#!documentDetail;D=PCLOB-2013-0005-0049	Elizabeth Goitein was a panel member at PCLOB Workshop
Jeffrey H. Collins	http://www.regulations.gov/#!docume	

	ntDetail;D=PCLOB-2013-0005-0043	
Jeffrey H. Collins	http://www.regulations.gov/#!documentDetail;D=PCLOB-2013-0005-0045	Amended
Steven G. Bradbury	http://www.regulations.gov/#!documentDetail;D=PCLOB-2013-0005-0012	Panel member at PCLOB Workshop
Human Rights Watch	http://www.regulations.gov/#!documentDetail;D=PCLOB-2013-0005-0036	
"Human rights organizations and advocates from around the world"	http://www.regulations.gov/#!documentDetail;D=PCLOB-2013-0005-0042	Dozens of countries represented
Steven M. Bellovin	http://www.regulations.gov/#!documentDetail;D=PCLOB-2013-0005-0021	Panel member at PCLOB Workshop
Board of the U.S. Public Policy Council of the Association for Computing Machinery	http://www.regulations.gov/#!documentDetail;D=PCLOB-2013-0005-0026	Eugene H. Spafford, was a panelist at the Hearing
Private citizen	http://www.regulations.gov/#!documentDetail;D=PCLOB-2013-0005-0066	
Caspar Bowden, Prepared for the European Parliament LIBE Committee	http://www.regulations.gov/#!documentDetail;D=PCLOB-2013-0005-0068	
Stephanie Pell	http://www.regulations.gov/#!docume	Panel member at hearing

	ntDetail;D=PCLOB-2013-0005-0069	
Congressman Bennie Thompson	http://www.regulations.gov/#!documentDetail;D=PCLOB-2013-0005-0071	Ranking Member, Committee on Homeland Security
Government Accountability Project	http://www.regulations.gov/#!documentDetail;D=PCLOB-2013-0005-0072	

This Report is the Privacy and Civil Liberties Oversight Board's effort to analyze and review actions the executive branch takes to protect the Nation from terrorism to ensure the proper balancing of these actions with privacy and civil liberties.